THE LAY OF ALHA

THE LAY OF ALHA

WILLIAM WATERFIELD

GYAN

Published by

Gyan Publishing House
5, Ansari Road
Daryaganj, New Delhi-110002
Phone: 011-47034999, 9811692060
E-mail: books@gyanbooks.com

Distribution Network
gyanbooks.com
India, USA, Canada, UK, Australia

ISBN: 978-93-7133-201-9 (HB)

First Published, 1923

2nd Impression 2025

Printed at: Gyan Press, Delhi.

THE LAY OF ALHA
Author: WILLIAM WATERFIELD

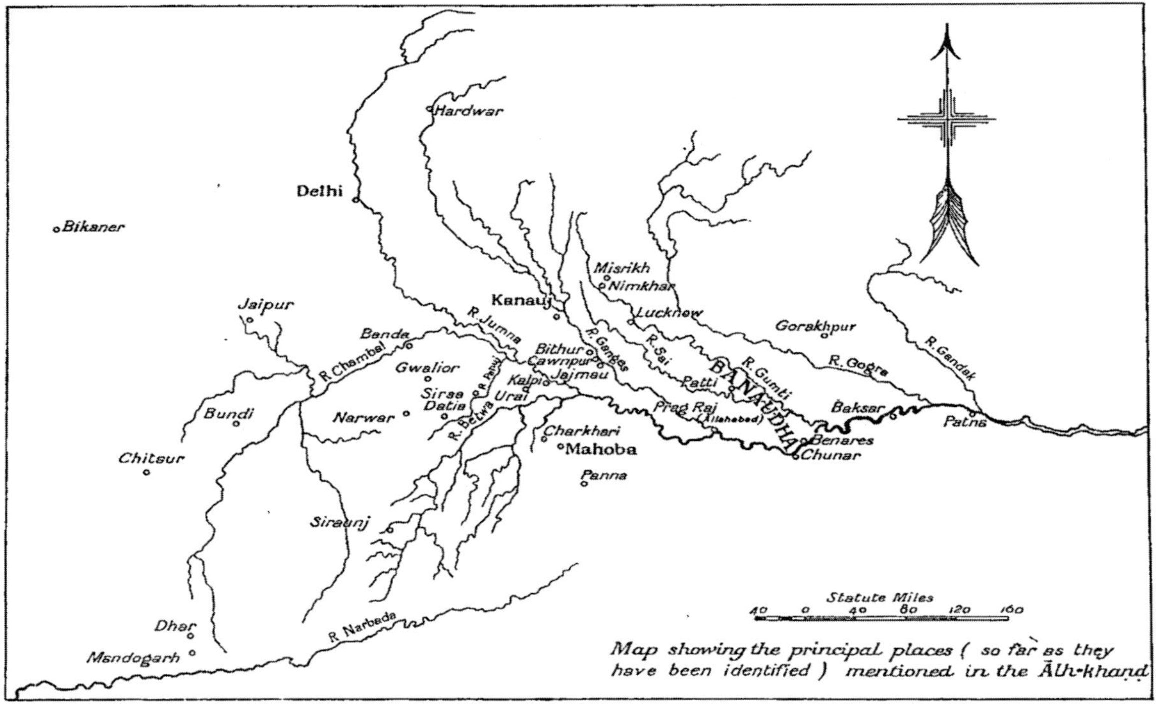

Map showing the principal places (so far as they have been identified) mentioned in the Ālh-khaṇḍ

The Lay of
ALHA

A Saga of *Rajput Chivalry* as sung by Minstrels of NORTHERN INDIA

Partly translated in English Ballad Metre
by the late WILLIAM WATERFIELD
of the *Bengal Civil Service*

With an Introduction and Abstracts of the
untranslated Portions
by SIR GEORGE GRIERSON, K.C.I.E.

OXFORD UNIVERSITY PRESS
HUMPHREY MILFORD
1923

PREFACE

My father, Mr. William Waterfield, the translator of these Ballads, was born in 1832, and was the eldest son of Thomas Nelson Waterfield, who for many years was Chief Clerk in the Political and Secret Department of the Board of Control, which was the predecessor of the India Office.

He was educated at Westminster School, of which he was Captain in 1849–50, and thence, having obtained a Bengal Writership, he went to Haileybury, then the training college for Service under the East India Company. He passed out Head of the College in June 1852, having been awarded many medals and prizes in Sanskrit, Persian, Bengali, Hindī, and other Indian languages, &c., and arrived in Calcutta in November 1852.

His training was completed at the College of Fort William, where he gained Certificates of High Proficiency in Persian, Hindī, Urdū, Sanskrit, and Bengali, and was awarded medals for Urdū, Bengali, Hindī, Persian, and Arabic, and Degrees of Honour in Bengali, Sanskrit, and Hindī.

His first two Degrees of Honour were presented to him in the Council Chamber by the Governor-General, Lord Dalhousie, in person, a practice which had fallen into disuse, but which Lord Dalhousie had for some time wished to restore; and, as he said, 'the remarkable performance of Mr. Waterfield offered the best occasion that could be hoped for'.

In June 1854 Mr. Waterfield was appointed Assistant Magistrate and Collector of the twenty-four Parganas, and having been transferred to the Survey in 1856, he became Superintendent of the Northern Division of Survey in 1858. In 1859 he was removed to the Financial Department and appointed First

Assistant to the Accountant-General, Madras, and then First Assistant to the Accountant-General to the Government of India. In 1867 he became Accountant-General of the North-West Provinces, and in 1877 Comptroller-General of India, retiring from the Service in 1881.

He was the author of 'Indian Ballads and other Poems' and 'Hymns for Holy Days and Seasons', as well as other poems that have not been printed. One of these has been added as an appendix to this volume; since, though it is not a part of the Lay of Ālhā, it deals with the predecessor of Prithīrāj, who takes a prominent part in the Lay.

After my father's return to England he settled in Devonshire, residing near Exeter at first and subsequently near Dawlish, where he died in 1907. It was, unfortunately, not until after this date that the work on which Sir George A. Grierson was engaged led him to address a letter to my father to ask where he could obtain a copy of his translation of 'The Nine-Lākh Chain' (the second canto of the Lay of Ālhā), which had been printed in the 'Calcutta Review'; and thus much information of interest regarding my father's compilation of his translation has been lost and I am unable to state his reasons for selecting certain cantos for translation, or for not completing those which he began but left unfinished. But I put my father's MSS. and papers dealing with the Lay in Sir George Grierson's hands, and I take this opportunity of expressing my indebtedness to him for his labours in preparing this volume for the Press and in writing abstracts of the remaining cantos, thus presenting the substance of the Poem as a whole and giving coherence to my father's translation.

For the benefit of readers who may be unfamiliar with old-fashioned English words on the one hand, or with Indian manners and customs on the other, I have thought it better not to omit any of my father's numerous explanatory footnotes.

PHILIP G. WATERFIELD.

CONTENTS

INTRODUCTION

Every reader of that fascinating classic, Tod's 'Rajasthan', will remember how much its author depended on the bardic chroniclers of Rājputāna for his materials. In old times each Rājpūt monarch kept his court bard, who recorded the deeds of his master and celebrated the virtues of his ancestors. The most famous of the epics so composed is the 'Prithīrāj Rāsau' of Chand Bardāī, who died beside his master, Prithīrāj the Chauhān of Delhi, in the 'Great Battle' of A.D. 1192, when India fell under Muslim domination. It comprises a hundred thousand stanzas in sixty-nine books, and Tod[1] accurately describes it as a universal history of the period in which its author wrote. It, and many other similar works, were composed by educated men, familiar with the traditional rules of composition and of poetics. Such chronicles were carefully preserved in manuscript and exist in that form to the present day.

The work of which an account is given in the following pages is of a somewhat different character. No old manuscripts of it have ever been discovered. Parmāl, whom it celebrates, disappeared from history in ignominy, and Mahōbā, his capital, ceased to exist as a royal town only eleven years after the death of Chand and Prithīrāj. The very name of its author is unknown except for a tradition of little value that it was composed by Jagnaik, sister's son of Parmāl. Nevertheless, it is, without doubt, the most popular poem of its kind in Hindostan. It is the property, not of educated men, but of illiterate minstrels who are found scattered over northern India from Delhi to Bihār. These 'Ālhā Gānēwālās', as they are called, make it their profession to recite the Ālh-khaṇḍ, or 'Lay of Ālhā', handed down to them from generation to

[1] Ed. Crooke, vol. i, p. 297.

generation by their predecessors. Under such circumstances the text varies from place to place, and the language has changed as time elapsed. It now presents the singular appearance of a poem composed in the twelfth century, yet containing such English words as 'pistol', 'bomb', and 'Sappers and Miners'.

It had never been reduced to writing till Mr. (afterwards Sir Charles) Elliott, when in Farrukhabad in the late sixties of the last century, found some three or four minstrels, and employed one of them to compile a complete set of the entire cycle from their joint memories. Farrukhabad is close to Kanauj, one of the places with which the heroes of the cycle were closely connected, and so the text, as we have it, may be called the Kanaujī recension of the poem. This is the only complete version of the cycle of which I am aware. The popularity of the Kanaujī edition, which has been several times reprinted, has induced other publishers to produce sections of the poem from the mouths of other reciters, and I myself have published portions collected by me in Bihār[1] and by Mr. Vincent Smith[2] in Bundelkhand. Mr. Elliott drew the attention of Mr. W. Waterfield, of the Bengal Civil Service, then Accountant-General of the North-West Provinces, to the cycle which he had had compiled, and that gentleman undertook the task of translating the whole into English ballad metre. A portion of this translation appeared in instalments in vols. lxi to lxiii (1875–6) of the Calcutta Review, under the name of 'The Nine-Lākh Chain or the Maro Feud', but that periodical was read by few people whose home was not in India, and it followed that Mr. Waterfield's spirited version did not acquire more than a local reputation. The style adopted by him, that of the English Border ballads, is excellently suited to the subject, and the occasional use of antique words and phraseology gives just the right idea of the rough and somewhat antique Bundēlī Hindī dialect of the original.

[1] 'Indian Antiquary', vol. xiv, pp. 209, 255.
[2] 'Linguistic Survey of India', vol. ix, i, pp. 502 ff.

Mr. Waterfield retired from the Indian Civil Service in 1881, and died in the year 1907. 'The Nine-Lākh Chain' was the only portion of the poem which had up to then appeared in print, but some years ago I was fortunate enough to get into touch with members of his family, and his son, Mr. Philip Waterfield, very kindly placed at my disposal his father's papers dealing with the whole cycle. Among them I found a good deal more of the verse-translation, viz. the whole of the first, fourth, and thirteenth cantos, and portions of the eighth and of the fifteenth. It will be convenient here to give, in Mr. Waterfield's own words, his account of the poem, and of his methods of translation :—

'The original Ālh-khaṇḍ was, no doubt, as appears from its name, a single book of Chand's great Hindī epic of the twelfth century upon the exploits of his master, King Prithī of Delhi. Whether it was the same with the Mahobā-khaṇḍ, or whether these form the groundwork of the two parts of the Kanauj collection, I must leave to the students of the ancient poem to determine. Those who are learned in Hindī must decide also how much of the old poem has been handed down to the modern minstrels, each of whom, probably, has gradually modernized the language and introduced his own improvements. The comparison would be interesting, and might help to throw light on the question how much of the original Homer survived through his rhapsodists to the days of Pisistratus; but the Greek language and metre were far more conducive to permanency of diction than the Hindī, which is a simple grammar and a loose measure and rhyme more like that of the Spanish ballads: while the manners of Greece probably underwent no such violent changes as those which have in these ballads not only planted Muhammadan barons, mercenaries and devotees along with the Hindū before the days of Muslim invasion, and filled the battle scenes with cannon, rocket, and pistol, side by side with arrow and spear, but even have, evidently within the present century, added regimental officers, and sappers and miners to the other constituents of the armies. The differing versions of our English ballads preserved from the recitations of the minstrels of distant parts of the country offer a truer comparison; but in their case we have no original standard for reference; and I shall not be surprised if little is to be found here of Chand's poem except the story, and even that with much variety and addition of incident.

The cycle of ballads which is collectively known as the Ālh-khaṇḍ, has only been printed within the last two years, and was reduced to writing for the first time from the version current at Kanauj under the instructions of Mr. C. A. Elliott, B.C.S., to whom I am indebted not merely for my introduction to the poems, but for a native translation in his possession, and some valuable notes and illustrations of his own, as well as for advice and assistance in my own share of the work. In fact the present portion of my version was written before I had had an opportunity of seeing the original, and what little acquaintance I ever possessed with the vernacular and folk-lore of India was acquired in the provinces of Lower Bengal.

It will be seen that I offer this contribution not to the antiquarian or philologer, but to the student of folk-lore. It cannot but be interesting to know something of the tales which, next to versions of the great Sanskrit epics, and perhaps I should add the adventures and transmigrations of the famous King Vikramāditya, are the favourite subject of recitation at all Hindū gatherings throughout the middle and lower Doab and Bundelkhand. The memory of the heroes, Ālhā and Ūdan, is yet preserved at their native Mahoba, where a clan of Banāphars still claims them as ancestors, and where the ruins of their pleasure-house are still to be seen towering on one of the hills above the beautiful Madan Sāgar Lake (and, indeed, most of the antiquities are attributed to them by the less instructed peasantry). This is even more the case in the seat of the other school of Ālh singers, Kanauj, the land of their exile, where I suspect the hereditary jealousy of Delhi is still cherished, and King Prithī depreciated and his rivals exalted in proportion.

I do not profess, therefore, to give a perfectly literal translation, though, I believe, my version is quite near enough to show the spirit of the original. Indeed, I think my variations are chiefly omissions of catalogues of weapons and the like, reduction of the lists of casualties reckoned by lacs to rather more possible numbers, and compression of the accounts of battles. After all I am afraid there is a great deal of monotony in these last, but I suppose it is scarcely avoidable in the description of a series of combats; even those in Homer have a strong mutual resemblance. It will be remembered, too, that the ballads, though bound up together, are recited by the minstrels on separate occasions, and no doubt come with all the interest of novelty to the unsophisticated audience.'

In the above Mr. Waterfield suggested that the original of this cycle is to be found in the Mahōbā-khaṇḍ of Chand's Epic, the 'Prithīrāj Rāsau'. Since then the latter work has been published, and I have been able to compare the two, and can state that it is certain that they are quite independent works. Chand's poem deals with the story from the point of view of Delhi, and the Ālh-khaṇḍ from the point of view of Kanauj and Mahōbā. Chand's story can be put in a few words—Parmāl of Mahōbā enrages Prithīrāj of Delhi, by cutting up a number of his wounded troops returning from a raid on Samētā. Ālhā and Ūdan being away from Mahōbā, Prithīrāj attacks Malkhān at Sirsā, kills him, and defeats his army. There is then a two months' truce, during which Parmāl recalls Ālhā and Ūdan. The war is resumed, Ūdan is killed, Ālhā disappears, Parmāl flees, and Mahōbā is captured. Except that the battle of Sirsā and the death of Malkhān occur in both stories, it therefore altogether disagrees with the version of the Ālh-khaṇḍ. In the latter, it is true, Ālhā and Ūdan return from Kanauj, but in other respects the tale of the fall of Mahōbā is quite different. This will be evident from the following summary of the contents of our present poem:—

It is concerned with the fortunes and rivalries of three famous Indian principalities of the twelfth century A.D.—Delhi, ruled by Prithīrāj the Chauhān; Kanauj, ruled by Jaychand the Rāṭhōr[1]; and Mahōbā, ruled by Parmāl the Chandēl. Chauhān, Rāṭhōr, and Chandēl are all names of Rājput clans.

[1] Once for all, I am giving what the poem says, and not the facts which are necessarily historically true. Jaychand appears really to have been a Gahaṛwār.

Of these three, Jaychand of Kanauj was by far the most powerful. Musalmān historians tell us that his kingdom extended so far east as Benares, and we shall see that the present poem makes him overlord also of Bihār, Assam, Bengal, and Orissa. He claimed suzerainty over the greater part of Rājputāna, and Parmāl of Mahōbā was one of his numerous vassals.

Prithīrāj, the first and last Chauhān king of Delhi, is still celebrated in India for his gallant deeds and warlike adventures. He not only refused to accept Jaychand's suzerainty, but claimed himself to be a rival suzerain. There was hence great jealousy between Kanauj and Delhi, which culminated when Jaychand called in his vassal kings to attend a great assemblage at Kanauj, in order that his daughter Sanjōgin might choose one of them for her husband. Prithīrāj was one of those summoned, but would not attend, and, instead, forcibly carried off Sanjōgin, a not unwilling captive, in the face of Jaychand's armies. This abduction forms the subject of the first canto of our poem. The result was continued war between Delhi and Kanauj, which lasted for several years, and ended, as we shall see, in the destruction of both kingdoms, and in the subjugation of India to Muslim domination.

Kanauj, as shown in the map facing the title-page, was situated on the Ganges, and Delhi some two hundred miles to the north-west, on the Jumna. About 120 miles south of Kanauj, across the rivers Jumna and Bētwā, in Bundelkhand, lay the city of Mahōbā. Its territory was separated from that of Kanauj by these rivers, and was originally in the hands of the Parihār Rājpūts till they were conquered by the Chandēls in the middle of the eighth century. The Parihārs remained subject to the Chandēl king, their chiefs being allowed to hold subordinate fiefs. Parmāl, or Paramardī, the last Chandēl king, succeeded to the Mahōbā throne about the year 1185, and at that time the fief of Uraī, beyond the Bētwā, was held by Māhil Parihār, whose sister, Malhnā, Parmāl married. Māhil, though openly on friendly terms with Parmāl, being indeed his and Malhnā's trusted adviser, never forgot the grudge which he, as Parihār, owed against the Chandēl dynasty. He was an unscrupulous traitor, and whenever opportunity offered, he secretly plotted with Parmāl's enemies to compass his ruin.

Parmāl, as said above, acknowledged Jaychand's suzerainty. Indeed, if we are to accept the statement of our poem, he seems to have been a kind of viceroy on Jaychand's behalf, and to have been empowered to act for him in his absence. He is represented in the poem as an effeminate coward, the real ruler of his kingdom being his wife Malhnā, too ready to accept the advice of her treacherous brother, but upheld in authority by certain Banāphar chieftains.

There are many legends as to the origin of these Banāphars. According to the poem the founders of the clan in Mahōbā were four chieftains of Baksar (Buxar) in Bihār, named Dasrāj, Bachrāj, Rahmal, and Ṭōḍar, who happened to be in that city when it was attacked by Karinghā, prince of Māṛō. They stoutly defended the gate and defeated Karinghā. Parmāl then took them into his service. They married, and Dasrāj begat Ālhā and Ūdan, and Bachrāj Malkhān and Sulkhān. There is some mystery about the birth of these boys. One story says that their mothers were respectively Dēbī or Diwal Dē, and Birmhā, daughters of Raja Dalpat of Gwālior. Another, and more romantic, version is that these wives were of cowherd (*Ahīr*) origin. It was said that Dasrāj and Bachrāj were one day out hunting, when they came upon a fight between two wild buffalo-bulls. Seeing that their way was obstructed, two Ahīr girls stepped up, and each taking a bull by the horns thrust it aside. Considering that such strapping wenches would breed mighty sons, Dasrāj and Bachrāj there and then married them. Whether this story was true or not, it was widely spread, and with it the belief that the Banāphar youths were not of pure Rājpūt origin, a cause of much of the fighting described in the poem. Whatever may have been the origin of these two wives, they were on most affectionate terms with Queen Malhnā, who treated them as sisters. The four boys, with a son each of Rahmal and Ṭōḍar, grew up in the palace as companions of Brahmā, Parmāl's son, and the whole seven treated each other as brothers. All this is described in Canto II.

In Canto III we learn that some years afterwards, before the birth of Ūdan and Sulkhān, Karinghā, to avenge his defeat by the Banāphars at the gate of Mahōbā, makes a sudden raid on them in their home at Daspurwā near that city. He murders Dasrāj and Bachrāj in their sleep, and carries off some of their most valued possessions, the most noteworthy of which was a nine-lākh chain, or necklace worth nine hundred thousand rupees. When Ūdan is but twelve years old he hears the story for the first time, and he and the other Banāphar boys determine to take revenge. With Parmāl's aid they collect an army, attack Māṛō, kill Karinghā, his father Jambay, and all his family, and devastate the country, bringing back in triumph to Mahōbā all the property that had been carried off. This campaign establishes the reputation of the Banāphars as heroic warriors. Cantos IV to VII describe the marriages of Ālhā, Malkhān, Brahmā, and Ūdan respectively. The two following cantos are episodes, the first dealing with a misunderstanding and consequent war, due to the instigation of Māhil, following an invitation to Parmāl's married daughter to visit her parents' home. In the second episode, we are told how Indal, Ālhā's son, is changed by a sorceress princess into a parrot and carried off to Bukhārā, and how he is rescued and married to his captor. This concludes the first part of the poem.

With the tenth canto, we are told of Ālhā's banishment. Prithīrāj has his quarrel going on with Jaychand, and at Māhil's instigation, sends word to Jaychand's vassal Parmāl, claiming suzerainty over him, and demanding tribute. The cowardly Parmāl is ready to comply, but Ālhā and Ūdan object so strongly that at last, stung by their reproaches, he banishes them from his kingdom. They take refuge with Jaychand of Kanauj, who, after some hesitation on the ground that they have been banished by his vassal, receives them into his service. The eleventh canto celebrates the Banāphars' exploits in their new sphere of action. Here they conduct and win the war waged by Jaychand against the Rājā of Būndī, in connexion with the marriage of Lākhan, Jaychand's nephew and heir, to that Rājā's daughter. In the following canto Ūdan and Lākhan are dispatched by Jaychand to collect tribute from the recalcitrant kings of Bihār, Assam, Bengal, and Orissa. Ūdan successfully accomplishes this task, but the main result is that he and Lākhan become sworn brothers.

In the meantime Prithīrāj has not forgotten his claim against Mahōbā. Parmāl, long before this, had established Malkhān in a fief at Sirsā, an important strategic point on the direct road from Delhi to Mahōbā. Māhil informs Prithīrāj that, owing to Ālhā's and Ūdan's banishment, Mahōbā is now without champions and that if he can capture Sirsā, the way to it will be open. Prithīrāj accordingly sets forth. Sirsā, left unsupported by Parmāl, is taken, and Malkhān is killed after a most gallant defence. Prithīrāj marches against Mahōbā. News of this reaches Ūdan, who with Lākhan steals away from Kanauj, and raises the siege. All this is described in Cantos XIII and XIV.

In the fifteenth and sixteenth cantos Ūdan and Lākhan have returned to Kanauj, and Prithīrāj has brought a new army to besiege Mahōbā. The city is on the point of falling and Malhnā writes to Ālhā entreating him to return and save them. He has been driven from Mahōbā with every accompaniment of ignominy, and at first he refuses, but at length, stung by his mother's reproaches, he sets out with Ūdan and Lākhan and strong forces lent by Jaychand to defend his vassal. They defeat Prithīrāj decisively in the Battle of the Bētwā, and he retreats to Delhi. Mahōbā is thus relieved, and the second part of the poem is concluded. Here is inserted Canto XVIII, an episode having nothing to do with the main story. It tells how Ūdan, like Indal, is changed by a sorceress into a parrot, and how he is released. The canto is wrongly placed, and should have appeared at an earlier stage of the narrative, for Malkhān here appears alive and taking an active part in the fighting.

The third and last part of the poem consists of Cantos XVIII to XXIII, and narrates the final catastrophe and the circumstances that led up to it. In Canto VI, we have been told of the marriage of Brahmā, Parmāl's son and heir, to Bēlā, the daughter of Prithīrāj of Delhi. This was long before the attack on Sirsā, and Delhi and Mahōbā were then, at least nominally, at peace. When the marriage was concluded, Prithīrāj had claimed that, according to the custom of his house, his daughter should remain with her parents for a year before she is sent to her husband's home, and this was agreed to. The year has now long elapsed, and the Mahōbā court determines to call upon Prithīrāj to redeem his promise and to send Bēlā to her husband. It is a noteworthy fact, which appears over and over again in Rājpūt bardic tales, that once a girl is married—no matter where she happens to be—if a quarrel takes place between her husband and her father's people, she invariably sides with her husband. In this way, though Bēlā lives in Delhi in Prithīrāj's palace, during all this time she sympathizes with Mahōbā, and actively intrigues on its behalf. When it is determined to ask Prithīrāj for her, Ūdan volunteers to be the messenger, but Brahmā insists on going himself, and starts for Delhi at the head of his army. Prithīrāj refuses to give her up, and attacks Brahmā's army, but is defeated. At Māhil's instigation he takes to treachery, and under pretence of dispatching Bēlā he sends his general, Chauṇṛā, dressed as a woman, who with the help of Tāhar, Prithīrāj's son and Bēlā's brother, and others, attempts to assassinate Brahmā and sorely wounds him. The news reaches Mahōbā, and Ūdan and Lākhan with a large army start out to avenge him. They gain access to Bēlā's palace by a stratagem and with her full consent carry her off. After fierce fighting they bring her to the camp where she finds Brahmā dying of his wounds. She vows vengeance against her brother Tāhar, who had been the leading spirit in the assassination,[1] and after visiting Mahōbā and being formally recognized as the wife of the heir apparent, she dresses herself in Brahmā's armour, rides out on his horse at the head of an army, and in single combat defeats Tāhar and beheads him. She carries back the head and presents it in a charger to Brahmā, who now declares that he can die happy, and straightway breathes his last. Bēlā determines to become Satī on her husband's pyre, but it must be made of sandal-wood from the sandal-grove near Delhi, which is owned by Prithīrāj. Ūdan and Lākhan set out, cut down the grove, and in the face of great opposition, bring it to camp. The wood is, however, too fresh and will not burn, so, at Bēlā's urgent request, they go again, force their way into Delhi, and cut and carry away the sandal pillars of Prithīrāj's own throne-room.

The funeral pyre is arranged. Brahmā's body is laid upon it, and Bēlā ascends it. At her request, Ūdan is about to set it alight, when Prithīrāj appears at the head of a large army. He declares that he cannot allow Ūdan—a Banāphar of doubtful caste—to light the pyre, and demands that this should be done by a member of Parmāl's own family. Ūdan refuses, and the armies join battle in what is the Armageddon of Mahōbā. While it progresses, fire bursts from Bēlā's hair and sets the pyre alight, and she is consumed with Brahmā's body. The fight is terrific. Thousands of soldiers on both sides are slain. The remaining sons of Prithīrāj and all his best generals are killed, and so are Ūdan, Lākhan, and, except Ālhā and his son Indal, all the great champions of Mahōbā. Not one of Mahōbā's soldiers escapes, and Prithīrāj retreats to Delhi with the meagre remnants of his army.

The news reaches Mahōbā, where all the wives of the knights of the army find themselves widows. Headed by Sunwā, Ālhā's wife, and Phulwā, Ūdan's widow, they hasten,

[1] He was a stickler for the rules of Rājpūt chivalry, and so he would not disguise himself as a woman; but he accompanied Chauṇṛā, who was not a Rājpūt, and dealt the fatal blow.

weeping, to the battlefield and search among the piled corpses each for her husband. Sunwā finds Indal, her son, alive, and in the agitation of the moment asks him where Ālhā is, mentioning him by name in the presence of her son, a thing which is forbidden by one of the strongest Rājpūt taboos. Ālhā hears this, and bids her farewell for ever. Accompanied by Indal, he sets out for the mysterious Kajarī-ban, the 'Land of Darkness', and, immortal, he is still there waiting for the moment when he is to issue forth to avenge the woes of Mahōbā. Sunwā, Phulwā, and all the widows then throw themselves into the fiery pit which forms the remains of Brahmā's funeral pyre and are consumed to ashes.

In Mahōbā no one remains but Malhnā and her husband, the craven Parmāl. Malhnā takes the wondrous Philosopher's Stone, the treasure of the house, and casts it into the city lake, to abide there for ever. Parmāl, refusing to be comforted, starves himself to death, and so Mahōbā disappears from history.

Thus ends this saga of Rājpūt chivalry. Besides Prithīrāj, the only prominent character who escapes unharmed is, by an Atê worthy of a Greek tragedy, the traitor Māhil. It is a noble story, replete with incident and with characters well contrasted. The rustic bards have succeeded in bringing before us alive and in the flesh Ālhā, the Indian ideal of a sagacious general, *dhīravīra*, slow to anger, but terrible and invincible when roused; the gallant and impetuous Ūdan—lover ardent yet chaste, foe implacable yet chivalrous—whom, in spite of his wayward temper, it is impossible not to love; the brave faithful Malkhān; and Lākhan, that truest of knights, worthy of a seat with the noblest heroes at the Arthurian table. The women, too, excite our admiration, even when, as in the case of Bēlā, their vengeance appals us. There is the queenly Malhnā, fated to yield her trust to her traitorous brother, but still the mainstay of Mahōbā, and bravely coming to the forefront of its defence in place of her unworthy husband. Her fate is not mentioned in the poem, but it is impossible to suppose that it was other than that of any brave Rājpūt wife when her husband dies. Well can we picture her unfaltering step as she approaches the funeral pyre of him, whom, in spite of his weakness, she loved. Dēbī, too, the heroic mother of Ālhā and Ūdan, appears ever spurring them on to new deeds of chivalry, and careful lest their knightly scutcheons should be fouled with ingratitude even to the king who, though he once cherished them, had banished them in disgrace. Finally there is the piteous tale of Ūdan and the fair Bijaisin, not mentioned in the preceding abstract, but told by Mr. Waterfield in the third canto. The pathetic story of her death and of her burial by Ūdan in the deep waters of the Narmadā is one that cannot be read without emotion. Even the unworthy characters are not less clearly portrayed. What contrast can be greater than that between the weak, hesitating Parmāl, and the crafty treacherous Māhil—both of them cowards, and yet how different! Chauṇṛā, on the other hand, a Brāhman unscrupulous and treacherous, twice guilty of cowardly assassination, is a valiant warrior, who fears not death for himself, and who receives it with a welcome when he finds it on the field of battle.

The cycle has its weak points. Like others of its class all over the world, it abounds in repetitions. There are stock descriptions of single combats and of general battles, which are repeated over and over again as occasion occurs, with only a change in the names of the combatants. The first or second time they are read they are interesting enough, and not without poetic charm, but when they are met again and again, the reader must confess to a feeling of weariness. For this reason, as Mr. Waterfield has given more than one such account in full in his translations, I have omitted all reference to them in my abstracts of the other portions, and have left them to be supplied by memory.

The reader must be warned not to expect too much consistency in the various cantos of this cycle. The bards' ideas of geography are most elastic, and few of the places mentioned by them can now be identified. The singers themselves do not help, for their traditions, when they have any, are of little value. We must also allow for exaggeration. The poem describes armies of hundreds of thousands, and slaughters thousands and thousands without hesitation. Assuming that the battles described did occur, we may safely conclude that they were much smaller affairs than as we find them described.

Attention must also be drawn to the very remarkable marriage customs depicted. These will be found of great interest to all students of the subject. There seems to have been a regular routine, of which a full account is given in Mr. Waterfield's version of Canto IV, and which can be found repeated with very slight variation in the succeeding cantos. The procedure was as follows. A king has a marriageable daughter, and sends round a letter of invitation to all princes with marriageable sons, the terms of which are practically a challenge to let him take her who dare. The more powerful the sender of the letter, the fewer people there are ready to accept the invitation. At last it is accepted by some hero. The usual rites are performed at his home, and then he sets out with his marriage procession, which consists of a large army strengthened by contingents supplied by friends and relatives. When the army arrives at the frontier of the bride's father, a herald is sent to acquaint him with the fact. The herald is received with contumely and has to fight his way out of the city and back to the camp against overwhelming odds. The bride's father refuses to give his daughter, and there is a pitched battle in which thousands of troops are represented as being engaged on each side. If the bride's party are worsted, they resort to treachery, as for instance, when they pretend to give in, and send poisoned food to the bridegroom's camp. In our poems this stratagem is always detected, and the bearers of the food are dismissed with a beating. But there is nothing to lead us to suppose that in other cases the stratagem may have succeeded, and the whole bridegroom's party put to death. When this fails other stratagems are tried. Attempts are made to get the bridegroom alone or accompanied only by a few near relations all unarmed, and then they are set upon by armed men and have to fight for their lives with what weapons they can improvise. At length the bride's father admits defeat, and the bridegroom and a few of his friends are invited into the fort for the wedding ceremony, during which the bride and bridegroom make the orthodox seven circuits of the marriage post and arbour. Here again, in the presence of the bride, they are attacked by her relations, and, when these fail, by concealed armed men. If the attack is successful, those of the bridegroom's party (including the bridegroom himself) who survive are taken away and cast into prison. If the attack fails, the seven circuits are completed, but the arbour and post having been wrecked in the *mêlée*, a spear is substituted for the post, and the roof of a new arbour is made by joining shields together. The marriage ceremony having been completed, the bridegroom is invited into the female apartments to eat the wedding breakfast with the bride. Here again an attack is made upon him, in which he is now protected by his wife, and if he survives it, all further opposition is given up and he goes off, taking his bride with him or not, as may be arranged.

It must be observed that, as described above, the battles are not sham fights. They are real bloody combats, in which hundreds of men on both sides are slain. That such fighting was a pundonor before a Rājpūt wedding is plain from the fact that on two occasions[1] Ūdan refuses to countenance any marriage which is not accompanied by bloodshed. The most extraordinary thing about the whole affair is that once the marriage is completed, the contending parties become quite friendly again, and, on the next occasion of a marriage, they are ready to take out their armies and go to each others' assistance. We can admit that the accounts given by the bards are grossly exaggerated. But the story would not be told if at least the main facts did not resemble a true state of affairs or what is

[1] Canto III, iv, verses 57–8; Canto IX, p. 214.

traditionally accepted as having once been such. No body of auditors would listen to story after story in great detail of their own country and their own kith and kin if they were not told what had at least a groundwork of truth. So far as I can ascertain, there is no trace of such customs as those described above to be found in Rājputāna at the present day, but I think that the poem does contain memories of customs which were in full use in ancient times. Here I must leave the matter in the hands of anthropologists to explain the origin and meaning of this curious picture of marriage and of warfare.

In the following pages I have reproduced Mr. Waterfield's translation exactly as given by him. The only alterations which I have made have been the correction of evident misprints in the sections which appeared in the 'Calcutta Review'. The other sections were made by him in later years, and apparently at fairly long intervals. During this time he did not always adhere to the same system of spelling of Indian words. I have taken his latest spellings as the model, and have endeavoured to follow them uniformly throughout. In other respects his translation is so accurate and follows the original so closely that I have not thought it necessary to alter a single word. In the case of one or two slips which seemed important, I have drawn attention to each in a foot-note, to which I have added my initials. In order to preserve the sequence of the story I have myself prepared abstracts in prose of all those portions not translated by him, and in doing so have freely utilized some accounts of the contents of the first ten cantos and of the thirteenth canto, which had been prepared by Sir Charles Elliott, and which I found in Mr. Waterfield's papers. These I have carefully compared with the original, and have freely altered where it seemed advisable, as they were certainly not prepared for publication. The remainder of the abstracts I have made myself, and must thus accept responsibility for the whole. The present version of the Ālh Khaṇḍ, therefore, consists of five cantos translated, and two partially translated by Mr. Waterfield; seven abstracts based on Sir Charles Elliott's papers;

and nine abstracts prepared entirely by me. Everything not by Mr. Waterfield is printed in smaller type. I hope that this arrangement will serve to elucidate Mr. Waterfield's admirable version, and will at the same time draw attention to the merits of the bardic literature of Rājputānā.

A few words may be added as to the pronunciation of Indian names occurring in the Saga. English readers may pronounce all vowels as in Italian. In the prose passages, when a vowel is long it is so marked. All other vowels are to be pronounced short. In the parts in English verse, vowels should be pronounced long or short as suggested by the metre. The letter *n̠* has the nasal sound of the *n* in the French word *bon*. No attention need be paid to the dots under the consonants *ḍ*, *ṛ*, and *ṭ*. These have been inserted for the benefit of persons familiar with Indian languages, and indicate shades of pronunciation not employed in this country.

GEORGE A. GRIERSON.

LIST OF CHARACTERS
APPEARING IN THE CYCLE

WITH the published version of the 'Nine-Lākh Chain' Mr. Waterfield gave a list of the characters appearing in those cantos. In substitution for this, I here give a similar list for the whole cycle. It must, however, be explained that in the original, proper names appear with no systematic spelling. Not only are full forms, such as Uday Singh, and shorter forms, such as Ūdan, used to indicate the same person; but the same word appears at one time with one spelling, and at another with another, as the cadence of a sentence may require. In his verse-translation, Mr. Waterfield has availed himself of this poetic licence, and, as he himself points out, he writes such words as 'Māhīl' or 'Māhil' according to the exigencies of the metre, and follows the original in nasalizing vowels *ad libitum* in cases such as 'Ṭōḍar' or 'Ṭōṇḍar', 'Māṛō' or 'Māṛōṇ', or in inserting an *i* to give an extra syllable, as in 'Parmāl' or 'Parimāl'. In my own prose abstracts, no such liberty was required, and I have endeavoured, so much as was possible, to adhere to one spelling for each name. In the following list, the Roman numerals indicate the cantos in which the names occur:

Abhai, the Parihār. Son of Māhil. He was as faithful as his father was treacherous. III, XIV (killed by Tāhar).

Abhinandan, Rājā of Balkh-Bukhārā. His Queen is Champā. He has seven sons, of whom three, Hansāmal, Sukkhā, and Mōhan are named. His daughter is Chittar-rēkhā, who marries Indal. IX.

Ādibhayankar, name of the elephant ridden by Prithīrāj. XIX, &c.

Agmā, Queen of Prithīrāj. VI, VIII, XVIII, XIX, XXII.

Ahmad, an old Muslim Fakīr. He tries to dissuade Gajmōtin from becoming Satī. XIII.

Ajaipāl, father of Jaychand and Ratībhān. No longer alive when the story opens. I, &c.

Alāmat and **Alī,** two of Mīrā Tālhan's nine sons. IV.

Alī Bahādur. A Mahōbā champion. IV.

Ālhā or **Nūn Ālhā,** the Banāphar. Son of Dasrāj and Dēbī and brother of Ūdan. In the earlier cantos he rides the winged horse Karilyā, and in the later cantos the elephant Pachsāwaḍ, the horse being taken by his son Indal, and now called Hansāman. Mentioned in nearly all cantos. In canto XXII he is granted immortality, and in canto XXIII he kills Chauṇṛā and disappears, with his son, into the Kajarī-ban.

Angad, of Gwālior. A champion of Prithīrāj. VI, XIII, XVI,

XIX. His fate is uncertain. In canto XIII he is said to be killed by Malkhān before Sirsā, but in canto XXII he is said to be killed by Parsū in the battle for the Sandal Pillars.

Anūpī. Son of Jambay of Mārō. III (killed by Ūdan).

Bachrāj (properly Bachhrāj), the Banāphar of Baksar. Comes to Mahōbā with Dasrāj, Rahmal, and Ṭōḍar his brothers. Marries Birmhā, daughter of Dalpat of Gwālior, and has two sons, Malkhān and Sulkhān, the latter posthumous. Murdered by Karinghā of Mārō. II, IV.

Banaudhā, the twelve princes of Banaudhā join Ūdan and Lākhan in the relief of Mahōbā and the subsequent fighting. XIV, XV, XXII. Banaudhā is the tract of country comprising Southern Oudh and the Districts of Jaunpur, Āzamgaṛh, and Benares.

Bangā, a Paṭhān general of Jambay of Mārō. III (killed by Ḍhēwā).

Bans Gōpāl, of Datiā. One of Prithīrāj's champions. XVI (killed by Lākhan).

Baunā, in charge of Kuṛhar during Gangā Pamār's absence. XV.

Bēlā or **Bilam Dē,** daughter of Prithīrāj and Agmā. VI (an incarnation of Draupadī. Married to Brahmā, son of Parmāl), XVIII, XIX (list of her previous incarnations), XX (beheads her brother Tāhar), XXI, XXIII (becomes Satī).

Bēn Chakbai (Vēṇa Chakravartī). An ancient mythical King of Kanauj. I, &c.

Bēndulā or **Rāsbēndul,** name of Ūdan's winged horse. III, IV, VI, &c.

Bēnī Brāhmaṇ, the Kanauj Astrologer. XI.

Bhaurānand, name of the elephant ridden by Dhāndhū. XVI, &c.

Bhōgā, see **Jōgā.**

Bhūrā, 'Brown'. Name of the elephant ridden by Bīr Sāhi of Baurīgaṛh, VIII. Name of that ridden by Sātan of Paṭṭī, XII.

Bhūrā Mughul, one of the champions of Prithīrāj. VI, XIV, XV, XVI, XIX, XXIII (killed by Mīrā Tālhan).

Bhūrī or **Bhuruhī,** 'Brown'. Name of the she-elephant ridden by Jaychand (XV) and by Lākhan (XII, XVI, XIX, XXIII).

Bijai Singh, of Bijahaṭ. VII (an ally of Narpat of Narwar).

Bijai Singh, of Bīkānēr. A champion of Prithīrāj. XXI (kills Hir Singh and Bir Singh, and is killed by Gangā).

Bijaisin or **Bijmā,** daughter of Jambay of Mārō. II, III (killed by Malkhān). VII (after her death becomes reincarnate as Phulwā).

Bijyā, one of the sons of Naipālī of Naināgaṛh. IV.

Bilam Dē, see **Bēlā.**

Bilundin, name of the mare ridden by Dhanuā Tēlī. XI.

Bīr Bhugantā, of Jagnik. A champion of Prithīrāj. VI, XXII, XXIII (kills Mīrā Tālhan, and is killed by Gangā).

Birmhā or **Brahmā Dē,** daughter of Dalpat of Gwālior and wife of Bachrāj. Mother of Malkhān and Sulkhān. II, IV, XIII (with her sons at Sirsā, and is not heard of again after the sack of that place). XIV (referred to).

Bīr Sāhi, the Jādōṇ (Yādava) Rājā of Baurīgaṛh. V (with Malkhān's wedding party), VI (with Brahmā's ditto), VII (with Ūdan's ditto), VIII (he rides the elephant Bhūrā. His Queen is Sundarī. He has seven sons, Jōrāwar, Sūraj Mal, Indrasēn, Mōhan, Jagman, and two others. Of these Indrasēn is married to Chandrābal, the daughter of Parmāl), XI (with Lākhan's wedding party).

Bir Singh and **Hir Singh,** brothers, Rājās of Biriā, near Gōrakhpur. XII (taken prisoners by Ūdan), XIV and XVI (accompany the Kanauj forces in both the reliefs of Mahōbā), XXI (both killed by Bijai Singh of Bīkānēr).

Brahmā or **Brahmānand,** he rides the horse Harnāgar. II, V, VI (an incarnation of Arjuna. Marries Bēlā, daughter of Prithīrāj), VIII, XI, XII (merely mentioned), XIV, XV, XVIII (assassination attempted by Chauṉṛā, Tāhar, and Dhāndhū), XIX (lying sorely wounded. He is an incarnation of Arjuna), XX (Bēlā avenges him), XXI (dies of his wounds), XXIII (his cremation).

Brahmā Dē, see **Birmhā.**

Champā, Queen of Abhinandan of Balkh-Bukhārā. IX.

Champā Rānī, Queen of Gajrāj Bisēn of Jhunnāgaṛh. V.

Chand, Prithīrāj's bard and Ambassador. I.

Chandan, a son of Prithīrāj. V (invited to Malkhān's wedding), VI, XIII, XV.

Chandan of Datiā, XIV (aids Ūdan and Lākhan in the first relief of Mahōbā.)

Chandrābal, Chandrāvali, or **Chandra bel.** VIII (daughter of Parmāl and Malhnā, and married to Indrasēn, son of Bīr Sāhi of Baurīgaṛh). In the subsequent Cantos she is apparently an unmarried girl in her parents' home. XIV (claimed by Prithīrāj as a wife for Tāhar), XV, XVI, XX.

Chauṉṛā, a Nāgar Brāhmaṇ, Prithīrāj's General. He rides a one-tusker elephant. VI (is an incarnation of Drōṇa), VIII (accompanies Ālhā to Baurīgaṛh), IX (accompanies the Mahōbā army to Balkh-Bukhārā), XIII—XVI, XVIII (assassinates Brahmā), XIX—XXII, XXIII (kills Ūdan, and is killed by Ālhā). He is the Chāmuṇḍ Rāi of the Prithīrāj Rāsau, the epic describing Prithīrāj's exploits.

Chintāman, of Gōrakhpur. XIV (accompanies Ūdan and Lākhan on the first relief of Mahōbā).

Chintā Ṭhākur, of Rusnī. XII (taken prisoner by Ūdan), XIV and XVI (accompanies both the reliefs of Mahōbā).

Chittar-rēkhā, daughter of Abhinandan of Balkh-Bukhārā. IX (she changes Indal into a parrot and subsequently marries him).

Chūṛāman, a paṇḍit and astrologer of Mahōbā. IV, VI.

Dalganjan, name of the horse ridden by Tāhar the son of Prithīrāj. VI, &c.

Dalpat, of Gwālior, father of Dēbī and Birmhā. II.

Daryā Khān, one of Mīrā Tālhan's nine sons. IV.

Dasrāj (or **Dassrāj**), the Banāphar of Baksar. Comes to Mahōbā with Bachrāj, Rahmal, and Ṭōḍar, his brothers. Marries Dēbī or Diwal Dē, daughter of Dalpat of Gwālior, and has two sons, Ālhā and Ūdan, the latter posthumous. Murdered by Karinghā of Māṛō. II, III (his ghost speaks), IV (referred to).

Dēbī, Dēvī, or **Diwal Dē,** daughter of Dalpat of Gwālior, and wife of Dasrāj. Mother of Ālhā and Ūdan, whom she accompanies in their banishment. II, III, IV, IX, X, XV, XVI (accompanies them on the second relief of Mahōbā), XXIII (spoken of as dead). In Cantos VI and XXII Dēbī is given the name of 'Machhulā'.

Dēbī, a Marāṭhā of the South. A champion of Prithīrāj. VI, XVI, XXII (killed by Ūdan).

Dhāndhū, son of Khāṇḍē Rāi, Prithīrāj's brother. One of Prithīrāj's foremost champions. He rides the elephant Bhaurānand. VI, XIV, XVI, XVIII (shares in the assassination of Brahmā). XIX, XXI, XXII (kills Dhanuā Tēlī), XXIII (kills Gangā, and is killed by Lākhan).

Dhanuā Tēlī, of Rijigiri. One of the Kanauj champions. Rides the mare Bilundin. XI (accompanies Lākhan's wedding party), XV (accompanies the Kanauj army on the second relief of Mahōbā), XIX, XXII (killed by Dhāndhū).

Ḍhēwā, the Banāphar, son of Rahmal. He rides the horse Manurthā, and is a skilled soothsayer. II–V, VI (kills Sahmat), VII–XII, XIV, XV, XVII, XIX, XXII, XXIII (killed, the poem does not say by whom).

Gajmōtin, daughter of Gajrāj Bisēn, of Jhunnāgaṛh. V (married to Malkhān), XIII (becomes Satī with her dead husband), XIV (her ghost addresses Ūdan), XV (mentioned), XX (her ghost consoles Bēlā).

Gajrāj Bisēn, Rājā of Bisēn, the capital of which is Jhunnāgaṛh, and which has an outlying fortress at Pathrīgaṛh. V (his daughter, Gajmōtin married to Malkhān), VII (accompanies Ūdan's marriage party), XI, XVII.

Gangā Ṭhākur, Pamār, of Kuṛhar, mother's brother of Lākhan. He rides the she-elephant Shērsinghinī. XI, XV (steals Jagnaik's horse), XVI (accompanies the Kanauj army on the second relief of Mahōbā), XXI (kills Bijai Singh of Bīkānēr and Hīrāman of Charkhārī), XXIII (kills Bīr Bhugantā, and is killed by Dhāndhū).

Gangādhar, Rājā of Būndī. VI (accompanies Brahmā's wedding party), XI (he has two sons, Jawāhir and Mōtī, and a daughter Kusum Dē, Kusumā, or Kusmā. The daughter is married to Lākhan).

Gānjar, the four Rājās of. XIV & XV (they join the relieving forces for Mahōbā), XXII (fight on Mahōbā's side). Gānjar is apparently Bihār, Assam, Bengal, and Orissa.

Gōvind Rāj, a champion of Prithīrāj. I (killed by Hamānjamā).

Gōpī, one of Prithīrāj's sons. VI, XV.

Gurūkhā, Rājā of Bengal. XII (taken prisoner by Ūdan), XIV & XVI (accompanies both expeditions to relieve Mahōbā).

Hamānjamā, one of Jaychand's champions. I (kills Gōvind Rāj).

Hansāmal, a son of Abhinandan of Balkh-Bukhārā, IX.

Hansāman, Rājā of Kāśī (Benares). XII (taken prisoner by Ūdan).

Hansāman, name of the winged horse ridden by Indal. Apparently the same as Karilyā, ridden by Ālhā before he regained Pachsāwaḍ. XII, XVII, XXIII.

Harinandan, of the Sundarban, brother of Naipālī of Naināgaṛh. IV.

Harnāgar, name of the winged horse of Brahmā, Parmāl's son. IV (ridden by Jagnaik), VI (ridden by Rūpnā), XV (ridden by Jagnaik), XVIII (ridden by Brahmā).

Harsingh Ṭhākur, a champion of Prithīrāj. I (kills Sudhit, and is killed in battle).

Hīrāman, of Charkhārī, a champion of Prithīrāj. XXI (killed by Gangā Ṭhākur).

Hīrāman, name of the parrot of Sunwā, of Naināgaṛh. IV.

Hīrāman, name of the parrot of Chandrābal. VIII.

Hiraunjin, name of the horse of Sulkhān. VI, VII.

Hiriyā Mālin, the wife of the gardener of Phulwā, the daughter of Narpat, who was subsequently married to Ūdan. She was brought up in Naināgaṛh with Sunwā who married Ālhā, as her sister. Like Sunwā, she is a sorceress. VII.

Hir Singh, see **Bir Singh**.

Indā, Parmāl's barber. III.

Indal, son of Ālhā and Sunwā. His horse is Hansāman. V, VII, IX (changed into a parrot by Chittar-rēkhā, daughter of Abhinandan of Balkh-Bukhārā, whom he subsequently marries), X, XII (rides Hansāman), XV, XVII (rides Hansāman), XXIII (ditto. Indal disappears).

Indrasēn, son of Bīr Sāhi of Baurīgaṛh. He rides the horse Surkhā. He is married to Chandrābal, Parmāl's daughter. VIII.

Jagman, son of Bīr Sāhi of Baurīgaṛh. VIII.

Jagman, Rājā of Jinsī. XII (taken prisoner by Ūdan), XIV (joins Ūdan and Lākhan in the relief of Mahōbā).

Jagnaik, sister's son of Parmāl. IV (he rides the horse Harnāgar, which belongs to Brahmā, Parmāl's son), V, XV (he lives at Argal. Rides Harnāgar), XVII, XVIII, XXII, XXIII (killed, but not stated by whom).

Jambay, the Baghēl Rājā of Māṛō. His Queen is Kuslā or Kushlā. His sons are Karinghā or Kariyā, Anūpī, Ṭōḍar Mal, and Sūraj. His daughter is Bijaisin or Bijmā. II, III (taken prisoner by Ālhā and crushed to death in a mill by Ḍhēwā).

Jān Bēg, son of Mīrā Tālhan. IV.

Jawāhir, son of Gangādhar, Rājā of Būndī. XI.

Jaychand (Jayachandra), the last King of Kanauj, traditionally said to be a Raṭhōr. He was son of Ajaipāl, brother of Ratībhān, and uncle of Lākhan. I, II, V (invited to Malkhān's wedding), VI, X (receives Ālhā and Ūdan), XI, XII, XIV, XV (his elephant is Bhuruhī).

Jōgā and **Bhōgā**, sons of Naipālī of Naināgaṛh, and brothers of Sunwā, Ālhā's wife. IV, V (help Malkhān at his wedding), VI (accompany Brahmā's wedding party), VII (accompany Ūdan's wedding party), XII (both killed by Sātan at Paṭṭī), XV (mentioned as dead).

Jōrāwar, son of Bīr Sāhi of Baurīgaṛh. VIII.

Kabutrī, the mare of Malkhān. IV, XVII.

Kālnēm, one of the champions of Prithīrāj. XVI.

Kamlāpat, a champion of Prithīrāj. VI (killed by Jagnaik).

Kamlāpat, Rājā of Kamlā in Kāmrū (Assam). XII (taken prisoner by Ūdan).

Kānhkunr, left in charge of Delhi during Prithīrāj's absence. I (killed by Ratībhān).

Kāntāmal, son of Gajrāj Bisēn, of Jhunnāgaṛh. V, IX (accompanies Ūdan to Balkh-Bukhārā).

Karilyā, name of Ālhā's winged horse, III, IV (ridden by Rūpnā and Ālhā). It appears that this horse is afterwards called Hansāman, q. v.

Karinghā or **Kariyā,** son of Jambay of Māṛō. II, III (killed by Malkhān).

Kēśarī, Queen of Naipālī of Naināgaṛh. IV.

Kēsarī, a maid in the Baurīgaṛh palace. VIII.

Kēsarī Naṭin, a maid of Chittar-rēkhā. IX.

Khunkhun Kōri, a Mahōbā champion. V (at Malkhān's wedding), XI (accompanies Malkhān's relief force at Lākhan's wedding).

Khāṇḍē Rāi, brother of Prithīrāj and father of Dhandhū, VI.

Kunjarbad, a champion of Prithīrāj. I (killed in battle).

Kuslā or **Kushlā,** Queen of Jambay of Māṛō. III.

Kusmā, wife of Makrand of Narwar. IX.

Kusumā, Kusmā or **Kusum Dē,** daughter of Gangādhar of Būndī. XI (married to Lākhan), XV (bids farewell to Lākhan).

Lākhan, son of Ratībhān, and nephew and heir of Jaychand of Kanauj. He rides the she-elephant Bhūrī or Bhuruhī. V (a guest in Malkhān's wedding party), VI, X, XI, XIV–XVI (accompanies both forces relieving Mahōbā), XVII, XVIII, XIX (he is an incarnation of Nakula), XX–XXII, XXIII (kills Dhāndhū, and is killed by Prithīrāj).

Lākhā Pātar, Dasrāj's dancing girl. II (carried off by Karinghā), III (brought back by Ālhā and Ūdan).

Lalā Tamōlī. XI, XV (accompanies the second force relieving Mahōbā), XXII (joins in the capture of the Sandal Pillars).

Langarī Rāi, a champion of Jaychand of Kanauj. I (killed by Gōvind Rāj).

Lillī, name of the mare ridden by Māhil. III, &c.

Machhulā, another name of Dēbi or Diwal Dē, mother of Ālhā and Ūdan, VI, XXII.

Madan Gaṛariā, a Mahōbā champion. V (at Malkhān's wedding), XI (accompanies Malkhān's relief force at Lākhan's wedding).

Madan Gōpāl, Rājā of Pataunj, always coupled with Rūpan of Siraunj, both allies of Mahōbā. V, XIV.

Madhukar, of Chitaur. An Ally of Mahōbā. XIV.

Māhil, the Parihār, Ṭhākur of Uraī, a fief of Mahōbā. Brother of Malhnā Parmāl's wife, and Parmāl's chief advisor. The traitor.

His son is the loyal Abhai. Rides the mare Lillī. II, IV–XV, XVIII, XIX.

Makrand, son of Narpat, Rājā of Narwar, and brother of Phulwā, Ūdan's wife. VII, VIII, IX (his wife is named Kusmā. He accompanies Ūdan to Balkh-Bukhārā).

Makund, a champion of Prithīrāj. I (killed by Ratībhān).

Malhnā, sister of Māhil, and Queen of Parmāl. II, IV, VI, VIII, X, XI, XIV, XV, XVI, XVIII, XX, XXIII (casts the Philosopher's Stone into the lake).

Malkhān or **Malkhay**, the Banāphar. Son of Bachrāj and Birmhā. His brother is Sulkhān. He rides the mare Kabutrī. II, III, (kills Karinghā), IV, V (marries Gajmōtin, daughter of Gajrāj Bisēn of Jhunnāgaṛh, VI (in charge of fort at Sirsā), VII, VIII, IX (shuts the gates of Sirsā against Ūdan), X (stays at Sirsā after Ālhā's banishment), XI (leads a relieving force at Lākhan's marriage), XIII (he and his mare are killed), XIV (his ghost addresses Ūdan), XV (dead), XVII (joins the forces rescuing Ūdan. This Canto is wrongly placed), XXIII (dead).

Maniyā Dēvī, the patron goddess of Mahōbā. IV, &c.

Mannā Gūjar, a Mahōbā champion. IV, V, VI (kills Rahmat), VII, XI.

Manōhar, see **Murlī**.

Mān Singh, Rājā of Jagnik. V (ally of Gajrāj).

Manurthā, name of horse ridden by Ḍhēwā. III, IV, XII, XVII.

Mardan, a son of Prithīrāj. VI, XIV (killed by Brahmā), XVIII (killed by Brahmā). There is something wrong in the text, as he is killed twice, in two different battles.

Mīrā Tālhan, the Saiyid of Benares. Comes to Mahōbā with the Banāphars. He has nine sons and eighteen grandsons. The nine sons are Alī, Alāmat, Daryā Khān, Jān Bēg, Sultān, Miyān Bisārat, Surmā Khān, Kārē, and Kalyān. He is the Nestor of the cycle, and a brave warrior. He rides the mare named 'Lioness'. II, III, IV, X (accompanies Ālhā and Ūdan on banishment), XI, XIV (accompanies the first relief of Mahōbā), XV–XVI (also the second relief), XVIII, XIX (he is an incarnation of Bhīmasēna), XXII, XXIII (kills Bhūrā Mughul, and is killed by Bīr Bhugantā).

Mōhan, one of the seven sons of Abhinandan of Balkh-Bukhāra. IX.

Mōhan, of Hardīgaṛh. XIV (accompanies first relief of Mahōba).

Mōhan, son of Bīr Sāhi of Baurīgaṛh. V (accompanies Malkhān's marriage procession). VI (similarly for Brahmā), VIII.

Mōtī, a son of Prithīrāj. VI.

Mōtī, a son of Gangādhar, Rāja of Būndī. XI.

Murlī and **Manōhar**, brothers, Rājās of Cuttack. XII (taken prisoners by Ūdan). In XIV they accompany the first relief of Mahōbā, but are described as of Kalpī (almost certainly a misprint), not as of Cuttack.

Naibā, a maidservant of Dēbī or Diwal Dē. III, XV (accompanies her to Kanauj).

Naipālī, the Baghēl, Rājā of Naināgaṛh. His Queen is Kēsarī. His three sons are Jōgā, Bhōgā, and Bijyā. His daughter is Sunwā, Sunmā, or Sōnmatī, who becomes the wife of Ālhā. His brother is Harinandan of the Sundarban. He possesses a magic drum, which, when beaten, restores the dead to life. IV.

Narpat, Rājā of Narwar. VI (accompanies Brahmā's wedding party), VII (his Queen is mentioned, but not named. His son is Makrand, and his daughter is Phulwā, who becomes Ūdan's wife), VIII (his garden visited by Chandrābal's parrot).

Nūn Ālhā, see **Ālhā**.

Pachsāwaḍ, name of Dasrāj's elephant. II (carried off by Karinghā), III (recovered by Ālhā, and henceforth ridden by him), IV, X, XII, XXIII.

Paǰūn, one of Jaychand's champions. I (killed by Kunjarbad).

Papīhā, name of Dasrāj's winged horse. II (carried off by Karinghā), III (recovered by Ālhā), IV (ridden by Rupnā), XII (ridden by Jōgā at Paṭṭī, and wounded by Sātan), XV.

Parmāl, the Chandēl, Rājā of Mahōbā. His Queen is Malhnā. His two sons are Brahmā and Ranjit, and his daughter is Chandrābal. II (Viceroy of Jaychand), III–VI, VIII, IX, X (banishes Ālhā and Ūdan), XIV–XVI, XVIII, XXIII (starves himself to death).

Parsū, Rājā of Parhul. XI (accompanies the wedding party of Lākhan), XV (he and his brother Singhā are Rājās of Parhul. At the summit of his fortress there is a beacon which can be seen from Kanauj), XVI (he and Singhā accompany the second relief of Mahōbā), XXII (kills Angad, and is killed by Bīr Bhugantā).

Phuliyā Mālin, Gajmōtin's maidservant. V.

Phulwā, daughter of Narpat of Narwar. She is a reincarnation of Bijaisin. VII (married to Ūdan), IX, XVII, XX, XXIII (throws herself into a fiery pit).

Pithaurā, see **Prithīrāj**.

Prithīrāj, **Prithī**, or **Pithaurā**, the Chauhān Rājā of Delhi (sometimes called 'Bādshāh'). His Queen is Agmā. He has seven sons, viz.—Sūraj (twice recorded as killed), Chandan, Mardan (twice recorded as killed), Sardan (killed), Gōpī, Mōtī, and Tāhar (killed). His daughter is Bēlā. His brother is Khāṇḍē Rāi, the father of Dhāndhū. He rides the elephant Ādibhayankar. I (abducts Sanjōgin), V (invited to Malkhān's wedding), VI (list of his sons; Bēlā married to Brahmā, son of Parmāl), VIII (helps Ūdan on his way to Baurīgaṛh), X (demands Parmāl's submission), XI, XIII (captures Sirsā), XIV (besieges Mahōbā), XV (opposes Ālhā's return), XVI (defeated in the Battle of the Bētwā), XVII, XVIII–XIX (refuses to send Bēlā to her husband), XX–XXII, XXIII (kills Lākhan; his standard carried off by Ālhā. Ūdan states that all his seven sons have now been slain).

Puhpā Mālin, a maid in the Baurīgaṛh palace. VIII.

Pūran, Rājā of Paṭnā. IV (an ally of Naipālī of Naināgaṛh). XII (taken prisoner by Ūdan), XVI (an ally of Prithīrāj in the Battle of the Bētwā).

Pūran, of Pūrā. XIV (accompanies the first relief of Mahōbā).
Rahmal, the Banāphar of Baksar. Comes to Mahōbā with his brothers Dasrāj, Bachrāj, and Ṭōḍar, and is taken into Parmāl's service. His son is Ḍhēwā. II, IV (dead).
Rahmat, of Jinsī, a champion of Prithīrāj. VI (killed by Mannā Gūjar), XVI (again appears at the Battle of the Bētwā). There is, hence, confusion here. On both occasions he is mentioned together with Sahmat.
Randhīr, a champion of Prithīrāj. VI.
Ranjit, son of Parmāl, a younger brother of Brahmā. XIV (killed by Tāhar).
Rangā, a Paṭhān general of Jambay of Māṛō. III (killed by Ūdan).
Rāsbēndul, see **Bēndulā.**
Ratībhān, brother of Jaychand of Kanauj. His wife was Tilkā. Their son was Lākhan. I (killed by Kānhkunr), VI (mentioned).
Rūpā, maid of Queen Kuslā of Māṛō. III.
Rūpan, Rājā of Siraunj. An ally of Mahōbā. XI. Coupled with Madan Gōpāl of Pataunj in V and XIV.
Rūpnā (or **Rupnā**) **Bārī,** the Mahōbā herald. III–VII, IX, XI, XVI.
Sabjā, 'Iron grey', VIII (name of the horse of Sūraj, son of Prithīrāj), XI (name of horse of Lalā Tamōlī), XII (name of horse ridden by Bhōgā).
Sahmat, of Jinsī, a champion of Prithīrāj. VI (killed by Ḍhēwā), XVI (again appears at the Battle of the Bētwā). There is some confusion here. On both occasions he is mentioned together with Rahmat.
Sahuā, brother of Subhiā Biṛinī. XVII.
Sanjōgin, daughter of Jaychand of Kanauj. I (abducted by Prithīrāj).
S'āradā, a name given to Dēvī, as the patron goddess of Mahōbā III, &c.
Sardan, a son of Prithīrāj. VI, XIV (killed by Brahmā).
Sātan, Rājā of Paṭṭī. He rides the elephant Bhūrā. XII (kills Jōgā and Bhōga and wounds Papīhā; taken prisoner by Ūdan), XIV (accompanies the first force relieving Mahōbā).
Sēmā Bhagtin, a sorceress at Jhunnāgaṛh. V.
Shērsinghinī, name of the she-elephant ridden by Gangā Ṭhākur, Pamār, of Kuṛhar. XV.
Singhā, brother of Parsū, q.v. XV, XVI (accompanies the second force relieving Mahōbā).
Subhiā Biṛinī, a gipsy girl. XVII (changes Ūdan into a parrot and carries him off).
Sudhrit-hari or **Sudhit,** a champion of Jaychand. I (killed by Harsingh).
Sukkhā, one of the sons of Abhinandan of Balkh-Bukhāra. IX.
Sukhiā Barain, of Purwā. XX.
Sukhyā, a female slave of Prithīrāj, who absconded to Kanauj. I.
Sulkhān or **Sulkhay,** the Banāphar, posthumous son of Bachrāj and Birmhā. His brother is Malkhān. His horse is named

Hiraunjin. II, III, V, VI (in charge of Sirsā during Malkhān's absence), VII (horse named).

Sultān, one of the nine sons of Mīrā Tālhan. II, IV.

Sundarī, Queen of Bīr Sāhi of Baurīgaṛh.

Sunwā, Sunmā, or **Sōnmatī**, daughter of Naipālī, Rājā of Naināgaṛh. She is skilled in magic. Her parrot is named Hirāman. IV (married to Ālhā), V (defeats Sēmā Bhagtin in magic), VI, VII, IX, XIV (approves of Ūdan's setting out to relieve Mahōbā), XVII (her necklace stolen at Biṭhūr. She conquers Subhiā Biṛinī in magic), XX, XXIII (throws herself into a fiery pit).

Suphnā, Lākhan's elephant-driver. XVI, XXIII.

Sūraj, son of Jambay of Māṛō. III (killed by Ūdan).

Sūraj, son of Prithīrāj. He rides the horse Sabjā. VI, VIII (accompanies Ūdan to Baurīgaṛh), XIV (killed by Abhai), XVIII (killed by Brahmā). Here there is confusion, as he is twice reported killed, each time in a different battle.

Sūraj, Rājā of Gōrakhpur. XII (taken prisoner by Ūdan).

Sūraj, Rājā of Bāndā. XIII (killed by Malkhān).

Sūraj Mal, a son of Bīr Sāhi of Baurīgaṛh. VIII.

Sūrat, the Hāṛā, a champion of Prithīrāj. XIII (killed by Malkhān).

Surjā, a son of Gajrāj Bisēn of Jhunnāgaṛh. V.

Surkhā, 'Roan', name of the horse of Indrasēn, the husband of Chandrābal, and son of Bīr Sāhi of Baurīgaṛh. VIII.

Tāhar, son of Prithīrāj. He rides the horse Dalganjan. He is an incarnation of Karṇa. VI, XIII, XIV (kills Ranjit), XV, XVI, XVIII (helps to assassinate Brahmā), XIX, XX (killed by his sister, Bēlā).

Ṭankbai (Rājā), a champion of Prithīrāj. XIV (killed by Abhai).

Tēgh Bahādur, a Mahōbā champion. IV.

Tilkā, Ratībhān's wife and Lākhan's mother. XV.

Ṭōḍar, the Banāphar of Baksar. Comes to Mahōbā with his brothers Dasrāj, Bachrāj, and Rahmal, and is taken into Parmāl's service. His son is Tōmar. II, IV (dead).

Ṭoḍar, a champion of Prithīrāj. XVIII (killed by Brahmā).

Ṭōḍar Mal, a son of Jambay of Māṛō. III (taken prisoner by Ūdan and killed).

Tōmar, son of Ṭōḍar, the Banāphar. II.

Ūdan or **Ūdal**, his full name being **Uday Singh**. So called in this recension of the poem, which spells his name indifferently Ūdan or Ūdal. Mr. Waterfield prefers Ūdan, and I have followed him in this respect, using Ūdan throughout. In Bihār he is called Rūdal, i.e. Rudra Singh. He is a Banāphar, a posthumous son of Dasrāj and Dēbī, and brother of Ālhā. He rides the winged horse Bēndulā or Rāsbēndul. II (his parentage), III (attacks Māṛō; kills Anūpī, Rangā, and Sūraj), IV (accompanies Ālhā's marriage procession), V (ditto for Malkhān; list of his conquests), VI (ditto for Brahmā; treacherously stabbed by Chaunṛā), VII (marries Phulwā of Narwar), VIII (brings home Chandrābal), IX (Indal is carried off from him and Ḍhēwā), X (accompanies Ālhā in banishment), XI (accompanies Lākhan's marriage procession), XII (conquers Gānjar; claims to have conquered a number of other countries; becomes sworn brother of Lākhan), XIV (leads first relief of Mahōbā), XV–XVI (accompanies second relief of Mahōbā), XVII (is changed into a parrot, and carried off by Subhiā Biṛinī), XVIII, XIX (brings Bēlā away from Delhi), XX, XXI (cuts down Prithīrāj's Sandal Grove), XXII (carries off Prithīrāj's Sandal Pillars; kills Dēbī Marāṭhā), XXIII (killed by Chauṉṛā).

Canto I

THE WOOING OF KING PRITHĪ

The subject of this canto has no direct connexion with the rest of the Ālhā cycle. It makes no reference to Mahōbā, but tells how King Prithīrāj Chauhān of Delhi (or Dihlī) carried off Sanjōgin the daughter of Jaychand the Rāṭhōr,[1] king of Kanauj. This is a favourite subject of Rājpūt bards, for Sanjōgin, 'like another Helen, fired another Troy'. In the ensuing war, Jaychand, hard pressed by Prithīrāj, called in to his assistance the Musalmāns who had already invaded India, and who had established themselves with some success at Lahore. Prithīrāj, lulled in the arms of Sanjōgin, and neglectful of his princely duties, paid little heed to the threatening storm. When he awoke it was too late. The storm had burst in all its fury, and Prithīrāj was routed in 'The Great Battle' of A. D. 1192 at Ṭhanēsar. He was made captive and slain, and Sanjōgin ended her life upon the funeral pyre. Nor did Jaychand escape. In the following year he was driven from his kingdom by Shahabu'd-dīn, and found a watery grave in the Ganges. Thereafter North India remained subject to Musalmān domination, and Delhi became, and continued till it was captured by the English in the Mutiny, a Muhammadan capital.

The Ṛape of Sanjōgin is thus looked upon by the bardic chroniclers as a turning-point in the history of India, and as the original cause of Musalmān domination. It also explains why Jaychand espoused the cause of Parmāl of Mahōbā, when the latter was attacked by Prithīrāj. It hence forms a fitting preface to this cycle of poems.

I CALL on thee, Sandōhin fair;
  Thee, Phūlmatī, I name;
Gōvardhanī, whose guardian care
  Gained Ajaipāl his fame;

Bhaurārin, thee, who dwellest where
  Bēn Chakbai reigned as king;
To all the gods I make my prayer;
  A deed of arms I sing.[2]

[1] The tradition that Jaychand was a Rāṭhōr is incorrect. He was really a Gahaṛwār, but throughout the cycle he is called a Rāṭhōr.

[2] Sandōhin, Phūlmatī, Gōvardhanī, and Bhaurārin are all guardian goddesses of Kanauj. Ajaipāl, a famous king, was, according to the bards,

FYTTE I

King Jaychand sate in his council hall,
Long was he wrapped in thought;
'It is time,' he said, 'that my child were wed.
A bridegroom must now be brought.'

He sent his messengers through the land
To every king to go:
He held a feast for his daughter's hand:
Right goodly was the show.

All the rājās of Hind were met
That tide in the King's abode;
Carpets of price in the palace were set
When into Kanauj they rode.

The Princess' fame did thither bring
The chiefs of every race;
Only for Prithī, Dihlī's king,
There was left an empty place.

To each that met there was duly set
In the royal rites a share;
But the task of Prithī, the brave Chauhān,
Remained untaken there.

When word of this was to Jaychand brought,
His pride was angered sore;
An image in Prithī's likeness he wrought,
And set it to keep the door.

The princess came pacing through the hall,
A garland in her hand;
He, on whose neck she lets it fall,
Is her choice of all the band.

Then each in hope bent down his head,
As Sanjōgin paused beside;
And each for very shame blushed red,
As she to the next did glide.

Jaychand's father. Bēn Chakbai, or Vēṇa Chakravartī, was an ancient king of Kanauj of mythic times, and was said to have ruled the whole earth.

She sought in vain for Prithī bold,
The king of the fearless breast;
The garland she cast on the image of gold
Was there as a porter dressed.

'If one alone of the sitters on throne
Dares slight my father's word,
But one, I vow, is lofty enow
For his daughter to take as lord.'

The brows of the kings did with anger lower,
The Rājā's wrath did burn,
He bade his daughter seek her bower
And then on the morn return.

Then high their hopes on the morrow swelled
As they sat in their places all;
The garland of choice Sanjōgin held
As she moved around the hall.

By every king she silent passed,
Nor stopped, nor checked her pace;
On the image of gold her garland she cast
That stood in the porter's place.

'If only one of the kings,' she said,
'Dares slight my sire's command,
Then either his daughter will die unwed,
Or to Prithī will yield her hand.'

The brows of the kings with rage did lower,
Then Jaychand's wrath did blaze;
His daughter he shut in the prison tower,
And the rājās rode their ways.

Now in high Kanauj a day there fell,
The court of the King was set;
Rājās and chiefs a many to tell
In the chamber of presence met.

A stranger chief to the hall there came,
And fair was he in face;
King Jaychand welcomed and asked his name,
And gave him an honoured place.

But, when the stranger was seated there,
The chiefs 'gan smiling all;
'Methinks,' quoth the eldest, 'that good it were
For a mirror, O King, to call.' 20

When the mirror was brought, he gazed a space;
Then on to his neighbour passed;
Each did in turn his features trace,
Till it came to the stranger last.

And, when the mirror displayed his face,
Behold by the nostril there
The button of gold was left in place
Which none but women wear.

'Yea, sooth,' she cried, 'a woman am I,
And to Prithī the king a slave;
But to Jaychand's court for refuge I fly—
To his suitors he alway gave.'

'And if thou from Prithī the king art fled,
And reason hast had to flee,
Then thou shalt be ward of my child,' he said,
'Till she heal of her fantasy.'

Now to Prithī the king were tidings brought
How the choice of the maiden fell;
Counsel of Chand the bard he sought,
Whom ever he honoured well. 25

'And if of me thou askest a rede,
Be boune for Kanauj, I say;
And choose thee champions ready at need
To busk them with no delay.'

Then for Harsingh Thākur he called with speed,
Who did on his war array:
And Prithī was dight in a varlet's weed;
So wended the three their way.

A hasty ride they rode that tide—
Was nought their course should let;
And when they came to high Kanauj,
The court of the King was set.

Closely ranged were the seats by the wall,
  Thronged were the nobles there;
Dancers danced before them all
  With beauty beyond compare.

Behind the bard did Prithī stand,
  As he passed to hail the King;
Across his moustache the King passed hand,
  Then did Prithī's bracelets ring.

But Chand the bard, who his gesture saw,
  'Now hold, O King,' did cry;
'Thy hand o'er thy lip thou must not draw
  For such is Pithaurā Rāi.'

Quoth one of the chiefs, 'A varlet stout
  There goes with Chand, I wis:'
'Nay,' quoth another, 'I rather doubt
  King Prithī's self is this.'

'Now welcome, thou best of bards that sing,
  And see thou tell me true,
What manner of king is the Dihlī king
  Whom I so fain would view.'

'Like my servant here is the Dihlī king,
  A brave Chauhān is he;
He hath no fear what fate may bring,
  And death he laughs to see.

'And to him the gift Mahādēva gave,
  No shaft of his should err.'
Then Jaychand called for Sukhyā the slave,
  The betel to bring with her.

Into the hall fair Sukhyā came
  The betel roll to bring;
Down she cast her eyes with shame,
  For well she knew the King.

'Were I to say whom now I see,
  Pithaurā's life were shent;'
The roll to Jaychand offered she,
  And tingling back she went.

'In my garden, O bard,' the King began,
  'A place is prepared for thee;'
But Pithaurā was then an angry man,
  The porter's image to see.

Their tents were pight in the garden bright,
  The Kshatrīs their meal prepared;
To water his steed Pithaurā Rāi
  To the garden basin fared.

The fish for food came crowding round,
  So tame he could not pray;
He brake the lace his neck that bound,
  With pearls to pelt them away.

Sanjōgin stood at the casement high,
  And Sukhyā the slave also;
'See, Lady,' she cried, 'Pithaurā Rāi
  Is he who stands below.'

'His body is clad in a servant's weed;
  Can that be Dihlī's king?'
'Ay! but the swarming fish to feed
  He royal pearls doth fling.'

The princess hath taken a platter of gold
  With pearls of price heaped high;
She gave it to Sukhyā the slave to hold,
  And sent to Pithaurā Rāi.

When all the pearls of his chain were spent,
  The Rājā turned to go.
There Sukhyā stood with her head down bent,
  And her he well did know.

'Who sent thee hither, O runaway mine?'
  'I am sent by Sanjōgin fair.
Pearls I bring for the use of the King;
  She sits at the casement there.'

He raised his eyes, to the tower he passed;
  And the princess to meet him rose;
A flowery chain on his neck she cast,
  Saying, 'Thus I my husband chose.'

King Jaychand rose in the early morn
  His gifts to the bard to bring;
Chains of coral and pearls were borne
  With many a precious thing.

Shawls and kerchiefs and broidered weeds,
  Turban and crest and ring,
Elephants thirty, two hundred steeds,
  As fitted a mighty king.

When Chand on the Rājā's train set eyes,
  To Prithī he straight 'gan say,
'To mix the betel leaf, arise,
  And seemly service pay.'

Five leaves he rolled, as bade the bard;
  He handed it to the King,
But Jaychand's hand he pressed so hard
  That the blood from the nails did spring.

Thought he, 'I wis, no servant this;
  Pithaurā Rāi is his name.'
The goods he brought to the bard he gave,
  Then in wrath to his palace came.

The drum of battle to sound begun;
  He called his warrior band.
'The men of Dihlī must die each one,
  Let none of them 'scape our hand.'

For gauds and jewels Sanjōgin sent,
  And clad her in royal array;
With her maidens around to the litter she went,
  And to Prithī she took her way.

A golden censer she took in hand,
  O'er the head of the King to wave;
With a fan of flowers his face she fanned,
  And a pledge of the betel gave.

'To no house but one, will I go as a bride,
  To the Dihlī king am I plight;
But mighty the host on King Jaychand's side,
  And few are with thee to fight.

'If thou at Kanauj be in battle slain,
  O whom have I for stay?
My heart is heavy with doubt and pain.'
  Then comforted he that may.[1]

'Have thou no care though friends be few,
  Nor fear for me, sweet flower,
For this good sword a road shall hew
  To show thee Dihlī's tower.'

Then Sanjōgin went in her litter back,
  While her maidens laughed with glee;
And Prithī in mounting did not slack;
  As it were to the chase rode he.

Three kōs to the north he pitched his tent,
  Took Kālpī[2] paper and pen;
A letter in haste to Dihlī he sent,
  And summoned his bravest men.

'Gallants a hundred and champions sixteen,
  I bid you come with speed;
King Jaychand with me is at strife, I ween,
  And sore is now my need.'

The messenger took the letter in haste,
  And rode to Dihli town;
In open court was Kānhkunr placed,
  And there he bowed him down.

The letter that Prithī had given in charge
  Before the throne he cast;
Kānhkunr read the lines at large,
  Then called for his men full fast.

'Be boune for Kanauj, O Kshatrīs each;
  Do on your arms with care.'
Their hearts rose high to hear his speech,
  And soon they armour ware.

Some on elephants, some on steeds
  Took to Kanauj their way;
They were six score but wanting four
  From Dihlī rode that day.

[1] Maiden.
[2] A town on the Jumna, still famous for the manufacture of paper.

A hasty ride they rode that tide,
  Short time for rest they had;
And, when they bowed at Prithī's side,
  Their greeting made him glad.

So Harsingh then with Jaychand's men
  He bade some quarrel make;
And bring Sanjōgin's litter there
  The fire of his breast to slake.

FYTTE II

King Jaychand called for Langarī Rāi,
  And these were the words he said;
'Let none of the men of Dihlī fly;
  Go smite them every head.'

The troops were dight at the kettledrum's call,
  The din of armour rang;
And Sudhrit-hari rode forth withal,
  While loud the minstrels sang.

They had ridden of furlongs four times ten,
  A goodly sight to see;
When Harsingh with King Prithī's men
  Came marching o'er the lea.

'Thākur,' quoth Harsingh, 'hear my say!
  Sanjōgin's litter take,
And twixt us lay, the while we play
  To win so fair a stake.'

Rai Langarī with wrath waxed wode,[1]
  And redly blazed his eyen;
'If that should take the Dihlī road,
  Then shame to me and mine.'

Then strife sprang up and swords flashed out,
  And rose the mingled fray;
The Rājpūts raised the battle shout
  With cries of 'Slay' and 'Slay.'

[1] Mad.

There were some who feared, and some who fled,
And some were fighting slain;
Yea! lacking the head they rose from the dead
To deal their blows again.

Friend from foe might no man know,
So close the warriors stood;
King Prithī's men laid hundreds low
Left weltering in their blood.

When horse and foot a many fell,
Then Sudhit loud did cry,
'I rede thee, Thākur, guard thee well,
For now thy death is nigh.'

Then Harsingh spurred to meet his foe;
His sword has Sudhit ta'en,
And thrice he dealt a doughty blow,
But thrice he dealt in vain.

So when in two his falchion flew,
'Mine hour is come,' he said.
Then Harsingh drew and whirled his sword,
And smote off Sudhit's head.

Yet still they waged the lusty fray,
And still they slaughtered on;
They did not hold their hands that day
Till stars above them shone.

When tidings were to Jaychand brought
How Sudhit fell in fight,
The camp was all with grief distraught;
None cooked his meal that night.

'Bring the litter now, Rāi Langarī, thou
To the field,' did Jaychand say;
'But when Prithīrāj would bear it off,
Then set thou on and slay.'

And the Rājā called for Hamānjamā,
'If the litter to Dihlī go,
It will be a shame to my fathers' fame
Seven ages back and moe.'

In haste arose Sanjōgin fair
  When the news to the palace spread;
Robes and jewels she donned with care
  And dyed her feet with red.

Soon as she sat in the litter then,
  They bore away the bride;
All Kanauj's bravest men
  Went marching by her side.

When to Prithī the King they did tidings bring
  That the litter in field was placed,
Gallants a hundred and champions sixteen,
  He called them forth in haste.

'Now,' quoth Prithī, 'now the hour
  But once in life we see;
And bring my bride unto Dihlī tower,
  Then rich shall your guerdon be.'

Merry of mood were Prithī's men,
  With spears were soon arrayed;
They mounted on horses and elephants then,
  There was not a man delayed.

Good swords twain each knight hath ta'en,
  They did not fear to die;
And, when they came to the battle plain,
  Stout Harsingh loud did cry,

'Set down the litter, Hamān̲jamā,
  So back to Kanauj ye fare.'
'And where', cried he, 'may the Rājpūt be
  Can this litter to Dihlī bear?'

'Now speak not wildly, Hamān̲jamā,
  But set the litter down;
And he whose play shall gain the day
  Shall win it for his crown.'

'Lay on then,' quoth Rāi Langarī.
  'Let none go scatheless back.'
Then warshouts rang and swords outsprang,
  To close they were not slack.

And heads of men and necks of steeds
  And elephants' trunks were lopped;
Friend from foe might no man know,
  So fast the wounded dropped.

'King Prithī's champion here I stand,'
  Stout Gōvind Rāj 'gan say.
'Set down,' he cried, 'your bonny bride,
  And take your homeward way.'

With that Hamāṉjamā drew his blade,
  And stoutly they set to;
The heroes twain right deftly played,
  So fast their swordstrokes flew.

So keen a stroke Hamāṉjamā gave,
  He smote off Gōvind's head;
But still the corse whirled round its glaive:
  Good sooth! a sight of dread.

Full many a warrior there it slew,
  Rai Langarī's self as well;
Till o'er it they threw a banner of blue,[1]
  Then lifeless down it fell.

Three gallants of Prithī has Lākhan slain,[2]
  And fiercely swelled the fight;
The litter was stained with a crimson stain,
  I wis a goodly sight.

About it then thronged Jaychand's men,
  They fenced it round with shield:
And Prithī has called for Kunjarbad,
  Came hastening o'er the field.

'King Jaychand's armies press me sore,
  On thee my hopes are bent;
If the litter be ta'en to Kanauj again,
  Then is our Chauhānī shent.'

[1] This seems the orthodox procedure in such cases. In Canto XIV Bhūrā Mughul quiets the headless bodies of Abhai and Ranjit in the same way.—G. A. G.

[2] An error of translation. The passage means literally, 'The three gallants of Prithī were slain after killing lākhs of knights'. At this time Lākhan was only three years old. See Canto XXIII, p. 272.—G. A. G.

Never a word spake Kunjarbad,
He strode to meet the foe;
'Now one shall be slain on the battle plain,
And one shall victor go.'

Then Kunjarbad a red bow drew,
And a weighty bolt it cast;
He aimed full true, and dried it flew,
So far through the breast it passed.[1]

When the champion fell, then Kunjarbad
The litter raised on high;
Beating the drum the Chauhāns did come,
And they shouted Victory.

Five kōs[2] in turns they bare the load,
I wis they did not slack;
Following still with shouts of 'Kill,'
Came Jaychand on their track.

FYTTE III

All through the night till morning broke,
By moonlight pressed they on;
Then crows awoke and kōils[3] spoke,
And out the bright sun shone.

And even as sprang the morning tide,
King Jaychand barred their way;
'Shall they carry the bride to Dihlī?' he cried,
'Set on, my friends, and slay.'

Then bullets and shafts in deadly rain,
And swords and spears they ply;
The valiant hearts in the ranks fell slain,
The cowards from field did fly.

How should I tell what gallants fell
On either part that day,
As now toward Dilhī the litter moved,
And now did Kanaujward sway!

1 The man who was killed was named Pajjūn.—G. A. G.
2 A kōs is about two miles.
3 The Indian cuckoo.

Yet on and on their way they won,
  As knight by knight went down;
Hour by hour, kōs by kōs,
  Till they came to Sōrōṉ[1] town.

And, when they came to Sōrōṉ town,
  King Jaychand barred their way;
'Ho! Prithī, wouldst win a thief's renown,
  That thou stealest thy lady gay?

'Set the litter down by Sōrōṉ town
  For the best in the battle play.'
Then swords were drawn and ranks closed in
  And fiercely swelled the fray.

Quoth King Jaychand to his Rāthōr clan,
  'Now rouse ye, brethren all;
Full seldom birth in the body of man
  To the spirit of each doth fall.

'If ye flee the brave Chauhān before,
  And leave him unscathed to go,
When will ye meet him in field once more
  Your battle deeds to show?'

Then each was ready his life to sell,
  And closely swords were plied;
Foe from friend might no man tell
  As flowed the crimson tide.

There was no breeze from east or west,
  The air was heavy and wan,
The winds of heaven were all at rest
  As the pitiless steel clashed on.

O bitter and sore was waged the war
  At Sōrōṉ on Gangā's side,
Where thirty and five of Prithī's knights
  Midst slaughtered hundreds died.

Yet still the litter was moving on,
  Kanauj still following hard;
When seven kōs of the way were won,
  Again their path they barred.

[1] On the Ganges, about half-way to Delhi.

Now to Ratībhān[1] the news they bore
  That the litter was carried away,
That Lākhan was slain and many more
  At Sōrōṉ in fierce sword-play.

Scarce had he heard the messenger out,
  He called for his elephant straight;
The howda they bound with silk ropes stout,
  So mounted he at the gate. 15

First he blessed the great God's name
  And all the gods as well;
As through the gate of Kanauj he came,
  An evil omen fell.

Clouded with doubt was the Pandit's face,
  And many a word 'gan say;
'The omens bode thee an evil case;
  Thou must not ride to-day.'

'O what are omens of good or ill
  To Kshatrīs on steel that feed?
How in Kanauj can I hold me still,
  And the King my help doth need?

'If Prithī the litter to Dihlī bore,
  And I were alive to heed,
If folk called shame on Ratībhān's name,
  That, that were death indeed.

'Counsel me not a counsel base,
  Though the iron age this be;
From the open gate if I turn my face,
  I have broken my Rājpūtī.' 20

Now Prithī still with the litter fled,
  Still Jaychand followed hard;
Ratībhān thither his elephant sped,
  And soon the way he barred.

'No litter to Dihlī shall pass this way
  Till ye each his head shall lack.'
Quoth Makund, 'Try all the arts ye may,
  But ye shall not win it back.'

[1] Jaychand's brother. Lākhan was his son and Jaychand's nephew. The news of Lākhan's death is an error. The text should be translated 'that many lākhs of knights were slain'.—G. A. G.

Quoth Ratībhān, 'Set it betwixt us twain,
  A prize for the best in fight.'
Then he set the litter aside on the plain,
  And soon were the heroes dight.

'Strike first, Makund, or in paradise
  Thou wilt mourn for thy wasted chance.'
Then full at his face he aimed in a trice,
  But he warded off the lance.

With that Makund his good sword drew,
  And the name of the great God praised;
But the blade in his stroke to pieces flew,
  When Ratībhān's shield was raised.

When only the heft in his hand was left,
  He wist that death was near;
'That I stand this day of my sword bereft,
  'Tis the anger of God I fear.'

Then Ratībhān soon his good sword drew.
  He drew it from out his belt;
'Sore strokes of thine I have tholèd two,
  And now must mine be felt.'

With that he struck a stroke full sore,
  The shield was raised on the left,
Through the rhinoceros targe he tore
  And the bosses of silver cleft.

The rings of mail did the stroke divide,
  Shoulder to chine he hewed;
Thus Makund died the litter beside,
  And all men silent stood.

But, while they gazed like men amazed,
  To the rest king Prithī spoke,
'If the prize be won back from our very gates,
  Then our Rājpūtī is broke.'

Then all the gallants who lived as yet
  Grasped sword and shield in hand;
Around the bride they were steadfast set,
  And pressed to the Dihlī land.

The earth that day did tremble and shake
  And the guardian nymphs with fright;
King Indra all on his throne did quake,
  And Śiva on Kailās height.

'On whom will the wrath of God betide?'
  They looked in awe to tell,
As swords were yet more closely plied
  And many a warrior fell.

And the boundary flood ran red with blood
  Two kōs from Dihlī town;
But Ratībhān's onset none withstood,
  Chief after chief went down.

'To Dihlī', he cried, 'ye shall bear no bride.
  Try all your schemes in vain.'
At four fields' span from the city gate
  Was the last of the champions slain.

When tidings came to Kānhkuṇr tried,
  That the champions all are slain,
Only Prithī and Chand are left, and the bride
  Is borne to Kanauj again.

He made himself boune in his war array,
  And called for his elephant straight,
To the howda he mounted without delay,
  And rode through Dihlī gate.

'Ho! Thākur', he cried, 'set down the bride,
  And try the fight with me.'
Nor was Ratībhān slack the bout to bide.
  'Now warily sit', quoth he.

Ratībhān swung on the left his mace,
  And on Rāma's name did call;
As the elephant passed he smote at his face,
  And the blow on the shield did fall.

Then Ratībhān drew his falchion bright,
  And aimed from the right his blow;
On Kānhkuṇr's forehead he struck with might,
  And fast the blood 'gan flow.

'Now, hearken, Prithī,' Kānhkuṉr cried,
'And see thou take good tent,
If back to Kanauj they bear thy bride,
Then is our Chauhānī shent.

'Staunch for a time this wound so wide,
Until I have slain my foe.'
Then Prithī took an arrow in hand,
And fitted his good red bow.

He pierced the sides of the gaping wound
With the shaft that could not stray;[1]
When the red blood flow ceased from Kānhkuṉr's brow
He turned again to the fray.

At Dihlī's gate were swords well plied
By either chief that day;
Kānhkuṉr cleft through mail and side,
And hewed the shoulder away.

Through Ratībhān's stroke the crimson tide
From Kānhkuṉr's brow gushed down;
Side by side they dropped and died
At the gate of Dihlī town.

Prithī the king and Chand the bard,
The litter in they bore;
Sanjōgin passed to the palace at last,
And bade them close the door.

'Now go in peace and high renown,
Nor deem thy prowess vain;
All the champions of Dihlī town
King Jaychand's arms have slain.

'Now go in peace,' said Chand, 'O king,
Thou hast left to Pithaurā none.'
The wooing of Prithī thus I sing.
So Rājpūt brides were won.

[1] This was the famed magic arrow of Prithīrāj which never missed the mark. Even if aimed at a mere voice, it hit the unseen speaker.—G. A. G.

CANTO II

THE NINE-LĀKH CHAIN

THE story proper of the cycle begins with this canto. I give a brief abstract of its contents, as it displays the groundwork of the whole.

Kariyā or Karinghā, son of Jambay, the Baghēl Rājā of Mārō, proposes to go to the Jājmaū Ghāṭ on the Ganges (about five miles from Cawnpore) to bathe at the festival of the Dasahrā. His father dissuades him, saying that he (Jambay) has paid no revenue to Rājā Jaychand of Kanauj for twelve years, that Jajmaū belongs to Kanauj, and that the Rājā's people will take him prisoner there. Kariyā refuses to listen to him and sets out, his sister Bijaisin or Bijmā, as he starts, asking him to bring her some keepsake from Jājmaū. Arrived there, he bathes, gives gifts to Brāhmaṇs, and searches in the bazaar for a nine-lākh necklace (i.e. a necklace worth 900,000 rupees). There he meets Māhil, the Parihār, who was Ṭhākur of Uraī and brother of Malhnā, the Queen of Parmāl, the Chandēl Rājā of Mahōbā.[1] Māhil asks him what he, a prince, does in so petty a place. Kariyā explains, and he replies, 'My sister Malhnā has a nine-lākh necklace. She is married to Parmāl of Mahōbā. The Chandēls are weak and broken, and if you go there you can take the necklace and no one will oppose you.' So Kariyā sets off to Mahōbā.

Here the story turns back to tell of four brothers, Banāphars[2] of Baksar (Buxar in Bihār), Dasrāj (or Dassrāj), Bachrāj (or Bachchhrāj) Rahmal, and Ṭōḍar. They have had a boundary dispute with Mīrā Tālhan of Benares, a Saiyid who had nine sons[3] and eighteen grandsons, all mighty men of war. They first have a good fight over the dispute, and then set off amicably together to Rājā Jaychand's court at Kanauj, in whose rule this territory was, to have it settled. Their road leads through Mahōbā, and when they get there they are told that Rājā Parmāl of Mahōbā is Jaychand's viceroy, and that

[1] Mahōbā was once owned by Parihārs, but they had been expelled by the Chandēls. Māhil secretly bore the old grudge, and while openly friendly, spent his whole time in traitorously scheming against Parmāl, his own brother-in-law. Uraī was a fief of Mahōbā.

[2] The Banāphars are an old Rājpūt tribe, descendants of a Vanaspara who was a governor of Magadha under the emperor Kanishka, at about the time of the beginning of the Christian era. See 'The Journal of the Bihar and Orissa Research Society', vol. vi (1920), p. 150.

[3] The nine sons were Alī, Alāmat, Daryā Khān, Jān Bēg, Sultān, Miyāṉ Bisārat, Surmā Khān, Kārē, and Kalyān.

they can get their dispute settled there without going to Kanauj, where they might have to wait three years for a decision. So they put up in a house in the city gate, the four Banāphars on one side, and the Saiyids on the other. There they have been waiting three days when Kariyā arrives from Jājmaū.

He tells them to go in and call Queen Malhnā to come out with the nine-lākh necklace. They refuse, and he orders his attendants to hew down the gates. On this the Banāphar party reflects that they have drunk Mahōbā water for four days, and that any disgrace alighting on the Chandēls would affect them also; so they set upon Kariyā and his men, make a terrace of heads and a pile of bodies, and put the rest to flight. For this action Parmāl is very grateful. He appoints Mīrā Tālhan commander of his army, and adopts the Banāphars as sons, making them lords of his 'milk, sons, and riches', or of all that is dear to him. He also gets Dasrāj and Bachrāj married to the two daughters of Rājā Dalpat of Gwālior, Dēbī (or Diwal Dē, also called Machhulā), and Birmhā (or Brahmā), and gives them a hamlet, a mile from Mahōbā, to live in, which they call Daspurwā (or Dasrapur or Das'harpurwā). Here they dwell for some time, and sons are born to them, viz. Ālhā (or Nūn Ālhā) and Ūdan (or Uday Singh) to Dasrāj and Dēbī, Malkhān and Sulkhān to Bachrāj and Birmhā, Ḍhēwā to Rahmal, and Tōmar to Ṭōḍar. Parmāl and Malhnā also have a son called Brahmā (to be distinguished from Birmhā or Brahmā, the wife of Bachrāj), so that there are seven boys in all. But a month before the birth of Ūdan and Sulkhān, Kariyā comes by night at Māhil's instigation, attacks Daspurwā, sets it on fire, stabs Dasrāj and Bachrāj while they sleep and cuts off their heads, which he carries off and hangs up over the gate of Māṛō. He also takes away the elephant Pachsāwaḍ, the horse Papīhā, the dancing-girl Lākhā-pātar, and the nine-lākh necklace, and returns in eight days to his home.

The original compilation of the Ālh Khaṇḍ under (Sir Charles) Elliott's auspices was based on the joint memories of several professional reciters, and Mr. Waterfield had doubts as to the authenticity of this introductory canto. He says:—

> 'I strongly suspect this to be spurious, though not from the want of opening invocation, for it is admittedly incomplete and breaks off abruptly in the garden scene, verse 19 of the next canto, which begins really with the 37th verse. (I have rearranged some of the verses and divided them differently to make the hiatus less evident.) The suspicious points to my mind are the following:—King Jambay has nothing to do with the raid which is carried out in defiance of his instructions. He appears afterwards as the bitterest enemy of the Banāphars.
>
> Bijaisin, here not an infant, is still an unmarried girl some fifteen years after.
>
> Māhil's spite against his own sister is perfectly unaccountable. It had afterwards at least the excuse of Ūdan's outrages.
>
> Mīrā, who has already grandsons bearing arms before Dasrāj is married, appears afterwards as a brother in arms of the latter and was, probably, not very much older.

The wives of the Banāphars, here of noble birth, are afterwards said to be of the cowherd caste, and the family to be degraded in consequence.

The death of Dasrāj took place at Mahōbā according to one account, at Māṛō according to the other.

Though the geography of the ballads is somewhat vague, the whole incident would scarcely have been made to depend upon Mahōbā being in the direct road from Baksar (Buxar) to Kanauj.

The foreign origin of the Banāphars is quite opposed to Mahōbā traditions, in which they are said to have been the hereditary generals of the State, and at feud with the house of Māhil, the hereditary minister; but, as the Mahōbā legend makes Bachrāj an ancestor of Dasrāj, and Malkhān to be of a different family, we cannot accept this as a certain discrepancy.

The decisive point, however, in my opinion, is the description of Parmāl as the minister of Kanauj on leave in his own territories.

I do not think there is the least allusion elsewhere to Mahōbā being dependent on Kanauj. Indeed, if any suzerainty was claimed, it was by Delhi. This, then, added to the extension of the Kanauj State to Baksar and the claim at least of sovereignty asserted over Māṛō, leads me to affirm without hesitation that the whole ballad was concocted at Kanauj as an introduction to the real legend. Still it does serve as an introduction of a sort, and for the sake of the story therefore I have retained it.

Where Māṛō was I cannot say. It is certainly not Mārwār (Jōdhpur), as is, I believe, assumed by the bards. Nor is it Rīwā, the modern Baghēlkhaṇḍ. Its neighbourhood to and dominion over Jhānsī[1] I conceive to be a poetical embellishment, unless there is a second fort of that name. It was close to the Narmadā (Nerbudda) and on the further side. This may perhaps furnish a clue for identification to some one who is acquainted with that part of the country, which I am not.'

On the above I may be permitted to make the following remarks. I do not think that the question of Bijaisin's age need disturb us. The bards little heeded such discrepancies. As for Bijaisin, the point raised by Mr. Waterfield is not the only difficulty. It is true that she is described as born some years before Ūdan, and is yet a marriageable girl when he is grown up. But that is not all. At the end of Canto III she dies, and is subsequently born again as Phulwā, princess of Narwar. Phulwā has to grow up and become marriageable herself, yet when Ūdan weds her he is still young. In the same way we meet other discrepancies, such as that noted about Mīrā Tālhan, but I do not think that they suggest anything but heedlessness on the part of bards who wish to tell a good story.

Māhil's spite was directed not against his sister, but against Parmāl, the Chandēl. The Parihārs, of which clan Māhil was a leader, had once lorded it over Mahōbā, but had been ousted by the Chandēls. This fully accounts for his hate, though it does not justify his uniform treachery.

[1] Indeed the name of Jhānsī only dates back as far as the reign of Jahāngīr.

So far as I have studied the poem, it seems that the story that the wives of the Banāphars were cowherds (*Ahīrans*) by caste was spread by their enemy Māhil. Often in the poem whenever a marriage connexion with Mahōbā is mooted, it is not only the caste of the Banāphars, but that of Parmāl, the Chandēl himself, that is contemned. Now it is a fact that the origin of the Chandēls is suspect. They themselves claim to be descended from a Brāhmaṇ woman who was espoused by the moon, but unkind sceptics deny this and suggest that they are of mixed origin, partly Gōṇḍ and partly Rājpūt.[1] Nor do I see anything improbable in Parmāl being a vassal of the powerful Jaychand. The Mahōbā territory adjoined that of Kanauj, the two being separated only by the River Bētwā. The poem nowhere states that Mahōbā was subordinate to Delhi. The quarrel between Prithīrāj and Parmāl (in which the latter was helped by Jaychand) was due to an altogether different cause which will be explained in the introductory remarks to Canto XIII.

As to Māṛō, I would suggest that it is probably the ancient and famous town of Māṇḍū or Māṇḍōgaṛh (pronounced Māṇṛōgaṛh) in the Dhār State of Central India. It is within a short distance of the Narbadā River, but not on the further side. It is about 350 miles in a straight line from Mahōbā, and the poem represents the distance between Māṛō and Mahōbā as sixteen days' journey, but as eight days for a rapid foray.

On the whole I do not think that it is possible to speak of any portion of the Lay as spurious or as genuine. It is a collection of folk-ballads, dealing with the ancient history of Mahōbā and Kanauj, which were carried in the memory of professional bards and never reduced to writing, but came down to the present day through generations of singers in many differing versions. There was no religious impulse to ensure the retention of a correct text, and generation after generation has altered them and added to them (our present version speaks even of 'Sappers and Miners', and of 'shells') as fancy suggested, while always retaining the main thread of the story.

Before concluding these remarks, I may point out that Parmāl was celebrated as the possessor of the philosopher's stone and of five magic horses which could fly, named Harnāgar, Rāsbēndul or Bēndulā (given to Ūdan), Hansāman,[2] Papīhā (given to Dasrāj), and (a mare) Kabutrī (given to Malkhān). These are often mentioned in the following pages.

As in other cases, the chronology of the bards is careless about these horses, which are as fresh and trustworthy at the beginning of the story as at the end. This is specially the case with Dasrāj's Papīhā, which takes an active part in the campaign of Ālhā's marriage.

[1] See Hamīrpur Gazetteer (1909), pp. 126 ff.

[2] Elsewhere called Karilyā, and under this name was ridden by Ālhā.

It fell upon the Dasahrā[1] tide,
  When folk to the Gangā go,
To King Jambay his son did say,
  As they sat in the fort Marò:—

'Now let me ride to Gangā's side,
  To the Jājmaū[2] holy fair,
Give the Brahmans a gift and make my shrift,
  As I bathe in the waters there.'

His hand he caught—'That Jājmaū ghàt
  Is in Jaychand's[3] land, my son;
From the far sunrise to the western skies
  Doth Jaychand's lordship run.

'Twelve years my Mārō fort I keep
  And have paid no tribute in;
But thee will he cast in dungeon deep
  If into his land thou win.'

'The quarrel is thine, O Baghēl Rāi,[4]
  The quarrel is none of mine;
But if to Jaychand's court I hie,
  I well may quit the fine. 5

'I will bear thy load as a good son ought,
  Since I am King Jambay's heir;
But whoso shall bar me from Gangā's ghàt,
  Himself my sins must bear.'

The kettledrums sound and the trumpets bray,
  Karinghā hath his will;
But he took no heed of his father's rede,[5]
  So his journey shall be for ill.

[1] The great feast in October at the close of the rains, when kings go forth to battle and the exploits of Rāma are celebrated.

[2] Jājmaū on the Ganges, just below Cawnpur, which has now eclipsed the more ancient settlement.

[3] King of Kanauj, head of the Rāṭhōr clan now settled in Jōdhpur, and cousin and rival of King Prithī of Delhi. Their jealousies were the chief cause of the overthrow of the Hindū empire by the Muhammadans. This ballad, being the Kanauj version, loses no opportunity of magnifying its birthplace.

[4] Prince.

[5] Counsel.

Bijaisin fair came down the stair
To see her brother ride;
'What bring ye back from Jājmaū fair?
What bring ye me?' she cried.

'With a nine-lakh chain[1] will I greet thee again,'
So Kariyā rode away;
And he gave his gift, and he made his shrift,
And now will his promise pay.

He sought in the fair each rich booth there,
He searched each merchant's pack;
Quoth Māhil, 'How? and a King's son thou—
Dost chaffer for chains of lac?'[2]

'No chain of lac, but a nine-lakh chain
I seek for my sister dear.'
'A nine-lakh chain may a stout man gain,
And that with little fear.

'A nine-lakh chain my sister wears;
Mahōbā's Queen she hight;[3]
And there lives not a man in that Chandēl clan
To buckle on belt for fight.'

Far out in the east in Baksar[4] dwelt
The bold Banāphar crew;
There was Bachrāj tall, and Dasrāj withal,
And Rahmal and Tōdar too.

And Mīrā Tālhan the Saiyid[5]
In Banāras then abode;
And by his banner nine stoût sons
And eighteen grandsons rode.

Their clothes were black, their trappings black,
On horses black they rode;
And black upon the Saiyids' heads
The Mughul[6] turban showed.

[1] That is, worth £90,000.
[2] Sealing-wax. [3] Is called.
[4] Or Buxar on the Ganges, below Ghazipur and Banāras (Benares).
[5] Descendant of the Prophet.
[6] Of course that Tartar tribe, the Mughuls or Moguls, was not heard of in India till the invasion of Taimur in the fourteenth century.

They met and fought on a border feud,
Then dressed them to ride straightway,
All to the court of King Jaychand,
Where in Kanauj[1] he lay.

And, when they came to Mahōbā town,
The four Banāphars cried,
'What road is ours to Jaychand's court,
Where we are boune to ride?'

'And what would ye do in Jaychand's court?
And why do ye ride so far?'
'O! we fell out on a border feud
In the fat lands of Baksàr.

'We made good play with our swords all day,
Yet we were not a whit agreed;
So now to Kanauj we take our way
And there our cause will plead.'

'Now listen my rede and take you heed,
For good is my rede I trow;
To Kanauj if ye ride, ye may three years bide
And yet no sentence know.

'But hither is come Parmāl the King,
King Jaychand's viceroy he;
So plead your cause in the Chandēl's court
And abide you by his decree.'

Now void was then the gateway house,
And down they lighted there;
The four Banāphars took the right,
To left the Saiyids were.

They had not dwelt in Mahōbā town
A day but barely four,
When Jambay's son with his braves each one,
Came riding to the door.

[1] Kanauj, on the Ganges between Farrukhabad and Cawnpur, one of the most ancient cities of India, and shortly before the date of the ballad the most powerful among them.

'Ho warriors! hear, and my message bear
To these proud sons of the moon,[1]
That Malhnā the Queen must do homage, I ween,
With her nine-lakh necklace soon.'

'We dwell in this place but for four days' space;
Such message we may not bear,'
'Bring axes then to the gate, my men;
So win we a booty rare.'

Then axes were plied to the timbers wide,
Till beam and pillar shook;
Up rose the suitors from either side
And hasty counsel took.

'Four days have we drunk from the Chandēl's well;
Their shame must fall on us;
'Twere better dearly our lives to sell
Than to lose our honour thus.'

Wherever the ranks stood thickest,
The Banāphars' swords flashed out;
What horseman charged the bravest,
The Saiyids turned to rout.

They made a terrace of heads that day
And piled a heap of slain;
So Kariyā took his homeward way
Without his nine-lakh chain.

When the King Parmāl and Malhnā heard
What champions saved their State,
They greeted them well with grateful word
As they sat by the city gate.

They took their hands and led them up
To Mahōbā's palace fair;
And where stood the throne of the moonsprung race,
They seated Bachrāj there.

'Ye are lords of my milk, my son, and my wealth,'
To the brothers the Rājā said;
And captain of all his host of war
Stout Mīrā Tālhan was made.

[1] The Chandēls of Mahōbā were said to derive their name and descent from the moon-god.

'Now hear, my lord, a woman's word,'
  Queen Malhnā then did say,
'Find them fair wives in the Chandēl land,
  And here will they dwell for aye.'

Then King Parmāl did the barbers[1] call,
  And he gave the bridesmen's fee;
And, 'Who', he said, 'hath daughters to wed,
  Let him know there are sons with me.'

King Dalpat in Gwālior held his state,
  He sent gifts to the Chandēl's door,
His daughters Dēvī and Birmhā to mate,
  And both one mother bore.

For Dasrāj and for Bachrāj
  They were taken by King Parmāl;
Queen Malhnā sang the marriage songs:
  'Twas joy and gladness all.

Beneath one roof two brides were made;
  King Parmāl brought them home;
The Queen to her daughters welcome bade,
  At the gate of the painted dome.

The nine-lakh chain that day full fain
  On Dēvī's neck she hung;
The younger queen a necklace gave,
  And marriage songs they sung.

'Now hear, my lord, thy Rānī's word;
  Our sons are fully grown;
Scant room have they got in our palace, I wot:
  They need a home of their own.'

So a hamlet a mile from Mahōbā wall
  They gave the Banāphars to dwell;
And Dasrāpur[2] to this day they call
  Where Ālhā's birth befell.

For within that year did on earth appear
  Of the stout Banāphar race,
Ālhā and Malkhān, Dhēwā and Tōmar,
  Four boys of a goodly grace.

[1] The barber is always the most important personage in marriage negotiations.
[2] Or Das'harpurwā, or Daspurwā, a hamlet near Mahōbā.

Now from Māhil the news of Mahōbā town
  To Mārō's fortress came;
On a midnight mirk came Karinghā down,
  And the hamlet he set aflame.

He stabbed Bachrāj while the hero slept,
  And he Dasrāj' head did smite;
And the treasures of price in the palace kept
  He carried away that night.

The elephant Dasrāj rode has he ta'en,
  And Lākhā the dancer sweet,
The caskets twain with the nine-lakh chain,
  And Papīhā the charger fleet.

And he has fixed the Banāphars' skulls
  On the gate of Mārō wall;
And the Queens did sing to his welcoming;
  'Twas joy and gladness all.

Yet within a month the widows bare
  Sulkhān and Uday too;
And these with Brahmā, Parmāl's heir,
  Seven lads together grew.

Canto III

THE MĀRŌ FEUD

This canto describes the vengeance taken by Ālhā and Ūdan on Jambay and Kariyā of Mārō for their father Dasrāj's murder. As explained by Mr. Waterfield in the introduction to Canto II, the division here differs slightly from that of the original. The earlier verses of this canto as here printed form the conclusion of Canto II of the latter. No abstract of the story is necessary; but an allusion may be made to the pathetic story of Bijaisin. As she lay dying she prophesied concerning Malkhān, who slew her:

> So shalt thou die with no brother by,
> Unhelped in an open plain.

This prophecy is fulfilled in Canto XIII, when Malkhān falls on the bloody field of Sirsā. Bijaisin and Ūdan were reunited. She was born again as Phulwā, princess of Narwar, and, as told in Canto VII, there Ūdan won her for his bride.

Ganēś,[1] with thee begins my rhyme;
  To thee I raise the psalm;
Right early in the morning time
  I praise the name of Rām.[2]

I sing to thee, Saraswatī,[3]
  I worship Durgā's [4] feet,
Whose Kāngrā,[5] spread with robes of red,
  Glows down each stately street.

I duly bade the flower-maid,
  Her mulsari [6] chain to bring,
For the Queen whose delight is in Dhauragir [7] height,
  Who shall teach my lips to sing.

[1] The elephant-headed god of wisdom, invoked at the beginning of every undertaking.

[2] Rāma, King of Ayōdhyā or Oudh, the modern Faizabad. The most popular incarnation of Vishnu in the Upper Provinces.

[3] Goddess of learning and poetry and wife of Brahmā.

[4] Wife of Śiva, also known as Kālī, the destroyer.

[5] Kōṭ Kāngrā, a famous fort in the mountains of the Punjab.

[6] *Mimusops elengi*, the fragrant, white, star-like flowers of which are much used for garlands.

[7] I suppose the same with Dhaulāgir or Dhawalgiri, the White Peak, the highest point of the western Himālaya. Durgā is the daughter of the Himālaya Mountain.

From the south she came with her eyes aflame,
And thundered along her way;
Her trident she bare, and the flesh she tare
Of the demons she made her prey.

On a lioness she rode to the curst ones' abode,
Mahishâsur[1] and Raktbīj she slew;
As to Kāśī[2] she did come, she struck the battle drum,
And the tyrants of the earth overthrew.

FYTTE I

It fell on a day as the boys would play,
Quoth Ālhā to the Queen,
'Of all thy sons, dear mother, say
Am I not the swordsman keen?'

She laughed and blessed him where he stood—
'Long live my dearest son;
My boys shall all be swordsmen good;
I drink[3] to every one.'

Then the seven with robes did Malhnā deck,
On each wrist a bangle of gold;
A sword for each hand and a shield for each neck,
Dakhnī[4] turbans and plumes all told.

She called to Indā, the barber:
'Take these for my lord to see.'
Up rose Parmāl and kissed them all,
And gave them sweetmeats free.

But when the court was risen,
The Rājā called the Queen,
'Now woe to thee, O Rānī,
That thou let these boys be seen.'

Queen Malhnā cried, 'Now do not chide,
Sweet lord, nor hold this wrong;
Milk, sons, and riches who can hide,
Or cage such eaglets long?'

[1] Mahisbāsur, the buffalo demon, and Raktbīj, two Titans slain by Durgā in the wars of the gods. Under her name Śāradā she seems to have been the tutelary deity of Mahōbā.

[2] A name of Benares.

[3] Only water, be it understood, but it seems to have been considered as efficacious as our drinking of healths in wine.

[4] Made in the South or, as we have called it, the Deccan.

A right good steed of the fairy[1] breed
  She hath given to each to ride ;
'My swordsman boy shall I count him indeed,
  Who brings game from the forest wide.'

They have ta'en their way ere break of day,
  They have spurred ere rise of sun ;
Three watches they ride through the forest wide,
  But wild deer find they none.

They turned them homeward one by one,
  They reached Mahōbā gate ;
Only Ūdan, the youngest son,
  Doth still in the forest wait.

'How can I go to Mahōbā town
  And before my mother stand ?
I have promised her game ; it were lasting shame
  To go with an empty hand.'

Queen Śāradā[2] lo ! in the form of a doe
  From a thicket beside up starts ;
And away they fly to proud Urai,[3]
  And into a garden she darts.

And over the wall flies Rāsbēndùl,
  And on channels and blossoms treads ;
And his hoofs raise the dust in that garden cool,
  And trample the dainty beds.

Quoth the gardener, 'Now what Rājā art thou,
  Or else what Rājā's son ?
That in Māhil's despite, in the broad daylight,
  This mischief thou hast done.'

[1] This, be it remembered, is part of the spurious Kanauj addition. The Mahōbā version is, that the horses were won for Parmāl by Ālhā himself, who delivered his master from a Gandharva (Southey's Glendoveer) or fairy king, who used to outrage him. The fairy steeds were the prize of the contest. It will be observed that, when the heroes start on their expedition, they seem to be presented with their coursers for the first time.

[2] The name under which Durgā seems to have been invoked at Mahōbā —the giver of goodness.

[3] Chief town of Jalaun, between Cawnpur and Jhānsī.

'Ūdan am I of King Parmāl's town,
  Ālhā's brother I wot;
I have followed a deer for my mother here,
  So I rede thee stop me not.'[1]

He spurred his horse and galloped by;
  To the ghāt Rasbēndul flew,
All in the plain of proud Urai
  Where the girls the water drew.

'Ho! maidens, weary and hot are we:
  So water my horse, I crave,'
'And who may'st thou be that askest so free
  Of Rājā Māhil's slave?

'What dost thou here in proud Urai?
  And which way art thou boun'?'
'Ūdan, Ālhā's brother, am I,
  And I dwell in King Parmāl's town.'

'Now listen my rede, and take with speed
  To Mahōbā thy homeward way:
Or Rājā Māhil will seize thy steed,
  And send thee afoot to-day.'

Then Ūdan's ire blazed up like fire,
  He snatched his pellet-bow;
With stroke on stroke the vessels he broke,
  As the damsels walked arow.

He struck his horse and galloped back,
  I wis[2] he never blan[3];
The maidens crying 'Out alack!'
  To Māhil's palace ran.

'Now art thou a Rājā, Māhil,' they cried,
  'That Ūdan, Dasrāj' son,
At thy palace door hath flouted us sore,
  And broken our jars each one?'

[1] Here breaks off the Kanauj fragment which I have called the first canto. The next seventeen stanzas are transferred from Ūdan's later adventure to conceal the hiatus.

[2] I wis or I wot. I know, certainly.

[3] Lingered.

An angry man was Māhil then,
  Seized Kālpī[1] paper in haste;
Next the pen-stand he took in hand,
  And the title in order traced.

'Hear, King Parmāl! thy servants rule,
  And curb these boys I pray;
At my water-gate they breed debate,
  And break the pots each day.

'Since when is Ūdan a man of war?
  Since when has he buckled on brand?
Has he vengeance wrought for his father's skull,
  That on Mārō gate doth stand?'

The messenger rode and drew not rein,
  Till he reached Mahōbā town;
The camel knelt when he pulled the chain,
  Then slowly he 'lighted down.

King Parmāl sate on his throne of state;
  It was wrought of the red, red gold;
The court was thronged with a gathering great,
  And a slave did the chaurī[2] hold.

Seven paces off the messenger bowed,
  Then the letter he gave Parmāl;
Troubled was the king as he cut the string
  And let the cover fall.

His visage changed as the lines he read,
  He took a gold-wrought reed;
'Let Dēvī's son be as thine own,
  But see my words thou heed.

'Pots of gold, all duly told,
  I give for thy pots of clay;
But tell not the tale of Mārō here,
  Or ruin will fall that day.

'Were the story told to Ūdan bold,
  Dasrāj' true son is he,
He would fearless march to the Mārō hold;
  Then woe for the child and me.'

[1] On the Jumna, between Cawnpur and Uraī, formerly the capital of the province. It is still famous for the manufacture of paper.
[2] The fan made of a Yak's tail, the ensign of royalty.

The messenger mounted his camel again,
  And his way to Urai did take;
Māhil cut the thread and the letter he read,
  But never a word he spake.

Now[1] Ūdan the bold at twelve years old
  All weapons of war he knew;
When a month had gone by, he rode to Urai,
  And two deer in the garden slew.

The gardener ran and to cry began
  In Abhai's wrestling yard,
'Ūdan is here and has killed the deer,
  And the vines and dates has marred.'

Forth Abhai rushed and loud 'gan say,
  'What ho, Banāphar's son!
Thou goest not away till I make thee pay
  For the mischief thou hast done.'

Down Ūdan came with eyes aflame
  And hard he gripped Abhai;
With broken arm he dashed him down,
  And so he galloped by.

'Māhil, arise, here Ūdan hies,'
  The messenger cried in haste,
'With a broken arm prince Abhai lies,
  And the garden is all a waste.'

In wrath he called for Lillī, his mare,
  And forth at speed he went;
His son he raised with tender care
  And home in a litter sent.

And fast he rode to Mahōbā town,
  I wis the time was short;
Before the gate he 'lighted down
  And thronged was Parmāl's court.

He called for a seat and placed it nigh,
  And bade him tell his tale;
'What news', quoth he, 'from proud Urai?
  And why is thy face so pale?'

[1] The real commencement of the poem after the introductory invocation.

'Why hast thou fostered Ūdan here,
  This gate to work me harm?
He hath wasted my fruits, he hath killed my deer,
  He hath broken my son's right arm.

'If Ūdan now be warrior grown,
  Doth Jambay rule Mārò?
Who cast Dasrāj in the mill of stone,[1]
  And wrought Daspurwā woe?

'Lākhā, the sweet, and Papīhā, the fleet,
  Pachsāwad, the elephant good,
And the nine-lakh chain from Queen Dēvī ta'en,
  He ravished and none withstood.'

'Hush! speak no word of Mārō here,'
  Parmāl made quick reply,
'The son of Dēvī knows no fear,
  He would not dread to die.'

Thereon came Ūdan in and cried,
  'My father who did kill?
Tell me the truth and nothing hide,
  And is he living still?'

''Twas at Pairāgarh [2] in Silhat [3] far,'
  So King Parmāl did feign,
'And there we warred a mighty war,
  And there thy sire was slain.'

'Now hear, Māhil, and soothly show,
  Or bliss thy life forsake;
What is the truth of fort Mārò,
  Whereof but now ye spake?'

'To Dēvī go, and ask of her;
  I know but as others tell;
Raghunandan was king of Pairāgarh
  Where thy father fought and fell.'

[1] The mill for crushing sugar-cane.
[2] I do not know whether this is a real name or not.
[3] The far east of Bengal, now under the Assam Government.

Now Ūdan is come to the painted[1] dome,
His soul could take no rest;
A dagger from out his belt he drew,
And held it against his breast.

'O mother, who is the king Jambay?
And where is the fort Mārò?
Is my father's skull fixed there on high?
I will die òr the truth will know.'

Quoth Dēvī, the Queen, 'Now hold thee still,
And be guided by me, dear son;
But woe to Māhil, that counsellor ill,
Mine house he hath sure undone.

'The Mārō King, full stark is he;
Thou mayst not thole[2] his stroke.'
'O mother, I cannot be ruled by thee,'
So Ūdan in thunder broke.

'There is nought that can quench the fire in my heart
Till my father's blood I wreak.'[3]
Queen Dēvī pressed the boy to her breast,
And proudly did smile and speak.

'These twelve long years that a widow I go,
My bracelets[4] of wedlock I wore;
When my son has avenged me on false Mārò
I may leave them on Sāgar's[5] shore.'

FYTTE II

Dēvī, the Queen, in haste arose
And Ūdan with her led;
To Ālhā's court with speed she goes,
And thus to Mīrā said:

'Thou wert a brother to my lord,
Now teach his son to fight;
Ūdan no longer heeds my word,
And I fear King Jambay's might.'

[1] This seems always to mean the women's apartments.

[2] Endure.

[3] Avenge.

[4] When the widow performs her husband's obsequies, she leaves off her marriage ornaments.

[5] The sea or any large water. The great tanks of Mahōbā bear the name, as many of our English lakes are called seas.

Then out and answered brave Malkhay,
To Dhēwā thus did speak:
'Now search thy books, our wise one,
How we may our father wreak.'

So Dhēwā took his war-art book,
And turned his Vēdas[1] o'er:
''Twill be ill for Mārò if as Jōgīs[2] we go
And spy out the land before.'

They sent for cloths and dyed them red,
They quilted them fold on fold
(With pearls and jewels thickly shed)
Both sword and shield to hold.

Their hats were set with the diamond clear,
Their wrists had bangles of gold;
Earrings of pearl in every ear,
And sandal-wood beads they told.

With a tambourine Dhēwā, and Ālhā a drum,
Mīrā, the Saiyid, a lyre,
Malkhān a lute and Ūdan a flute,
And well mote[3] the people admire.

A glamour they fling as their songs they sing,
And of Rāma they chant alway;
Now, circling round, the glories they sound
Of Pārvatī's[4] marriage day.

Quoth Malkhān, 'First of our mother beg,
And if she know us none,
We will dance before Queen Kushlā's door,
And the secrets of Mārō are won.'

The Jōgīs came dancing into the court,
And they sang right lustily;
By threes and pairs tripped down the stairs
The maids that sight to see.

[1] The Hindū Scriptures. [2] Wandering devotees and jugglers.
[3] Might.
[4] The daughter of the mountain, a name of Durgā, wife of Śiva.

Naibā ran back where Dēvī sate
  All on a sandal chair,
'The prettiest Jōgīs are come to the gate,
  As it Rām and Lakshman[1] were.'

Queen Dēvī came to see the show,
  And O! but she was fain;
'Whence come ye, Jōgīs? whither go?
  And where will ye remain?

'My heart towards you yearns; I pray,
  Abide ye in this land;
Day by day, if here ye stay,
  I will serve you with my hand.'

'I am no Jōgī,' quoth Ūdan the bold,
  'I am thy son, thine own;
Nine months thy womb did my body hold
  Yet me thou hast not known.

'Now will we beg at Kushlā's gate,
  And how shall King Jambay know;
So stroke[2] my back and bless me straight,
  I will quit my sire on Mārò.'

She stroked him thrice, she kissed his eyes,
  And fondly did him halse;[3]
'Now well I wot shall mine injuries
  Be wroken[4] on Mārō false.'

She worshipped the might of the arms[5] of the lads;
  Her marks[6] their foreheads wore;
'When ye make your boune for Mārō town,
  My litter shall march before.'

Now the Jōgīs five to the camp are come,
  And they bade the drummer sound;
The betel[7] they gave, and he beat the drum,
  And the troops came gathering round.

[1] Brother of Rāma and his faithful attendant in his wanderings in the forest.

[2] A form of blessing. [3] Embrace. [4] Avenged.

[5] The strength of their arms, not armour.

[6] The sectarian mark on the forehead, affixed by a parent or superior.

[7] The accepting a roll of betel leaf ratified an engagement to undertake an enterprise.

And first they sent for the master of horse,
  And they gave him bangles free;
And they bade him saddle the wightest[1] steeds
  Were in all the south countrie.

They brought them steeds of all good breeds,
  From over the river, from either hand;
As pigeons flock when the housewife feeds,
  They drew to the camp from all the land.

Prancing, dancing, with hoofs in air glancing,
  They bathed them well and their saddles they dressed,
With buckles of gold fair to behold,
  Silken girth and pearlen crest.

Juice of henna[2] in cups they strained,
  Saffron colour they mingled and plied;
Every tail was brightly stained,
  Every hoof was fairly dyed.

And next they the master of elephants called,
  And they gave him bangles free,
And they bade him the strongest elephants bring
  Were in all the south countrie.

Of each good caste[3] like hillocks vast,
  They gathered them in and for battle dight,[4]
A velvet pad each tusker had,
  And a canopy sewn of the diamond bright.

Warriors four each howdah bore;
  Better spearmen were none I ween;
Hangings they brought with pearls inwrought,
  And the pinnacles, twelve, were of golden sheen.

And then they called for the captain of guns,
  Gave plume and turban free,
And they bade him bring the heaviest guns
  Were in all the south countrie.

[1] Ablest.

[2] The plant from which is made the orange dye used especially for hands and feet.

[3] The different breeds are fully detailed in the original.

[4] Prepared.

Basilic,[1] bombard and culverin,
  Heavy of carriage, heavy of ball,
Painted vermilion, came creaking in,
  And slowly they lumbered in front of all.

Then Ūdan, the bold, ranged his troops in line,
  And he spake words of fire;
'No servants are ye, but brothers of mine,
  If ye aid me to wreak my sire.

'But mighty of arm is the Baghēl King,
  And strong is the fort Mārò;
So he whose wife is the dearest thing,
  Let him take his pay and go;

'But he who loves the warrior's sword,
  Let him march with Ūdan now.'
The Kshatrīs[2] hailed him with one accord,
  And all of them vowed a vow.

'We have eaten[3] the salt of the Chandēl land,
  Our feet shall never fail.'
Then each made ready his armour of proof,
  And donned his shirt of mail.

Each on his head had a turban red,
  And an iron cap also;
With the hauberk[4] whereon no brand[5] would bite
  They made a goodly show.

Then Ūdan and Malkhān to Kālkā[6] Māi[7]
  And the blue-throat god[8] did pray;
And on Śāradā called, Mahōbā's ward,
  For help in the danger day.

And now in the hall of King Parmāl
  The five bow down and speak,
'The salt of the King has entered our bones,
  Now send us our sire to wreak.'

[1] All ancient forms of cannon.
[2] The warrior caste used as a synonym with Rājpūts.
[3] The well-known bond of loyalty in the East.
[4] Coat of mail. [5] Sword.
[6] Kālī, the terrific form of Durgā or Śāradā. [7] Mother.
[8] Nīlkanṭh, i.e. Śiva, whose throat was stained when he swallowed the flaming poison which would have consumed the world.

Then the King Parmāl for five horses sent,
And all of the fairy breed,
Karilyā first with Ālhā went,
Manurthā was Dhēwā's steed.

And Ūdan the bold did Rāsbēndul hold,
And Malkhān, Kabutrī the mare,
But Mīrā, the Saiyid, that warrior old,
The Lioness had for share.

And to Ūdan the bold, a bracelet of gold,
For a leader meet, gave he,
'The Rājā, my son, is a mighty one;
So walk thou warily.'

'Father,' he saith, 'come life, come death,
I still will face my foe,'
He bowed to greet King Parmāl's feet,
And to Malhnā's gate did go.

'Thou goest forth,' Queen Malhnā said,
'When, Ūdan, shall we meet?'
'Let eight months wax and eight months wane,
The ninth I am at thy feet.'

He hath taken his leave, he hath reached the camp,
He hath bidden the drums to sound;
At the first drum-beat they sprang to their feet
And saddled their steeds around.

At the second drum-beat they leapt to the seat,
At the third they marched straightway;
They stayed not for darkness, they recked not of heat,
They marched by night and by day.

And when they were come to the Mārō land,
Ere the seventeenth morning broke,
The day 'gan spring and the birds 'gan sing,
And the harsh-voiced crows awoke.

Ere skies grew light the standard was pight[1]
In th' acacia[2] woodland wide;
And steeds were unsaddled and men ungirt,
And the elephant howdahs untied.

[1] Pitched. [2] The Babul or gum-arabic tree.

Three kōs[1] were elephants, tusk by tusk ;
  Three kōs were horse and spear,
Three kōs were cannon and powder-bags,
  Three kōs the foot in fere.[2]

Twelve kōs the Banāphars' standards flew,
  I wot they made good cheer;
The tents were pight both red and white,
  And they boiled the flesh of deer.

And here the bards their legends sung,
  And the Pandits[3] their Vēdas here ;
And here their clubs the wrestlers swung ;
  And the dancers danced anear.

FYTTE III

Ten mornings rose, ten evenings set,
  Then forth burst Ūdan's fire;
'What sleep art sleeping, Ālhā, yet,
  And wreakest not our sire?'

'Ho! Dhēwā, see for signs thou look,
  How Mārō we may quell,'
Then Dhēwā took his star-time book,
  And thought the matter well.

'Take each his thick Bengali quilt,
  So hide your arms,' he cried;
Then all the five took quilts belive[4]
  Both sword and shield would hide.

They came from the tents with their instruments,
  They played as slow they went;
Their foreheads they painted with Rāma's mark,
  And their bodies with ashes besprent.[5]

When Dēvī saw the Jōgī band,
  She rose in trembling fright;
The golden censer she took in hand,
  And all its lamps did light.

[1] A measure of length, two miles in some parts of the country, but much less in others.
[2] Together.
[3] Learned, especially in the scriptures.
[4] Immediately.
[5] Sprinkled, a usual practice of devotees.

O'er every head she waved[1] it well,
  Then set it on the ground;
They joined their hands, at her feet they fell,
  'Now bless the way we are bound.'

'O dear ones, speed with wary heed,
  For the Mārō hold is strong;
What God will mend is mended indeed,
  But the mending taketh long.'

They touch her feet[2] and in silence part,
  So Ūdan leads the band;
From earth and its joys they loose their heart,
  And take their lives in hand.

And when they left the acacia wood,
  And drew to the gates anear,
A fire did they light, and they cried with might,
  That every house might hear.

'Whence come ye, sirs?' cried the porters all,
  'Where dwell and whither fare?'
'We go to Hinglāj[3] and we come from Bengal,
  And we beg for our daily share.

'In each king's hall ask we alms withal,
  So your doors wide open throw.'
'Then we pray you wait awhile at the gate,
  Till your words to the king we show.'

To Jambay's son did the messenger run,
  And cried in the palace there;
'At the gate there stand a Bairāgī[4] band,
  No tongue can tell how fair.

'These youths shall I bring to my lord the King?
  They may show a merry game.'
Quoth Anūpī, 'Yea, let us see their play;'
  So into the hall they came.

[1] Supposed to ensure good fortune.
[2] The usual Hindū reverence to a parent or superior.
[3] A famous place of pilgrimage and pagoda on the coast of Khelāt beyond the Indus.
[4] Wandering devotees.

But when they stood to hail the King,
  They raised their left[1] hands all;
The Rājā was wroth at their ill-greeting,
  And he drave them from the hall.

But Ūdan thundered from the gate,
  'Look, Rājā, to thine own;
Our curse is strong to mar thy State,
  Or shake thy father's throne.

'The hand that marks our beads[2] in tale,
  When Rāma's praise we sing,
With that no earthly prince we hail,
  Not an 'twere Dihlī's king.'

Then up and answered Tōdar Mal,
  Who sat at the King's right hand,
'These Jōgīs well know charm and spell:
  Strive not with the saintly band.'

'Well,' quoth Anūpī, 'tell your tale,
  And have it as ye will;
Then shall ye sport in the Rānī's court,
  And show them of your skill.'

So Dhēwā played his tambourine,
  And Ūdan leapt and danced;
Till all men cried that they there should bide,
  So every heart was tranced.

'Jōgīs, O Rājā,' Ūdan said,
  'Abide but for a day;
To-day from thee we beg our bread,
  To-morrow wend our way.'

Then Anūpī sent for silver store,
  And bags he told them down;
And now they have moved from the Rājā's door,
  And are come to Mārō town.

And shrill at the gate they 'gan to call,
  Till the porter asked their way;
'We go to Hinglāj, and we come from Bengal,
  And here for alms we pray.'

1 A gross insult according to all Hindū ideas.
2 The rosary, used to mark prayers by both Hindū and Muhammadan devotees.

'O Jōgīs, bide ye here with me,
  The four dull months[1] of rain :
And I will render for your fee,
  Whatever wage I gain.'

'O porter, sure', bold Ūdan said,
  'Thy wits are gone astray;
To Hinglāj we wend for our journey's end,
  And we count each hour's delay.

'And but that our belts of coin were bare,
  We had not turned aside :
Now go we to Mārō's palace fair.
  So fling thy portals wide.'

An alms he cast as the gate they passed;
  So hie they up Mārō street;
And begging their way from house to house,
  In the fifty marts they meet.

The stalls of sweetmeats, the shops of grain,
  To keep them none would stay;
As the Jōgīs danced, all hearts were fain,
  Both women and men that day.

They gave them a ring or a gold coin string,
  A necklace or else a shawl,
And now they are come to the water-gate,
  Where the girls stood watering all.

Their hearts were tranced as Ūdan danced,
  And the marriage of Pārvatī sang;
On head or in hand the pots did stand,
  Or down in the well did hang.

Now Rūpā, Rānī Kushlā's maid,
  At morning time she came;
To afternoon the watch drew on,
  Yet stood she there the same.

'What shall I say for this delay?'
  She hasted before the Queen;
'Past are three watches[2] of the day,
  Since thou at the well hast been.

[1] During which no one is supposed to travel.
[2] The watch is three hours.

'Now on thine eyes, and answer true.
  Has lover cast a spell?
Or hast thou chosen a husband new,
  Where thou stoodest by the well?'

She joined her hands and prayed for grace:
  'Now be not wroth, O Queen!
The fairest Jōgīs are come to the place,
  That ever these eyes have seen.

'Their colour is dark, their mouths are round
  As the fruit of the coco tree;
I have dwelt from a child on Mārō ground,
  Yet no such sight did see.

'Their eyes like gazelles, the youngest danced
  Like the peafowl [1] in forest green;
An my lady say, I will hasten straightway
  And bring them before the Queen.'

'O damsel, are thy wits astray,
  Thou tell'st a tale so wild?
What form on earth,' did Kushlā say,
  'Is fairer than my child?'

'O Rānī, hearken my advice,
  For all I say is true;
Might say these were come from Paradise,
  Or had burst the mountains through.

'One touch of these Bairāgīs' feet
  With bliss thy life had crowned.'
So Rūpā hastened to the street,
  And soon the Jōgīs found.

'Why beg your store from door to door,
  When Kushlā calls you nigh?
Ask her a boon, her bounty soon
  Would thrice your lives supply.'

'What the sick desires, the leech requires,'
  Thought Ūdan, 'this our aim.'
And gladly all the Jōgīs rose,
  And back with Rūpā came.

[1] Always the simile for a light and airy step.

But when they reached the outmost gate,
'I touch your feet,' quoth she,
'I pray you, Jōgīs, a moment wait,
Till I my lady see.'

Papīhā there stood and the elephant good,
And Pachsāwad wept that tide;
'That Dēvī's sons have shaven[1] their heads,
Do they yet worse fortune bide?'

Then Ālhā wept and quoth Ūdan, 'Tell,
My brother, why weepest thou?'
'Pachsāwad stands here and Papīhā as well,
And both of them know me now.'

'Brother, give leave,' bold Ūdan cried,
'On Papīhā's back to leap;
With our father's beasts to the camp I'll ride,
And them against all men keep.'

But Malkhān checked him, 'Art mad to risk
This stain on thy chivalry?
Were a Kshatrī chief to steal like a thief,
He had broken his Rājpūtī.

'Take vengeance first for thy father's fate;
Then ride his steed that day,'
So the Jōgīs came to the second gate,
And there the stone-mill lay.

Dark over head did a fig-tree spread,
And a skull its branches bare;
As underneath did the Jōgīs tread,
The skull 'gan weeping there.

'My sons would, I thought, have the Gayā[2] rites wrought,
And on Mārō would vengeance vow;
But such claims are nought in a Jōgī's thought,
What hope from Mahōbā now?'

[1] Abandoned the world for a religious life—in desperation, it might be supposed.

[2] The capital of Bihār, a great place of pilgrimage, to which, as to the Ganges, relics of the dead are carried when it is too far to carry the entire body.

When Ālhā heard, he wept at the word;
Then back turned Ūdan bold,
'Brother, why weepest beside the gate?
Or what in the tree dost behold?'

'O Brother, yon is our father's skull,
Which King Jambay hung on the tree.'
Then Ūdan leapt, o'er the skull he wept,
And he kissed it tenderly.

'With its kindred skulls shall this skull repose,
Or be set beside the sea;
And vengeance I vow on my father's foes,
While breath in my nostrils be.'

With that came the maid, 'On the skull why gaze?
And why with weeping eyes?
No Jōgīs are ye, sons of kings must ye be,
Though ye come in deceitful guise.

'This word must I bring to Jambay, the king,
Who will cut you asunder straight.'
Quoth Malkhān, 'Nay, O damsel, I pray,
I will tell thee all the state.

'There are goblins many lie hid in yon mill,
A child is our youngest here;
And whiles they shriek and whiles they are still,
So he started back from fear.'

'O youths, ye have had a causeless fright;
No goblins are here to dread;
But a chief of Mahōbā, Dasrāj hight,
Was hither a captive led.

'King Jambay crushed his bones in the mill,
And his skull on the tree hangs white;
Now on Ālhā and Ūdan. his two sons, still
The skull calls day and night.'

Quoth Malkhān, 'Now pardon us, maid, we pray,
That we do not thy command;
King Jambay Jōgīs will surely slay,
If before his Queen they stand.'

'I pledge my word, my life for yours;'
  So through the gate they passed,
And they came withal by the crystal hall,
  To the seven-storied tower at last.

Casements of sandal the air did take,
  Jewelled the posts of the rooms,
Peafowl on roof and swans in the lake,
  And the thatch was of peacock's plumes.

FYTTE IV

The buildings rang when Ūdan sang,
  So sweetly did he trill;
Kushlā, the Queen, behind a screen,
  Through the casement gazed her fill.

'Tell me the truth,' in wrath she cried,
  Whom hast thou hither led?
This port of pride, these chests full wide,
  Is that a Jōgī's tread?

'Their legs that slope like lions' loins,
  The fire that lights their eye;
Tell me the truth, or, slave, in sooth,
  This hour shall see thee die.'

'Lady, thou know'st not,' Ūdan cried,
  'The tale we have to tell;
An orphan I from mine infancy,
  When my sire in battle fell.

'A widow lone was my mother left,
  And the dearth fell black on the land;
Her children at length, of hope bereft,
  She sold to a Jōgī band. 5

'If God hath given us bodies fair,
  That fairness can we hide?'
'Where got ye, then, those quilts so rare,
  Those rubies and gems of pride?'

'In Jaychand's court at Kanauj to sing
  We stayed as we came from Bengal;
And we pleased the King that a gay gold ring
  He gave and these quilts withal.'

Quoth Kushlā, 'if your tale be true,
As true it well may be,
The arts the Jōgīs taught to you,
We pray you let us see.'

Then danced the rider of Bēndulā
And charmed them with his grace;
Then Malkhān's strain was raised to gain
All hearers in the place.

Then Dhēwā played and the Saiyid old,
And Ūdan's flute did sound;
Then Ālhā struck his lyre of gold
And rapt all senses round.

They brought them stools of the teak wood made;
They sat before the Queen;
'Now tell your story,' Kushlā said,
'And what your lives have been.

'Whither now do ye take your way?
What country saw you born?
And what ill fates, O Jōgīs, say,
Has thus your young heads shorn?'

Then Ūdan spake with sweet-toned wit,
'From far Bengal came we,
In Gorakhpur[1] our hut we quit,
The Hardwār[2] Fair to see.

'And when we have bathed at holy Hardwār,
To Hinglāj[3] must we wend;
To Sētbandh[4] thence the road is far,
But there must our journey end.

'Now lacking coin for our daily meat,
Have we passed through the city here,'
She joined her hands, 'I touch your feet,
I hold you lief and dear.

[1] South of Nepāl between Oudh and Bihār.

[2] The place where the Ganges breaks through the Siwālik range to enter the plain country; a place of pilgrimage for immense crowds at the Fair times.

[3] On the sea coast beyond the Indus.

[4] Our Adam's Bridge, the chain of rocks between the South of India and Ceylon.

'I will send for my son, Karinghā Rāi,
He shall stand and serve you best;
I will call my daughter, Bijaisin, nigh,
She shall stand and fan your rest.

'Bide here the four dull months of rain,
World wanderers though ye are;
And I'll load with wealth full many a wain,
When ye start for holy Hardwār.'

Quoth Malkhān, 'O Queen! in this I ween,
Thy sense is gone astray;
To-morrow must Jōgīs take the road,
If they beg at thy gate to-day.

'Waters that flow and Jōgīs that go,
What power can make them stay?
Bring forth the alms thy bounty gives,
And let us wend our way.

'On before did our master go:
We follow him as we may;
We gather the ashes his path that show;
He will not brook delay.'

'O Jōgīs, would you a royal throne?
I have thrones at my command;
Or seek ye lovely brides to own?
I can dower a maiden's hand.'

The flame flashed high in Malkhān's eye;
In words of wrath he spake,
'A sinful word our ears have heard;
Our vow wouldst have us break?

'We hunger not for a kingly throne,
And what do we to wed?
Bairāgī's sons the world disown,
And the pilgrim's pathway tread.'

Up rose they all in haste to go;
She caught their feet to stay;
'O wait ye yet, till my alms I get;
Nor empty wend your way.'

She sent for platters, all of gold;
  With pearls she filled them free;
All to the Jōgīs in alms she told,
  Said 'lives it will last you three'.

Then Ūdan feigned himself a fool,
  A handful he took to smell;
'Such fruit, O Queen, I have never seen,
  What tree may bear them, tell.'

'O God, were these for Jōgīs made?'
  She clasped her hands in thought,
'No fruit of tree I give,' said she,
  'They are pearls from the ocean brought.'

He strewed the pearls on the palace floor,
  And thus did Ūdan say,
'Pearls and jewels if hence we bore,
  Robbers would bar our way.

'If thou wouldst grant us a worthy sign
  That we thy favour gain,
Queen Malhnā's bounty then be thine;
  She gave a nine-lakh chain.'

'A nine-lakh chain will I bestow
  When ye have danced for me;
Go call my daughter to the show,
  The joy of her life 'twill be?'

Up Rūpā climbed stair after stair,
  She reached the topmost tower:
And there she woke Bijaisin fair,
  Was sleeping in her bower.

She joined her hands, 'The Queen doth call;
  Come down, my bonnibel;
Here have we Jōgīs from Bengal,
  So fair no words can tell.'

Up and rose Bijaisin fair,
  Her betel-case in hand;
Down then came she stair by stair,
  And before the Queen did stand.

Five leaves of betel had she rolled
  Ere to the court she came;
The roll she gave to Ūdan bold,
  And soon he chewed the same.

She turned and looked on Ūdan's face,
  She gazed with sidelong glance;
Love's sudden dart pierced Ūdan's heart,
  And down he sank in trance.

Then she on the ground too sank in a swound;
  It troubled and angered the Queen;
'He, Jōgī, is none but a king's wanton son,
  Who the face ot my child has seen.

'Go hasten hither, Karinghā, my son,
  And hold the gate meanwhile;
In the mill of stone will I crush them each one,
  Who have entered my palace by guile.'

'If our youngest die,' did Malkhān cry,
  'Thy palace shall burn to the ground'
'What ailed him then,' quoth the Queen again,
  'That he fell in such sudden swound?'

Quoth Dhēwā then, with ready wit,
  'The roll from thy daughter came;
If bitter drugs she mingled in it,
  For the fainting her's the blame.'

Now Ūdan came to himself and rose,
  Up rose the princess eke;
And straight she hied to her mother's side,
  Who spoke and smoothed her cheek.

'From the bitter drug did the Jōgī faint,
  But wherefore thou as well?'
'O mother! their beauty no words can paint;
  As I gazed from the stair I fell.'

Now all the women of Mārō town
  To see the dances crowd;
Young and fair were the maidens there,
  And each to each spoke loud—

'How blest is she to whom fate,' quoth one,
'Such goodly sons did give!'
'Nay rather, if Jōgī became such son,
What mother could bear to live?'

'Or let me ever unwed remain,
Or have husband like Ūdan here,'
'Is it Rāma who walks the earth again,
Or Krishna to maidens dear?'

'Were Ūdan my husband, how blest my lot;
I would sit and fan his face;
Like Vishnu's heaven would seem our cot:'
Thus a spell was on all the place. 45

Some gave silver and some gave gold,
Or the pearls on their necks that lay;
Queen Kushlā fain gave the nine-lakh chain;
So the Jōgīs went their way.

Fast through the courts did the princess hie,
And by the lattice stand;
And, as the Jōgīs five went by,
She caught young Ūdan's hand.

Him into her secret bower she led,
On the jewelled couch set down;
'So thou to take me with guile,' she said,
'Art come from Mahōbā town?

'Karinghā, the fierce, I will call anon,
Who will tear thy limbs apart;
I know thee, Rānī Dēvī's son,
And Ūdan named thou art.'

'O Lady Bijmā,' Ūdan cried,
'Thy sense is strayed, I trow;
There are many like me; the world is wide;
Like Ūdan many also. 50

'Where hast thou seen me? Lady, say.'
''Twas at Siraunj,'[1] she said;
'For I was called to the marriage day
When Māhil's son was wed.

[1] A town of Mālwā.

'And thou didst with Abhai the bridegroom ride,
  And Bēndulā thee bare;
Thou didst stand 'neath the canopy by my side,
  And a purple turban wear.

'And thou didst jostle me in the press
  That my bodice was rent also:
'Twas in that place I saw thy face,
  And well thy name I know.

'Now am I tending[1] a holy tree,
  And every Sunday fast:
If Ūdan my husband may not be,
  Let me die a maid at last.'

'What can withstand thine eyes?' he laughed,
  'Ūdan in sooth they see;
If I sing for my bread and have shaven my head,
  It is all for the sake of thee.'

'If so, shall I send for the priest?' she said,
  'The marriage pole to rear,
And teach us the seven[2] rounds to tread
  In the seven-storied tower here?'

'O Lady, where are thy senses now?
  Should I wed thee like a thief?
With sword in hand will I vow my vow,
  As becomes a Rājpūt chief.

'When the marriage cups shall with blood run o'er
  In a sword-play fair to see;
When the marriage pole shall be smeared with gore,
  Shall our bridal in Mārō be.

'But, if in truth thou dost love me now,
  The secrets of Mārō say;
I must wreak my father and hold my vow,
  And the rounds will we tread that day.'

[1] To water a fig-tree, banyan or pīpal, is still considered an act of merit, and no gardener likes to uproot the troublesome seedlings which spring up in the crevices of buildings.

[2] For the bride and bridegroom to walk seven times hand in hand round the consecrated pole is an essential part of a Rājpūt wedding.

'First swear thy truth on Gangā's tide,
  If the secrets thou wouldst know;'
He thrust his hand his quilt inside,
  And drew out his sword from below.

'If I prove false to my plighted word,
  And wed thee not, sweet flower,
Upon me turn then my good sword,
  And this false heart devour.'

'Fort Lōhāgarh[1] is a right strong fort,
  So go not there to fight;
Jambay, the King, there holds his court,
  And who can withstand his might?

'And go not down to Jhānsī town,
  Where dwells Karinghā Rāi;
And try not the power of the twelve-doored tower
  Where Suraj my brother doth lie;

'But plant your guns from th' acacia grove,
  If victory ye would know.'[2]
'Now give me leave to part, my love,
  For Ālhā waits below.'

Bijaisin joined her hands and said,
  'O be not in haste to go:
Rest on the bed, which here I spread,
  While I stand and fan thee so.'

'Princess, such words should not be said;
  Bear absence patiently;
Should I set foot on a maiden's bed,
  I had broken my Rājpūti.'

So Ūdan left Bijaisin fair;
  He would no longer wait:
Down then came he stair by stair,
  Until he reached the gate.

[1] That is, the Iron Fort.

[2] The bride's duty is to her husband from the moment of plighting her faith, and her family are forgotten thenceforth. This explains the apparent treason of the heroines of many of these ballads.

FYTTE·V

Now Ālhā stood in the roadway near,
  And thus did to Malkhān say:
'If I be robbed in the palace here,
  And my brother be stolen away:

'What in Mahōbā town shall I tell?
  Or what bring to Malhnā instead?'
With that came Ūdan and clasped him well,
  And Ālhā laughed and said,

'Now tell me, I pray, what made thee stay
  So long in the seven-storied tower?'
'King Jambay's daughter knew me well,
  And led me to her bower.

'And she has made me swear an oath
  To wed her on Gangā's tide;
And I have plighted to her my troth
  That she shall be my bride.

'And all the secrets of Mārō town
  Hath Bijmā told to me,'
But Ālhā heard him with a frown:
  'Say not such words,' quoth he. 5

'From our foeman's line we will take no spouse,
  And Bijmā we will not wed:
When she thinks of her kin and her father's house,
  She will slay thee in thy bed.'

'O hush, my brother,' Malkhān said,
  'Revenge is all our part;
We have no thought the maid to wed,
  We must quench the fire of our heart.'

Now forth together went all the five,
  I wis they did not wait;
To Lōhāgarh they came belive
  Beside the massy gate.

The three deep moats with water filled;
  Above, vast guns to fire;
Quoth Ālhā, 'Strong their forts they build,
  How shall we wreak our sire?'

'Brother, take heart,' dark Ūdan replied,
'From God all favours be.'
Then loud at the gate like beggars they cried,
Till the porter took his key.

'Whence come ye? Whither go?' he spake;
Quoth Malkhān, 'Hear and know:
From the eastern land our way we take,
And on to Hardwār we go.

'But now have we turned to the city here,
For the coin in our belts is spent.'
Then he flung the gate wide and they passed inside,
And up to the court they went.

Right thronged was the court of the Mārō King,
Scant room for seats they gat:
Shield on shield did frequent ring,
Where the Kshatrīs like lions sat.

Dancers danced for all to behold,
Girls and boys they vied;
Jambay sat on his throne of gold;
Huge chaurīs waved beside.

Kariyā sat on the right of the King,
His drawn sword on his knee;
Ūdan sang till the roof did ring,
So skilled a voice had he.

Rājā Jambay turned his eye,
And gazed upon the band;
He bade a messenger call them nigh,
Before his face to stand.

But when they stood to greet the King.
Their left hands raised they all:
Right angry was he at their ill-greeting,
Bade lash them from the hall.

'Speak not so high,' cried Ūdan bold,
'Our right hands Rāma praise;
The hands with which our beads are told
To thee we may not raise.'

'Now tell me, Jōgīs,' quoth the King,
 'If master true you taught,
Whence gat ye each his gay gold ring,
 His quilt with gems inwrought?'

'To beg our bread,' brave Malkhān said,
 'We in Kanauj did sing;
And we gained in that place from the Rājā's grace,
 Both quilt and gay gold ring.'

'And if your words ye do not feign,
 And true they well may be,
Where gat ye the purple turban stain
 On your foreheads so plain to see?'

'From Kanauj we went down to Mahōbā town.
 And danced in the Rājā's hall;
And the flute I bear, I gained it there,
 As a gift from the King Parmāl.

'There Ālhā and Ūdan, two brethren dwell,
 They do not fear to die;
They gave us turbans and plumes as well,'
 So Ūdan made reply.

'Our tents on the lake side kept they there
 The four dull months of rain;
Four months our heads their turbans wear,
 And so do the marks remain.'

'And if the truth is what ye say,
 As truth it well may be,
Show us your Jōgī's art this day,
 Your skill we fain would see.'

Then did Ūdan dance and the Jōgīs sing:
 Right glad was the Baghēl Rāi:
They were bidden to sit before the King
 On stools of teak-wood high.

'Whence come ye, Jōgīs? Whither go?'
 'To Hinglāj from Bengal.'
Turbans on each did the King bestow,
 And plumes of price withal.

'If ye, O Jōgīs, here abide,
  I'll serve you every day.'
'O Rājā,' Malkhān straight replied,
  'Now hear the words I say.

'Waters that flow and Jōgīs that go,
  What power can make them stay?
To-day we wait before thy gate;
  To-morrow wend our way.'

'O King, through Kāśi[1] as we came,'
  So Ūdan 'gan to tell,
'Of Lākhā, the dancer, we heard the fame,
  Who in thy court doth dwell.

'Fain would we now her dancing see,
  That we are to Mārō come.'
Then Jambay sent, and forth came she,
  While a Brijman[2] beat the drum.

To the sound of the tambour and castanet
  She danced before them all;
And so she came where the Jōgīs were set,
  And she circled round the hall.

Quoth Ūdan, 'the nine-lakh chain bestow:
  In our house she was dwelling long.'
Quoth Alhā, 'if Jambay the chain should know
  He would bind thee in prison strong.'

The counsel he got he heeded not;
  He cast her the chain to wear:
It was Dēvī's sons then well she wot,
  Were sitting disguisèd there.

She signed with her eye to bid them fly,
  Lest Jambay should them slay;
'Methinks, O dancer,' Ūdan said,
  'Thy sense is gone astray.'

'Twelve years though thou hast in Mārō spent,
  Thou shalt see Mahōbā again,'
So the Jōgīs rose, to the gate they went,
  And their way to Pachpērā[3] have ta'en.

[1] Benares. [2] A man of the country round Mathurā (Muttra).
[3] The five trees.

She hid the chain within her breast,
  As she danced toward the door;
A gust from the west blew back her vest
  As she passed the King before.

Out flashed the chain, the nine-lakh chain,
  And Jambay marked it well.
'The Mahōbā chain whence didst thou gain?
  I bid thee, dancer, tell.'

She joined her hands, 'my lord, forgive;
  'Twas the Jōgīs gave it me:
Twelve years within thy court I live,
  Yet never such chain did see.'

Then Jambay, the King, was sore adread,
  To think what might befall;
'Go, Kariyā, fetch the chain,' he said,
  'Where it lies in the painted hall.'

Up Kariyā rose, and in haste he goes,
  The Mahōbā chain to bring;
His long boots creaked as on he strode;
  And the shield on his back did ring.

Up Kushlā rose her son to greet,
  And by the door did stand;
She took a fan of blossoms sweet,
  And Kariyā's face she fanned.

'What wouldst thou of me, dear son?' said she;
  He joined his hands and spake:
'Oh, mother, give the Mahōbā chain,
  Which I to the King must take.'

Then Kushlā, the Queen, was sore adread,
  And she trembled her body through:
'The necklace thread is broken;' she said,
  'I am having it strung anew.'

'Be it broken or be it marred,
  To give thou must not fail;'
'I have done, my son, what should not be done,
  And how shall I tell the tale?

'There came five Jōgīs from Bengal;
  To them I gave the chain.'
Up Kariyā rose and left the hall,
  And ran to the court again.

King Jambay sat on his golden throne,
  And Kariyā loud 'gan cry;
'These Jōgīs are none but each a king's son
  Come hither the land to spy.

'They have learnt the secrets of every house,
  They have taken the nine-lakh chain.'
'Go quickly nor fail them hither to hale,[1]
  And bring those Jōgīs again.'

With sword and shield forth Kariyā went,
  To Pachpērā came speedily;
'Rājās, take tent,[2] the King hath sent,
  So up and back with me.'

'Our master, Kariyā,' Malkhān said,
  'On us the word did lay,
Till we see his face, we must not trace
  One step of a backward way.'

He drew his long sword from his waist,
  And an angry man was he;
'One foot on your forward way be placed,
  And I hew you in pieces three.'

Then Uday Singh waxed wode[3] and wroth,
  And his sword from his quilt he drew;
And Malkhān and Dhēwā marked him both,
  And their broad swords grasped they too.

And all the five with swords belive[4]
  On Kariyā set and cry,
'No Jōgīs we, we will Mārō raze,
  And make it a pool for aye.'

'These are the chief of Mahōbā's sons,'
  Thought Kariyā, 'sooth to tell;
And, if in their face, I keep my place,
  I may bid my life farewell.'

[1] Drag [2] Heed. [3] Mad. [4] Immediately.

So back he strode his homeward road,
He joined his hands and spake:
'Bairāgī 'tis none, but Dasrāj' son,
So do not, O Sire, mistake.' 55

King Jambay heard and turned his eye,
And Sūraj, his son, did call;
'Let none of the men of Mahōbā fly,
But seize and bind them all.'

To camp went Sūraj, the drummer he called,
Gave betel[1] and ring to wear;
And he bade him array, without delay,
The armies of Mārō there.

FYTTE VI

Now the five to their camp from Pachpērā went;
Little they lingered, I wot;
Then straight they came to Dēvī's tent,
And up in haste she got.

A censer[2] of gold in hand she took,
And lighted the lamps all round:
The censer o'er every head she shook,
Then set it upon the ground.

She halsed[3] them well, 'now, dear ones, tell
Of Mārō town the tale.'
'I, mother, will tell whate'er befell,'
Quoth Ūdan, 'without fail.

'We have been all through Kushlā's hall,
Gained the nine-lakh necklace there;
And mother, thy chain I gave again
To Lākhā, the dancer, to wear.'

Said Ūdan bold to Dhēwā then,
'Come, brother, a ford to seek.'
Then they went to the ghât[4] of the washermen,
And loud they 'gan to speak. 5

[1] As a pledge to bind him to fulfil the task. [2] A ceremony of welcome.
[3] Embraced. [4] Steps or passage down to the river.

'Fast westward doth your Narmadā[1] flow;
  Now show us the passage we pray.'
'Four fields below ye can lightly go,'
  Then soon the ford found they.

The twain did into the water wade,
  The stream but reached their waist;
Bamboos with strips of cloth displayed
  They cut and careful placed.

To Ālhā's tent then straight they went,
  And Ūdan bowed and said:
'Kōs full twelve is the wood's extent,
  And dark it throws its shade.

'No foot can pass through in order due,
  And how shall horseman go?'
'Then hither Chandan the woodman call,
  And nine hundred woodmen moe.[2]

'Bid them hew the wood with their axes good,
  That the army through may go;
But here and there a tree to spare
  For the wounded to rest below.'

Nine hundred axes rang in the wood,
  They hewed with might and main,
Till where the acacia forest stood
  Was now an open plain.

To Tōndāpur ran a messenger then,
  Where the prince Anūpī lay:
'The Mahōbā Rājā, with all his men,
  Is hewing the forest away.'

Anūpī, in wrath, for the drummer sent,
  Gave bracelets of gold to wear,
'Now beat on the drum, let the army come,
  And quickly let each prepare.'

Then messengers hurried through lane and street,
  Headmen were summoning ward by ward:
They leapt to their feet at the first drum beat,
  And saddled their steeds for Mārō's lord.

[1] The river Nerbudda. [2] More.

To stirrup they sprang at the second drum beat,
 Swinging the head-stalls the troopers came;
At the third drum beat, they were all complete,
 And ranged their ranks for the Mārō name.

Some rode in nālkīs,[1] some rode in pālkīs,[1]
 Some of them rode in the elephant wain;
Oxen white in the cars were dight,[2]
 And stirred the red dust over the plain.

They choose their steeds, good colours and breeds,
 Under the saddles the saddle-cloths fold;
Golden buckles on silken girths,
 Stirrups of silver and bits of gold.

He next to the master of elephants passed,
 Gave bracelets of gold to wear;
Of each good caste like hillocks vast
 He bade him straight prepare.

Of each good caste he brought them past,
 In goodly length did the beasts defile;
A velvet pad each tusker had,
 And the foot sank deep in the crimson pile.

Canopies silver and pinnacles gold,
 Bound with cord of a silken string;
Warriors four did each howda hold,
 Ready to fight for the Mārō King.

And then for the captain of guns he sent,
 Gave bracelets of gold to wear:
And he bade him bring for the Mārō King
 The heaviest cannon there.

Culverin, bombard and falconet,
 Heavy of metal, heavy of ball,
Each on his carriage was duly set,
 And they moved like the wind before them all.

The wheels did groan, and rattled the gun;
 Loud clattered the bolts of vermilion hue;
Or ever the beat of the drum was done,
 The troops of Anūpī were all in view.

[1] Forms of litters. [2] Ready.

Then he asked for a jar from the Gangā stream,
  And bathed in the gateway there;
And down he sat on a silken mat,
  And he sent for sandal rare.

In a golden cup he ground it up,
  And his forehead and arms he dyed;
But first he spake the name of Ganēkh[1]
  And on Rāma duly cried.

He girt his waist with a silken band,
  No time he lost, I wot;
Knives and swords all ready to hand,
  As a champion stark, he got.

And on his right side his dagger well-tried,
  'Twas carved with a lion's face;
And his spear did wield, and rhinoceros' shield,
  On his stout left arm did place.

He rode his red steed, and at his right side,
  Rode Tōdar Mal his gray:
There were thirty thousand horsemen tried
  With Anūpī rode that day.

The horses set forth, and their necks they arched,
  As they heard the war drum sound;
With prance and caracole on they marched,
  Till they came to the battle ground.

With the rider of Bēndulā there they met,
  Who spurred before his line;
And Dhēwā eke on Manurthā set,
  Was noting[2] every sign.

From ten fields off shouted Jambay's son,
  'Whence come ye? whither go?
And who of the earth is that mighty one
  Has laid my forest low?'

'I am Ūdan, a servant of King Parmāl,
  Who reigns in Mahōbā town;
To make way for my men did the forest fall,
  For we are to Mārō boune.'

[1] Or Ganēś, the God invoked at the commencement of all undertakings.
[2] He was the astrologer of the party.

'Now hearken, Ūdan, my counsel heed,
And back to Mahōbā go.'
'Then give me Papīhā, my father's steed,
And the nine-lakh chain also.

'Pachsāwad, the strong, and Lākhā, the sweet,
And Bijmā, thy sister, to wed;
And yield moreover in tribute meet
The Rājā Jambay's head.'

Then Rājā Anūpī, wroth was he,
Like a coal was his red eyeball;
'Let none of the men of Māhōbā flee,
Seize horses and cattle and all.

'The heaviest guns on their carriages bring
And fire on the low-bred hound.'
Then cannon were loaded and rammers did ring
And matches were lighted around.

The bullets did rattle, the cannon did roar,
The arrows whistled and flew;
The rockets hissed as their way they tore,
And the smoke hid all from view.

None yielded a jot nor left the spot,
As he was true Rājpūt born;
Till bows grew slack and guns waxed hot
And the archers' hands were torn.

They left the cannon they could not work,
And dashed the missiles by:
With lance and spear they faced more near,
And the javelins fast 'gan fly.

And no Rājpūt would yield a foot
When he stood his foe before,
Till spears were broken and shafts were bent;
And the howdas swam in gore.

Then every warrior bared his blade,
And line rushed in on line;
I wis a goodly play they played,
Drawn out for furlongs nine.

Footmen and footmen there were set,
  Horsemen 'gainst horsemen ride:
Tusk to tusk the elephants met,
  Howda by howda's side.

Full many a fair young soldier then
  His blood on the broadsword shed;
At every step were wounded men,
  A horse or an elephant dead.

Like a red, red river[1] the blood did run,
  With turbans for lotus gay,
For tortoise and snake there were shield and gun,
  And mantles for weeds that sway.

Then some did groan for sire or son,
  Or wife to be widowed soon,
Or mother old, who has left her none,
  To give the funeral boon.[2]

O water than gold was more precious then,
  And none could be found that day:
Of Anūpī's thirty thousand men
  One half on the greensward lay.

At length they broke from the trenches and fled,
  The coward and eke the brave;
Down each ravine ran swordsmen keen,
  If only their life to save.

'These are wolves,' they cried, 'from Mahōbā side
  Are loosed on the Mārō power,
Of sheep and of goats they seek no prey,
  But the flesh of men devour.

'We will quit the service of King Jambay,
  And as woodmen earn our bread.'
When Anūpī saw his warriors fly,
  To Ūdan he spurred and said:

'O man of Mahōbā, Dasrāj' son,
  Enough has thy valour wrought;
Go back content with the deeds thou hast done,
  Nor lose thy life for nought.'

[1] Such a simile as this is a great favourite with the Hindū bards.
[2] The funeral rites can only be performed properly by a son.

'The sun and the stars may cease to burn,
  The earth may leave her sphere:
But, cut Ūdan asunder, he will not turn,
  Ere he wreak[1] his father here.'

His eyes flashed fire, 'if fight we must,
  Then let the die be thrown;
Why should our servants bite the dust,
  When the quarrel is all our own?

'The war game I and thou will play,
  Till only one see light,'
Quoth Ūdan, 'Ay, and so I say,
  Let us have our fill of fight.'

'Strike, chief of Mahōbā, first in place.'
  Quoth Ūdan, 'Nay, not so;
There never was knight in all our race
  Who first would strike the blow.

'Deal then, Anūpī, deal thy blow,
  Yet know thy death is near.'
Then straight Anūpī seized his bow,
  Its bolt outweighed a seer.[2] 55

A four-pointed arrow he fixed in the string,
  He fitted the notch aright;
Twanging loudly the cord did ring,
  For he drew the bow with might.

But Ūdan turned his horse to the right,
  So God preserved him there;
Then Anūpī grasped a javelin light,
  And poised it high in air.

He marked when Ūdan was not ware,
  Then straight his javelin cast;
But the horse Rāsbēndul leapt in air,
  And the dart beneath him passed.

'Sure a fast on Sundays King Parmāl made,
  Or thy mother kept fast also;
Some holy work hath been thine aid,
  That twice thou hast 'scaped my blow.

[1] Avenge. [2] Two pounds.

'Yet be warned in time and turn to thy place,'
Then a light laugh laughèd he;
'Were I to turn back from my foeman's face,
I had broken my Rājpūtì.

'Thou hast stricken twice, now make it thrice,
Do all that is in thy power;
Or, when thou art sitting in paradise,
Thou wilt grieve thou hadst lost thine hour.'

From his waist-belt then he drew his brand,
He struck at his face a stroke:
But the targe was lifted in Ūdan's left hand,
And the sword of Anūpī broke.

When only the heft[1] in his hand was left,
He wist his death was near:
'I have hewn down elephants with this sword,
But now it hath failed me here.'

'Now,' Ūdan cried, 'Anūpī, hold,
And take mine answer free;
Three blows have I tholed[2] of thine well told,
Now bear thou one from me.'

He struck his spurs, he drew his sword,
He called on Ganpat's[3] name;
The sun he adored and the feet of his lord,
And so to Anūpī came.

The rhinoceros' shield the good blade rove,
And the velvet padding withal;
Anūpī's shoulder to chine he clove,
And his weapons clashed in his fall.

Now Tōdar Mal stood there beside,
And he came spurring in;
'Ho, Ūdan, guard thy life,' he cried,
'For hence thou shalt not win.'

He whirled his mace, but Ūdan bent
And clasped the neck of his horse;
Clattering it went to the ground, and spent
In empty air its force.

[1] Handle. [2] Endured.
[3] A name of Ganēś. Both signify lord of Gaṇas, bands of demigods or Genii.

His sword from his belt he quickly drew,
At his head a stroke let fly;
But on Ūdan's targe it to pieces flew,
Then he deemed that death was nigh.

Then Ūdan spurred; with the boss of his shield
He thrust him to the ground;
Quickly Ūdan leaped to the field
And fast his arms he bound.

'Ho, Dhēwā!' he cries, 'a worthy prize,
So guard him with all our power,'
Then Dhēwā is gone to the acacia wood,
And he to the twelve-doored tower.

FYTTE VII

To the twelve-doored tower, where Surāj dwelt,
There rode a messenger wight;
He drew the chain and the camel knelt,
And slowly he down did 'light.

Seven paces off he joined his hands,
'What sleep art sleeping yet?
When the forest is hewn by Mahōbā bands,
And ruin thy house doth threat.

'Tōdar Mal is a prisoner ta'en,
And—woe betide the day!—
Anūpī lies slain on the battle plain,
Till thou bear his body away.'

Like a man distraught was Sūraj then,
Gave bangles of gold anon;
Bade the messenger summon the Mārō men
To do their harness on.

There was shouting of criers by streets and lanes,
There was arming on every side;
There was strapping of horse-cloths and swinging of reins,
And tightening of girths that tide.

There was mounting of troopers good at needs,
For Mārō bound to ride;
There was champing of bits and prancing of steeds,
And curvetting in paces tried.

At the first drum-beat they saddle their steeds,
  At the second, their arms they don;
At the third, they follow where Sūraj leads,
  And the banners of red move on.

'Your bones are compact with the Baghēl salt;[1]
  Then who, my friends, dare flee?
Whose foot steps back from the field, the fault
  Will be marring his Rājpūtì.'

'A step on the field we will not yield,
  Though they hew us in pieces,' they cried:
And the Muslims took their oath on the Book,
  The Hindūs by the Gangā tide.

O it was a gallant sight that day
  To see the army ride;
With sticks of gold did the drum-boys play,
  Flutes, trumpets, and conchs beside.

The bards with song, as they marched along,
  Roused the warriors' hearts the while;
Before them all went the horse, Haryāl;
  So Sūraj rode a mile.

'Who has killed my kōil,[2] my wild goshawk?'
  Like a lion he roared amain;
'What Kshatrī stood at the acacia wood?
  And who has Anūpī slain?'

When Ūdan heard, in haste he spurred;
  'My mother a lion bare;
O son of the Baghēl, hear my word,
  My heart[3] is shaggy with hair.

'I am the son of Dēvī, the Queen,
  And Uday Singh am hight;[4]
It was I who hewed the acacia wood,
  And Anūpī I slayed in fight.

'Deem me no weakling as those who erst
  Before thine arms took flight;
Within nine days I Mārō raze,
  And a pool will I make its site.'

[1] The eating of which binds to faithful service.
[2] The Indian cuckoo, but in poetry it almost takes the place of the nightingale.
[3] A supposed characteristic of the brave.
[4] Called.

'Let none of the men of Mahōbā go:
  Let none unwounded fly!'
There was priming of cannon and bending of bow
  As Sūraj in wrath did cry.

But first he onward pressed his horse,
  By Anūpī he 'lighted down;
He raised in his arms his brother's corse,
  And sent it to Mārō town.

'Now blow,' he cried, 'these caitiffs away.'
  Then matches were lighted fast:
The smoke spread high and darkened the sky,
  And arrows went whizzing past.

Afar did the gunner begin, I wot,
  And then the arquebusier:
And arrows were shot, as they nearer got,
  And next the dart and spear.

But bright, bright swords were deeply dyed,
  As line on line was set;
And last the cruel daggers were plied,
  As in deadly gripe they met.

Elephants trunk with trunk enlaced,
  With their hooks the drivers fought,
Howda by howda so close was placed,
  The blows were with daggers wrought.

Swords, well plied on every side,
  Rang in the warsmith's play;
Brother on brother dropped and died,
  Friend on friend that day.

Coats of mail did nothing avail,
  Such wounds the wearers bore:
Princes, whose hurts were not to death,
  Rose to the fight once more.

Of all that marched with Sūraj then
  Half on the field did lie;
Ūdan spurred amidst his men
  And loudly 'gan to cry:

'O servants none, but brothers of mine,
  With you is mine honour bound;
Whose foot goes back from the foremost line,
  Seven ages his name is drowned.

'Creatures on earth full many have birth.
  But rare are the births[1] of men;
O use this hour, for the wilted[2] flower
  Cannot join to its tree again.

'In coming days with songs and lays
  Shall this battle day be spoken,
And armlets of gold shall to each be told
  When Dasrāj' death is wroken.[3]

'If man must die, why die in our bed,
  A prey to crow and kite?
While the name and the fame of the battle dead
  Shall be sung by bard and knight.'

Then on the men of Mahōbā pressed,
  And hardy strokes they laid;
There blew no wind from east or west,
  While that game of swords was played.

Full soon the corse of man or horse
  At every step was cast,
And like heaps of dung in the farmer's field
  Lay the bodies of elephants vast.

At Ūdan's attack did Mārō give back,
  Nor noble nor hind could stay;
When Sūraj saw, to the front he spurred
  And to Ūdan loud 'gan say.

'Why waste thy strength on a servant crew,
  When I or thou must fall?'
And Ūdan was nothing loath thereto,
  Bade sheath their weapons all.

'Strike then, bold Ūdan, strike thou first.'
  Quoth Ūdan, 'Nay, not so;
There never was man in Mahōbā nurst
  Would strike the foremost blow.

[1] That is the turn in the cycle of transmigration.
[2] Withered. [3] Avenged.

'Strike thou the first, or in paradise
  Thou wilt mourn thy wasted day.'
Then Sūraj drew his strong bow thrice,
  The bolt a seer did weigh.

The arrow, as the bowstring rang,
  At Ūdan's face did fly,
From left to right his courser sprang,
  The shaft went whizzing by.

A weighty dart then Sūraj grasped,
  He struck with careful aim;
But Ūdan the neck of Rāsbēndul clasped,
  So harmlessly down it came.

'Now mark, Banāphar Rāi, my word,
  Twice hast thou 'scaped my blow,
Be warned in time ere I deal the third,
  And home to Mahōbā go.'

'Now hear the terms that Ūdan saith,
  Prince Sūraj,' laughing he cried;
'Nought else will I take, come life, come death,
  By my father and Gangā's tide.

'King Jambay's head, and thy sister to wed,
  And Papīhā the courser fleet,
And Pachsāwad strong, and the nine-lakh chain,
  And Lākhā the dancer sweet.'

Then Sūraj waxed wode and his eyes grew red,
  And his sword from his belt he drew;
He rushed and struck at Ūdan's head,
  But the shield snapped the blade in two.

When only the heft in his hand was left,
  He wist his death drew near.
'This blade in my hand has elephants cleft,
  But now it has failed me here.'

Then on Maniyā,[1] fair Mahōbā's ward,
  And the World Mother Ūdan cried;
And he called on God, and he drew his sword
  And he charged on the right-ward side.

[1] The tutelary goddess of Mahōbā.

The flowers of silver went rattling down,
  As he rove the rhinoceros shield;
The head he cleft both face and crown,
  And the armour rang on the field.

Astonished were all who saw the fall
  Of Mārō's chief that day:
At once they broke, they scattered like smoke,
  So the army melted away.

FYTTE VIII

In Kariyā's camp his court was placed,
  His chiefs were there, a crowd:
There came a messenger pressing in haste,
  And his camel groaned aloud.

He drew the chain, the camel knelt,
  And down he lighted near;
He stood and bowed, he cried aloud,
  That all the chiefs did hear.

'Mahōbā men from Mahōbā are come,
  Thy house a ruin they make;
Sūraj lies slain on the battle plain,
  Till his body home thou take.'

Prince Kariyā started from his seat,
  And eke his captains all;
The hair of their head stood up with dread
  Such evil chance should fall.

His long boots creaked as he forth did come,
  And the shield on his shoulders rang;
'Give the drummer the pledge that he beat the drum,
  On his wrists gold bangles hang.' 5

From tent to tent the tidings went,
  Each warrior grasped his sword;
Camels were groaning, horses were girthed,
  And howdas with silken cord.

Twelve pair of kettledrums sounded alarms,
  The trumpets and conchs also;
The Mārō host stood ready in arms,
  At the beat of the drum to go.

The Pathāns[1] of Shāhābād[2] were there,
  Hight Rangā and Bangā bold;
Quoth the Prince, 'In Mahōbā a touch-stone[3] rare
  Turns iron and steel to gold.

'The Māhōba men to our borders came;
  To you I yield the prey.'
Then loud they shouted Alī's name,
  And soon to selle sprang they.

To his elephant-ward then Kariyā cried,
  'Make ready Pachsāwad strong;
And Papīhā beside, if a horse I would ride,
  Shall be led by his groom along.'

When Kariyā saw them at the yett,[4]
  He donned his harness fine;
As his foot on the howda stair he set,
  He was ware of an evil sign.[5]

'O Pandit, say what this sign may bode,
  My heart misgives me sore—'
Then the Pandit took his star-time book,
  And conned his Vēdas o'er.

'The Node the twelfth house darkens,' he said,
  'The eighth doth Venus fill;
The baleful Saturn stands o'erhead,
  In the tenth the Moon works ill.

'I rede thee back to Mārō go,
  Nor tempt, my prince, the fray;
The times are cross, the stars work woe,
  Stir not a step to-day.'

'Let pedlars' sons the omens heed,
  Who traffic and trade alway;
Let peasants stay the stars to read,
  Ere they crown for their marriage day.

[1] Afghāns, but of course at this date they had not passed beyond the Punjab.
[2] I suppose the district in Bihār is intended.
[3] This which was gained by a predecessor of King Parmāl, and the wealth it produced, are renowned in many of the ballads.
[4] Gate.
[5] Almost every incident in the ballads is foretold by omens. Sneezing is one of the most unpropitious.

'Are Kshatrī youths to fear a freit,[1]
  Who the warsmith's steel devour?
The force must march, the drum must beat,
  So Kariyā rode that hour.

A murmur of marching men there rose,
  The dust turned day to night;
With a creaking of cannon the army goes,
  With a rushing of chariots light.

The force swept on like a storm-cloud bank,
  And before went the banners of red;
Kariyā ranged his troops in rank,
  And slow to the ground did tread.

Silent he lifted his brother's corse,
  In a litter to Mārō sent;
But he roared amain as a tiger roars,
  As back to his seat he went.

'What child of man can equal my might?
  Is my match in the Rājpūt race?
Whose hand has been raised my Sūraj to smite?
  Let him answer me face to face.'

Bold Ūdan galloped forth a space,
  And loud he made reply,
'The Rājpūt who dares meet thy face,
  Thy match in fight, am I.

'No Dasrāj I, bound with a chain,
  Thy captive unaware:
Whom in the stone mill thou hast slain,
  His skull thy tree doth bear.

'Now am I come to avenge his fate,
  And the fire of my heart to slake;
When I beat down proud Mārō's state,
  And make of her site a lake.'

'Let none of the men of Mahōbā go,
  Be smitten every head;
Fire all my cannon and sweep the foe,'
  Cried Karinghā with eyeballs red.

[1] Omen.

There was loading of cannon and ramming of ball,
  And priming and lighting the pan;
His friend from foe might no man know,
  Such a smoke overhead began.

The rockets screamed, the guns roared loud,
  The arrows whistled and flew;
Headlong like bolts from Indra's[1] cloud,
  Fell many a warrior true.

Camel and horse fell one by one,
  The elephants screaming lay;
Too hot to touch was every gun,
  Yet none drew back from the fray.

Torn were the hands of the archers tried,
  And slack each good bow-string;
But lances were plied and garments dyed,
  So fast the blood did spring.

'O servants none, but brothers to me,'
  Bold Ūdan cried around;
'Your names, if from the fight ye flee,
  For ages seven are drown'd.

''The Sāwan[2] month must soon be past,
  The flower must drop to earth;
The mother's time must come at last,
  And rare[3] is human birth.

'The leaf that from the bough may part,
  It never more can grow:'
Thus Ūdan cheered his Rājpūts' heart,
  And led them on the foe.

As the wolves the sheep, as the lion the kine,
  As the schoolboys drive the ball,
So onward pressed the Mahōbā line,
  And drew their good swords all.

As the parrot pecks the woodland nut,
  As the leaf 'neath the betel knife;
So down was many a stripling cut,
  Ah woe to the widowed wife!

[1] God of the sky.
[2] July–August. It seems to be a month of holiday, especially for women.
[3] In the cycle of transmigrations.

There was weeping for father and weeping for child,
  And weeping for wife new wed;
And weeping for fate of mother mild,
  Whose son is before[1] her dead.

Both armies that day made right good play,
  And sore were the strokes they gave;
But Mārō at length fled scattered away,
  And few their lives could save.

When Kariyā saw his soldiers fly,
  His elephant forward he drave;
He loosed the chain from the canopy high,
  And there to Pachsāwad gave.

'Thou hast eaten the salt of the Baghēl long;
  Now help 'gainst this evil blast;
Let none of the foe to Mahōbā go,
  Take Ūdan and bind him fast.'

Rangā and Bangā stood thereby,
  And Kariyā turned and cried,
'Shall a mere boy my house destroy,
  And humble Mārō's pride?

'Let none escape of Dēvī's sons,
  Down from their horses smite:'
The two Pathāns then charged at once,
  With Kariyā on their right.

Through troop and line Pachsāwad raged,
  He whirled his chain around;
The stoutest chief who combat waged,
  He dashed him to the ground.

The host of Ūdan wavered and broke,
  For life did faint hearts fly;
'Now, Ūdan, now,' fierce Kariyā spoke,
  'Bold knight, prepare to die.'

'I would not fly,' quoth Ūdan high,
  'Were all my flesh beshred.'
The massy mace Karinghā bore,
  He dashed at Ūdan's head.

[1] And therefore cannot perform the funeral rites.

He 'scaped the blow, he spurred his steed,
That it reared to the elephant's crown;
So mickle of might did Ūdan smite,
Came the canopy shivering down.

'Pachsāwad, now thy lord obey,'
Fierce Kariyā thundered amain;
'Let him not take the Mahōbā way,
Bind fast with thine iron chain.'

He swung the chain on Bēndulā's mane,
He bound his arms full fast;
Ūdan he swept to the howda aloft;
Then all men stay'd aghast.

FYTTE IX

Ālhā's court and Dēvī's tent
Were in the acacia wood;
Saying ''Tis long since Ūdan went,'
She at her tent door stood.

'Why comes he not?' She strained her eyes
The distant road to see,
When she was aware of Rupnā there,
Mahōbā's herald he.

And when she saw he weeping stood,
She halsed[1] him tenderly;
'Why weep so sore, my Rupnā good?
And how may Ūdan be?'

'O lady, thou amiss hast done,
To trust such boys in fray;
They never smelt the smoke of gun,
Nor saw the swordsman's play.

'When Kariyā fierce set on our line,
Was none could stand his ground;
Pachsāwad strong who erst was thine,
Fast Ūdan's arms he bound.'

She fell to ground in deadly swound,
But soon for her litter sent;
The pennon flapped o'er the bearers twelve,
So fast to the field she went.

[1] Embraced.

A mother's yearning filled her breast,
For fear she nothing shrunk;
As it were a cow her calf caressed,
She clasped Pachsāwad's trunk.

'I reared thee up in my house from youth,
And gave thee milk good store;
O little of grace, was this thy truth,
My Ūdan to bind so sore?'

At her words a shame o'er Pachsāwad came,
'I was pledged to the King Jambay;
I have eaten his salt, 'twas in me no fault
I should bind thine Ūdan Ray.

'Were Malkhān now to the battle sent,
He would soon set Ūdan free;'
Then Dēvī quick to her litter went,
And straight to the camp came she.

'O Malkhān brave, thy younger save,'
She cried with streaming eyes;
'On the battle plain, by Kariyā ta'en,
A captive bound he lies.'

'Now Ālhā, hear,' brave Malkhān said,
'Let all thine army come;
I must go to the ground where my brother lies bound;'
Then loud they beat the drum.

He blessed the World-mother and Rāma's name,
The feet of the earth and the sun;
So forth from his tent brave Malkhān went,
And thus to his mare begun.

'If I boiled thee carrots in days of spring,
And gave thee oil in rain;
If Malhnā the Queen thy milk did bring,
Full bowls for the filly to drain;

'In Mārō here, this land of fear,
Be thou my stay, O mare!'
Then did she arch her neck and rear,
And proudly paw the air.

'A long farewell to all things dear,
  To life a long farewell!'
So all the army marched in fere[1]
  When Malkhān sprang to selle.

To the field of fight they came with speed,
  In Kariyā's front he spake;
'Upon herbs on which asps have breathed canst feed?
  The lioness' milk canst take?

'A ladder 'gainst Paradise gate canst place?
  Canst bind a brother of mine?
Let a Kshatrī answer me face to face,
  If one be in the Mārō line.'

'Now a pretty boy in sooth,' said he,
  'But I rede thee home return;
Lest I deal, as with Dasrāj I dealt, with thee:'
  Then Malkhān's eyes did burn.

His sword flashed bare, he spurred his mare,
  That she reared to the elephant's crown;
Pillar of sandal and pinnacles gold
  At his stroke came toppling down.

The driver laid on strokes well told,
  Not a step Pachsāwad went;
His trunk between his tusks he rolled,
  And down his knees he bent.

And Ālhā then with all his men
  Came charging o'er the plain;
With a battle shout their swords flashed out,
  Like the sweep of the hurricane.

'Pachsāwad doth play me false to-day;
  He quits the foremost line:'
Karinghā's soul was troubled sore,
  And round he turned his eyne.

Then straight he bade Papīhā bring,
  And lighted down to ride;
From his courser's back did Malkhān spring,
  And sat by Ūdan's side.

[1] Together.

Ūdan unbound he laid on the ground,
And Rupnā Bēndulā led;
Queen Dēvī down from her litter came,
And worshipped Pachsāwad's head.

With the sandal free, so fair to see,
She painted his frontal wide;
'Behold I entrust my sons to thee,
Now help in this perilous tide.

'Lo Ālhā, here thy father's beast,
Mount up, my son, and ride:'
He climbed and stood on the painted wood
And sat as he grasped the side.

'Fight on, my merry men,' Ālhā cried,
'Take each his fill o' the game:'
Though swords by both were briskly plied,
With a rush Mahōbā came.

They beat down all like a desert bare,
Nor high nor low could stay;
They, who long gowns were proud to wear,
Fled through ravines away.

Then fast did Ūdan to Kariyā go,
At the gallop he came and cried:
'My turn 'tis now to deal the blow,
Look thou my stroke to bide.'

Karinghā turned his cruel eye,
To Rangā called and said;
'Let none of the men of Mahōbā fly,
Go, smite them every head.'

'Ho! stand,' stout Rangā 'gan to cry,
'O son of Mahōbā's King;
Strike turn by turn till one of us die,'
Then together their chargers spring.

He struck him once, he struck him twice,
But never the buckler cleft;
At the third stroke the good blade broke,
And the hilt in his hand was left.

Then on Nārāyan Ūdan cried,
And on Kālī's feet also;
With drawn sword galloped to Rangā's side,
He smote and laid him low.

Now Bangā was near and his sword drew he,
But Dhēwā spurred from the right;
'Fight we and see what is God's decree,'
Then struck he with all his might.

The blow on Dhēwā's buckler fell,
And broken was Bangā's blade;
'A summons is come from the lord of hell,
And near is my death,' he said.

Then Dhēwā wheeled and smote on the right,
Nor buckler nor pad could save;
Through twelve mail rings did the good steel bite,
And from shoulder to waist it clave.

When Rangā fell and Bangā as well,
Karinghā was troubled sore;
He struck with his mace at Dhēwā's steed,
But his blow the buckler bore.

So Bhīkham's[1] son was wounded none,
But his horse seven paces reeled;
And Ūdan thereon with his good sword drawn
Came spurring over the field.

But Ūdan's steed he smote with his mace
That he reeled five paces back;
Was never a chief could hold his place,
'Gainst Kariyā's fierce attack.

Then Ūdan rode to the brave Malkhay,
He joined his hands and spake;
'No match for Kariyā's strength am I,
Or a captive in chains I'd take.'

When Malkhān heard, he onward spurred,
Eight paces off 'gan cry:
'Now Kariyā, sit thou warily,
For know thy death is nigh.'

[1] Apparently another discrepancy with the prologue where his father is called Rahmal.

His Bardwān[1] broad sword in wrath he drew,
He struck with all his strength;
But never a whit on Malkhān it bit,
Not even a barleycorn's length.

Then Malkhān drew sword and remembered his Lord,
And Nārāyan's[2] name he said,
And Maniyā fair, Māhōbā's ward;
So he smote off Kariyā's head.

Down Ūdan sprang and the head he took,
And thus to Ālhā spake:
'We have slain the foe and laid him low,
Then here we our camp should make.

'I mind when we marched from Mahōbā, then
Queen Malhnā spake from the door:
"I bless you my sons, and I bless you again,
But when shall we meet once more?"

'Then I gave her my word for eight short months,
And now is a year gone by;
And surely I fear she sheds many a tear,
"Why comes not Ūdan Ray?"

'Send Kariyā's head her heart to ease:'
Then his word liked Ālhā well;
In a litter he laid the head and he bade
The herald the tidings tell.

A young horse saddled was standing there,
And Rupnā leapt thereon;
The bearers were yare[3] and the litter they bare:
So he to Mahōbā is gone.

FYTTE X

Queen Malhnā looked over lake and hill,
On the topmost turret raised;
All day she was standing, standing, still,
All night she waked and gazed.

[1] These weapons are generally described as coming from this town in Bengal.
[2] Vishnu as the Supreme Being.
[3] Ready.

She watched the road where earth met sky,
  'My youngest long doth bide.'
If a distant traveller met her eye,
  ''Tis Ūdan at last,' she cried.

Queen Malhnā stood on the topmost stair,
  She looked over dale and down;
And she was aware of Māhilā there,
  Came riding to the town.

Slowly, slowly she down did win;
  'What ails my sister?' he said,
'And why is thy body grown so thin,
  And thine eyes with weeping red?'

'Ask not, O brother, what ill I fear,
  For how shall I bear to tell?
Ālhā and Ūdan from infants I rear,
  Malkhān and Sulkhān as well.

'To war in the Mārō land they went,
  And there come no tidings here;
They promised eight months should not be spent,
  But now there is past a year.'

'There are floating, O sister, such rumours of bale,
  It likes me not to say;
Two Mārō messengers told the tale,
  They passed by my garden way.

'The Banāphars, they said, were slain and each head
  Was hung on a fig-tree high:'
The Rānī fell to the ground as dead,
  And the twelve queens loud 'gan cry.

'Who will ferry us over this stormy sea,
  Since sunk is our golden isle?'
'Will weeping bring back the dead?' quoth he,
  'Be patient, my sister, the while.

'Go, bid thy Brāhman choose the day,
  And memory's rites provide;
For each wife her bracelets must cast away,
  A widow, the sea[1] beside.'

[1] As in English, used for a lake.

Now the litter to Parmāl's court was led,
Then out and spake the King;
'Ill rumours are spread that our youngest is dead;
O herald, whose head dost bring?'

He joined his hands, 'O speak not so;
The lads are in health,' he said,
'They have wroken[1] their father on false Mārò,
And have sent me with Kariyā's head.'

Up from his seat rose the King Parmāl
And drew the curtains apart;
'An thou tarry to go to the painted hall,
The Queen will have stabbed her heart.'

And, when the herald reached the yett,[2]
The Queen came hurrying soon;
She saw the litter with blood was wet,
And fell in deadly swoon.

'Ill rumours are spread that Ūdan is dead;
Now tell me the truth, my son:'
'O mother, four sons King Jambay had,
Now Ūdan hath slain each one.

'They have razed the fort of th' acacia trees,
They have wrought their work in the land;
Prince Kariyā's head, thy mind to ease,
They send thee by my hand.'

The litter curtains he drew apart,
Karinghā's head to show;
Then glad was Rānī Malhnā's heart,
To hear they had quelled the foe.

'O brother Māhil, thou shouldst have died,
Ere such false rumours tell;
My sons are living each one,' she cried,
'They have wroken their father well.'

'Come, eat in the palace, my Rupnā good:'
His hands did he join and say,
'By thy leave, O mother, I cook no food,
It would hinder my backward way.

[1] Avenged. [2] Gate.

'For well I wot our youngest will chide,
  Till my journey to Mārō is done:'
So forth with the litter did Rupnā ride,
  Till Ālhā's camp he won.

Down from his horse did he leap and stand,
  And thrice low louted he;
But Ālhā caught him by the hand,
  And halsed him tenderly.

'Say, how is it now with Mahōbā fair?
  How doth the King Parmāl?'
'Well do all fare by God's grace there;
  He sits and governs all.'

'Now hear, my brother,' bold Ūdan cried,
  'For Lōhāgarh be we boune;
Against the gate let our guns be plied,
  And so shall we win the town.'

The drummer they called and a pledge they cast,
  Gave bangles of gold to wear;
And they bade him sound the camp around
  That each might his arms prepare.

Through each camp street went messengers fleet,
  And soon the tidings passed;
To and fro did the marshal go,
  And the troops arranged them fast.

Howda on elephant, selle on steed,
  On Manurthā Dhēwā sprang;
On Rāsbēndul did Ūdan speed,
  And the targe on his left arm rang.

Kabutrī there, that right good mare,
  The brave Malkhay bestrode;
Ālhā sat on Pachsāwad strong,
  And his Lioness Mīrā rode.

With beating of drum did the army come,
  With flaunting of banners of red;
The guns were raised and the linstocks blazed,
  And the smoke to the gateway spread.

To Jambay's hall two messengers hied;
The King with his council sate;
'Lo here the Mahōbā host,' they cried,
'They have planted their guns at the gate.'

Up started the King astonied sore,
He went to the painted tower;
Queen Kushlā met her lord at the door
With her fan of the purple flower.

She joined her hands, 'O husband, say,
What evil chance hath passed?
Why droops the hair of thy lip to-day,
And thy lofty look downcast?'

'How shall I tell the tale, O Queen?
Thy race is all undone;
Four goodly sons my stem made green,
But now there liveth none.

'Mahōbā's chief, that Ūdan hight,
Queen Dēvī's younger son;
Good sooth a warrior skilled in fight,
He slew them every one.'

Fair Bijmā was standing the lattice behind,
And her father's words heard she:
'Bēndulā's rider now will I bind,
Whose fear lies so heavy on thee.'

To her bower anon is the Princess gone,
And her Bengal[1] casket hent;
She busked her in haste and forth she paced,
And soon to the camp she went.

O'er Ālhā she cast the Bhairav spell,
He could not speak nor see;
On Malkhān the Narsingh powder fell,
Then voice and sense lost he.

Bīr Mahamdī's charm did to Dhēwā fly,
Then darkness wrapped him round;
Through the whole wide camp not a mouse could cry,
By the spell of Silence bound.

[1] Kāmrūp in Assam, perhaps, which is considered the head-quarters of all magic. It is curious to find this a common part of a lady's education as in the old romances of Europe, and we have good as well as bad enchantresses, the Lady of the Lake as well as Morgan le Fay.

Bold Ūdan she turned to a ram that day,
  So mighty a charm she got;
To lone Jhārkhand[1] she led him away
  To her teacher Jhilmilā's cot.

She tied him fast with a silken string,
  At her master's feet she fell;
'A Mahōbā thief, my father, I bring,
  As thou lovest me, guard him well.'

To Mārō then and her painted dome
  In haste the Princess passed;
And all her spells she summoned home,
  Which on the camp she cast.

Then Ālha woke, to Malkhān spoke,
  'My brother's steed I see;
But on his back no rider sits,
  O where may Ūdan be?'

'Ho, Dhēwā wise,' brave Malkhān cries,
  'What sees thy prophet mind?
Mark sign and book, and soothly look,
  Our youngest how to find.'

So Dhēwā took his star-time book,
  And soon he 'gan to say,
''Tis Jambay's child, Bijaisin styled,
  Has stol'n our brother away.

'She has made him a ram by the spell she cast,
  Through the might of Gramarye;
In Jhārkhand lone she has bound him fast,
  Her master's cottage nigh.'

'Now rede we a rede, how best we speed,
  To set my brother free:'
'Let Malkhān don the Jōgī's weed,
  And doff his Rājpūtī.'

He hath signed his forehead with Rāma's sign,
  Smeared his body with ashes well;
He sang the praise of the name divine,
  And his sandal beads 'gan tell.

[1] The forest of Baījnāth or Baidyanāth, I believe, in the hill country on the railroad between Allahabad and Calcutta; but the ballad is quite independent of time and place.

He hath taken his flute and Dhēwā his drum,
  The feet of their Lord they adore;
And soon to the Jhārkhand wood they come,
  And stand at the hermit's door.

Then Malkhān sang and the cottage rang,
  So sweetly did he trill;
Forth to his door the hermit ran,
  And asked them of their will.

'O Jōgīs twain that roam the waste,
  Whence come ye? whither go?'
'Our master's steps we vainly traced,
  His road we do not know.

'So here we stay to ask the way
  To Hardwār's sacred flow.'
'First let me see your skill, I pray,
  Then I the path will show.'

Then loud was Dhēwā's tambour struck,
  And Malkhān danced and sprang;
The wood as they trilled was with rapture filled,
  While every change they sang.

'O Jōgīs, here in my hut abide,
  I'll serve your feet each day.'
'Waters that flow, and Jōgīs that go,
  What power can bid them stay?

'Bring forth thine alms whate'er it be,
  And let us wend our way.'
'Ask what ye will, an asking free,
  I will not say ye nay.'

'Now give this ram,' quoth Malkhān brave.
  He stopped in dumb dismay,
'The boon ye crave is Bijmā's slave,
  It must not pass away.'

'Thy holy deeds are all undone,
  By swerving from thy word.'
On that he gave the ram they won,
  Nor any more demurr'd.

'What do I with this ram, O sage?
  To man I pray thee turn;
The laws of fast and pilgrimage,
  My minister shall learn.'

Into his script he thrust his hand,
  A spell of might he drew;
The charm he shed o'er Ūdan's head,
  And made him man anew.

But when the three were passed from sight.
  Quoth Ūdan, 'Brother, hear;
If lady Bijmā learn my flight,
  She will steal me again, I fear.

'This hermit is a warlock hoar,
  Him, Malkhān, must thou kill.'
Then Malkhān turned him to the door;
  The hermit asked his will.

'A draught from out thy well I ask,
  On weary journey boune.'
The silken cord, the silver flask,
  He stooped to let them down.

And, as he raised the silken thread,
  His bright sword Malkhān drew;
He smote the hermit's hoary head,
  And in the cottage threw.

The spells and charms of Gramarye,
  They bore them all away;
So to the camp are come the three,
  I wis they did not stay.

When Ūdan went to Ālhā's tent,
  Right glad was he, I ween;
He hals'd him well and ask'd what fell;
  Great joy was them between.

FYTTE XI

They have planted their cannon against the gate,
  Proud Lōhāgarh to quell;
An hundred guns did in order wait,
  Till the word for the onset fell.

An hundred linstocks at once they ply,
  And the smoke to the welkin wins;
And word is brought to the King Jambay,
  The Mahōba attack begins.

He bade them fire from every gun
  That stood on the turrets high;
They light the matches for every one,
  And the cannon balls roar and fly.

The army of Ālhā was troubled sore,
  As the groaning warriors fall;
In vain did the cannon of Malkhān roar,
  They pierced not that iron wall.

Quoth Ūdan, 'Brother, hear my rede,
  Send to th' acacia wood;
And lade on all our wains with speed
  The thorn boughs there that stood.

'Then heap them high in the ditch to lie,
  And drive a mine also;
And many a bag with the powder fill,
  To place in the trench below.'

The matches they light, the flames burn bright,
  They melt the lead of the wall:
The guns that stood on the battlement height,
  Each toppling down doth fall.

Then Malkhān brave his onset made,
  His sword at the gate he drew;
Strokes with his blade full heavy he laid,
  And all the guards he slew.

Bold Ūdan sprang from selle thereby,
  Found clubs of the metals eight;[1]
The locks at his strokes to pieces fly,
  So the army forced the gate.

A messenger ran, a fearful man,
  Where Jambay held his state;
And thrice he bowed, and cried aloud,
  'The foe has forced the gate.'

[1] These are said to be gold, silver, copper, brass, tin, bell-metal (or steel), lead, and iron.

Up stert[1] the King and his nobles all,
  Who sat in the council room;
Eftsoons did he the drummer call,
  And turban he gave and plume.

At the first drum-beat they saddle the steed,
  At the second to selle they spring;
At the third drum-beat they are ready at need,
  To ride with the Mārō King.

The King to Gaurī[2] and Ganēś bowed,
  And in water of Gangā bathed;
The muslin they brought was in Egypt wrought,
  Wherewith his limbs were swathed.

His girdle was all of the velvet good,
  With many a gay gold ring;
Dagger and sword at his waist there stood,
  As fitted a Rājpūt King.

He took in his hand his mighty mace,
  To his elephant forth went he;
And he stept up the stair of sandal fair,
  Was carved so rich to see.

And when they reached the Banāphar force,
  From his howda he loud 'gan call:
'Let none of the foe unwounded go,
  Fight on, my merry men all.'

His sword each man of Mārō drew,
  And all did quit them well;
Shot and spear and arrow flew,
  And many a warrior fell.

The sand around was soaked with gore,
  Where thick the ranks did tread;
Wounded rose to fight once more,
  Yea, bodies[3] that lacked the head.

'Friends,' cried Ūdan, 'this our day,
  Glory all may reach;
Soon we take our homeward way,
  With honour and wealth for each.'

[1] Started.
[2] The fair manifestation of Durgā, wife of Śiva, as Kālī is the dark.
[3] Not an uncommon incident in these heroic combats

He cheered his men, and on they sped,
But the Rājā loud 'gan cry;
'Is there ever a Rājpūt Mahōbā bred,
Dares meet with the King Jambay?'

Then Ūdan struck with his bossy shield,
And the pinnacles clattered from place;
But backward soon his courser reeled
At the blow from the Rājā's mace.

Then Dhēwā smote, but the King was ware,
And a blow on the steed did lay;
He reared full high and fast 'gan fly;
No reining him could stay.

There was never a Chief his place could hold,
Where the Rājā's blows did fall;
Oh! bitter that day the war that rolled,
Round the fort of the iron wall.

Faint heart and brave, 'fore Mārō's King,
They scattered like morning cloud;
Down the ravine, to 'scape unseen,
Fled many a turban proud.

There were some who, holding their breath, did lie,
A heap of slain below;
When an elephant mad rushed trampling by,
They died without striking blow.

There were some who swaggered with sword before,
In street though never in tent;
Now only a string and a loin cloth wore,
Their bodies with ashes besprent.

They signed their foreheads with Rāma's sign,
With the blood-stained earth they found;
'We were begging our way to the Jagannāth shrine,
When the sword play closed around.'

And one on his back took of bucklers a pack,
Like a Jaipur[1] artisan;
'For selling of shield I had come to the field,
Nor wist ere the fight began.'

[1] This Rājpūt State seems to retain its fame in the arts to the present day.

The howdas were filled with blood that day,
  The horsemen dripped with gore;
Friend from foe might no man know,
  But the fight raged more and more.

Brave Malkhān stood a while dismayed,
  Then fast to Ālhā sped;
He joined his hands and asked for aid,
  'Brother, give ear,' he said.

'No chief can stand in the Rājā's sight,
  My strength is all in vain;
But thou art able to equal his might,
  And to bind him with iron chain.'

When Ālhā heard his brother's word,
  For chains he straight did send;
To his elephant then he gave them to hold,
  And, 'Pachsāwad,' he cried, 'attend.

'We must bind the foe and make him a show
  For the folk of Mahōbā town;
When to King Parmāl and to Malhnā we go,
  In our homeward triumph boune.'

Onward Pachsāwad pressed amain,
  The ranks he scattered wide;
As he whirled his chain, he strewed the plain
  Like a desert on either side.

The warriors staggered, they scattered and broke,
  In hope their lives to save;
When Jambay saw they fled, he spoke,
  And his elephant onward drave.

'Mahōbā's champion, Dēvī's son,
  Now settle thy cause with me;
Alive from the field shall go but one,
  So turn by turn strike we.'

'I may not strike, by the Chandēl law;
  Do thou strike first, O king:'
Then a good red bow did Jambay draw,
  And fitted the notch to string.

The aim was good, the string did twang,
  Fast did the arrow fly;
Across the howda Ālhā sprang,
  And the shaft went whizzing by.

Then his javelin flew, as near they drew,
  Now how may Ālhā bide?
Queen Śaradā's[1] care, at his right hand there,
  She turned the spear aside.

'Now hear, Banāphar,' Jambay spake,
  'Twice hast thou foiled my blow;
In peace thy way to Mahōbā take,
  For thrice thou 'scap'st not so.'

But Ālhā there his breast made bare,
  And did to the Rājā cry:
'No part of a Kshatrī's trade it were,
  From the battle trench to fly.

'There are homes in heaven stand ready for all,
  To-morrow if not to-day;
And if I in Mārō this tide shall fall,
  My name shall live for aye.

'One chance is left thee, King, to save,
  And see thou miss no more.'
Then drew the King his shining glaive,
  And thrice he smote full sore.

No hurt on Ālhā's body happ'd,
  His shield was lifted high;
At length the sword of Jambay snapp'd;
  Then wist he death was nigh.

'I have hewn down elephants with this blade,
  And lopped their limbs away;
Its master's need has it now betrayed,
  My life is lost to-day.'

'Now, Rājā, now my stroke take thou,'
  And his elephant on he drove;
Howda to howda, tusk to tusk,
  Close met the champions strove.

[1] The name given to Durgā at Mahōbā.

Then Ālhā forward dash'd his shield,
  With the boss he dealt a blow:
The elephant's driver was hurl'd to the field,
  And he waver'd to and fro.

Then Jambay drew his dagger keen,
  Long time their steel they plied;
On Ālhā's body no hurt was seen,
  'Now bind the foe,' he cried.

Pachsāwad whirl'd his iron chain,
  Dashed the howda to the ground;
Soon Ālhā lighted on the plain,
  And fast his arms he bound.

FYTTE XII

They sounded the drum of victory,
  And the conqueror's shout they rais'd;
They rendered thanks to Rāma high,
  And the feet of their Lord they prais'd.

They blessed the virtue of Malhnā the Queen,
  And named King Parmāl's name:
Thus onward Ūdan's horse, I ween,
  And Ālhā's elephant came.

On the right hand there was Malkhān's mare,
  And Dhēwā's courser proud;
And on their right side did the Saiyid ride,
  And 'Alī' he shouted loud.

To the house of treasure when Ālhā came,
  The guards with his sword he killed,
The locks he broke and the wains did yoke,
  And with stores of price he filled.

A plunder rich from Mārō town
  Brought Dasrāj' warlike son;
And the guns of weight of the metals eight,
  He took them every one. 5

Horses and elephants spoiled he there,
  And every weapon withal;
Fire he set to the palaces fair,
  And blackened the lordly wall.

But when he came to the painted hall,
  He stayed beside the gate,
And a messenger sent his mother to call,
  And bring from th' encampment straight.

In her litter she left th' acacia wood,
  Full hastily did she ride;
And when at the Lion gate she stood,
  The five stepped down beside.

'Now, mother, send,' quoth Ūdan bold,
  'And Rānī Kushlā call.'
Then Kushlā's slave her lady told,
  As she sat in the painted hall.

'What sleep art sleeping here?' she cried,
  'And sit'st on thy sandal chair?
Ālhā doth wait beside the gate,
  And bids thee meet him there.'

Dismayed was she to hear the same,
  Her heart it died away;
Joining her hands, in haste she came,
  And did to Ūdan say—

'O harm not woman, Ūdan Rāy,
  Though thine the power to-day.'
'I ne'er did smite my foes that fly,
  Nor hand on woman lay.

'But bring my father's turban and crest,
  That have long in Mārō lain;
And Lākhā, too, that dancer best,
  And eke the nine-lakh chain.

'And the litter prepare of Bijmā fair,
  With me as a bride to wend.'
Whatever he bade she yielded there,
  Until he made an end.

So they moved on to the mill of stone,
  With Dēvī and the Queen;
There did they wait by the inner gate,
  And the litter was set between.

But Ūdan rushed to the fig-tree old,
His father's skull to win;
A censer of gold he brought to hold,
And set the skull therein.

Then Ālhā and Malkhān the presser plied,
Yoked in the bullock's place;
Ūdan beside stood the roller to guide
Before Queen Kushlā's face.

And Dhēwā too King Jambay threw
Into the mill to bray;
All as he stood they crushed him there,
Then smote his head away.[1]

His skull they by Dasrāj' skull did lay,
Who laughed a ghastly laugh;
'Ālhā and Ūdan, blest be they,
Of Dasrāj' line the staff.'

Each of his sons by name he blest,
And the mother that bare them also;
'The fire of my breast this day may rest,
They have venged me upon my foe.

'An evil son will shame his kin,
An it were seven ages back;
But the parents, who a good son win,
Nor peace nor honour lack.

'My skull, O sons, to Kāśī[2] take,
The Gayā[3] rites to pay.'
Then out the skull of Jambay spake,
'Now, Ūdan, hear my say.

'Of four brave sons the water to pour,[4]
Thou hast not left me one;
My skull then cast on Kāśī's shore,
I charge thee, Dasrāj' son.'

[1] The murder of Dasrāj seems to have been peculiarly atrocious to have provoked this retaliation. It is but fair to mention that in most of the ballads the Banāphars are chivalrous to a degree towards their conquered foes, even after meeting with treachery themselves.

[2] Benares.

[3] The capital of Bihār, a famous place of pilgrimage, especially for the uneral rites.

[4] In the funeral ceremony.

For the litter of Bijmā Ūdan sent,
In the palace hard by to be placed;
A pole he had pight[1] of the sandal bright,
And he called for a Pandit[2] in haste.

'To Bijmā fair I my vow will pay,
And the seven rounds[3] will tread.'
'What! are thy senses gone astray,
My brother?' Ālhā said.

'With the house of our foe, I bid thee know,
No marriage feast I keep;
When she thinks of her father and brethren slain,
She will kill thee in thy sleep.

'No, Ūdan, lady Bijmā slay,
And smite her where she stands:'
'O spare me, brother, this I pray,'
He cried with joining hands.

'How can I break my Rājpūt's vow
And lift my hand on her?'
'Then smite the Princess, Malkhān, thou,
And see thou do not err.'

On Mahadēva[4] Malkhān cried,
His shining sword he drew;
He smote so sore Bijaisin's side,
He cleft her shoulder through.

Then said she, 'Ūdan, once I dreamed
To spend our lives in fere[5];
And sweet to me e'en death had seemed,
Had thy hand made it dear.

'But, cruel Malkhān, woe to thee,
Thy brother's wife hast slain:
So shalt thou die with no brother by,
Unhelped in an open plain.'

But Ūdan's soul in love was drowned,
When Bijmā's speech heard he;
He clasped her hand and raised from ground,
And rested her on his knee.

[1] Pitched. [2] A priest learned in the scriptures.
[3] An essential part of the marriage ceremony.
[4] The great god, Siva. [5] Together.

'Here must we part ere yet we wed,
But meeting canst none descry?'
'O lay me down, my love,' she said,
'Since I must a maiden die.

'Here it is best my body should rest,
But my soul new birth shall see;
King Narpat's daughter of Narwar[1] town,
And Phulwā my name shall be.

'And when thou, goodly steeds to buy,
To the Kābul land shalt ride,
Our meeting, O love, shall then be nigh.'
So Bijmā spake and died.

But Ūdan bare her body fair,
To Narmadā's[2] holy tide;
He cast her into the river there,
While the troops to the camp did ride.

The litter of Dēvī they took withal,
And Lākhā the dancer true;
And Ālhā did all his warriors call,
When they to the woodland drew.

A gay gold ring, a robe, a shawl,
A crest and turban blue,
Or a silver fee to some did fall,
Each had his largess due.

'Friends,' cried Ālhā, 'all prepare!
Load the wains each one;
Home to Mahōbā now we fare;
Ālhā's work is done.'

But Ūdan turned aside from the crowd,
At his mother's feet to fall;
Before the Saiyid old he bowed,
And eke his brethren all.

'An order, O mother, an order I crave,
The Gayā rites to pay.'
He went with the skulls, when her leave she gave,
And left the triumphal way.

[1] The town in the Gwālior state. The doctrine of transmigration must be very useful for poetical justice. Bijaisin's prophecy is fulfilled in Canto VII.

[2] The Nerbudda, one of the sacred rivers.

The sound of victory swelled from the drum,
  They marched full many a day;
At length did the host to the border come,
  And Ālhā to Rupnā say—

'Ride on to Mahōbā our news to bring.'
  Then he spurred till he reached the wall;
He lighted down and he passed the town,
  And he stood in the Rājā's hall.

Joining his hands the herald drew nigh:
  'Now the news of Ālhā say.'
'He hath venged Dasrāj and hath crushed Jambay,
  And is here on his homeward way.'

Then Malhnā the Queen right glad was she,
  She gathered her maidens all;
By this were arrived the brethren three,
  And stood at the city wall.

Madrigals singing, the women came there,
  They met them and blessed their name;
With a four-flamed lamp in a salver fair,
  Queen Malhnā to greet them came.

Seven times o'er Ālhā she waved the dish,
  O'er his body she passed her hand;
'Now blessed be my sons for fulfilling my wish,
  I welcome ye back to the land.'

'O mother, thy favour hath gained us all,'
  He joined his hands and spake;
'Now pay I my homage to King Parmāl,
  If I thy leave may take.'

She bade them go the King to greet,
  Then Ālhā before him went;
His turban of purple he cast at his feet,
  And they stood with their heads down bent.

The Rājā took their hands each one,
  And there he set them down;
'Come, quench the fire of my breast, my son,
  And tell me of Mārō town.'

'O, a fearful fight was foughten, I wot,
  Round Mārō city wall;
Four sons that the Mārō King begot,
  In the war-field each did fall.

'We bound the arms of the King Jambay,
  And crushed in the mill of stone;
Bijaisin too with the sword we slew,
  And her corse in the stream was thrown.

'All that from us was plundered of yore,
  We have brought to our home again;
And Jambay's treasures, a goodly store,
  Have laden on many a wain.'

The King rejoiced and blessed them oft,
  And bade the cannon to play;
From an hundred guns spread the smoke aloft,
  Till the folk were deafened that day.

And all the crowd cried, 'Victory' loud,
  And alms did free bestow;
Gold gifts there did no man spare,
  Since Ālhā had quelled the foe. 55

Lend ear, my friends, to the song I write,
  So give you mirth and glee!
I have told the tale of the Mārō fight,
  As it was told to me.

CANTO IV

THE MARRIAGE OF ĀLHĀ

THE following canto describes how Ālhā won Sunwā (or Sōnmatī), daughter of Naipālī, the Baghēl Rājā of Naināgaṛh. The site of this town has not been identified, and nothing is known about it, except that it was seven days' march from Mahōbā. The reciters of the poem identify it with the fort of Chunār in the Mirzapur district, but this does not seem likely, nor can they give any grounds for their statement.

This canto gives a good example of the Rājpūt marriage customs to which attention has been drawn in the introduction. The father of the bride dares suitors to come, and when one does come, he has to meet force by force, and is treated with the foulest treachery. The most solemn oath of friendship, not to speak of safe conduct, is taken with no intention of its being kept, and is broken without hesitation. Ālhā succeeds, after many perils, in bringing away his bride, and it would naturally be expected that, in future years, his relations with his wife's people would at least be strained. Yet we find them subsequently on the most friendly terms, and fighting side by side as allies.

I HAIL thee, Evening, whose sweet hands
  The bonds of toil undo,
And house to house through all the lands
  The cheerful lamp renew.

Forth from the wood the grazing herds
  Thy voice doth summon home;
Thou bringest thoughts of nests to birds
  On weary wing that roam.

Queen Śāradā,[1] to thee I bow,
  I touch my master's feet;
Rāma, to thee I vow my vow;
  O make my work complete.

[1] The Mahōbā name of Dēvī.

FYTTE I

In Naināgarh Naipālī reigned,
  Rich in King Indra's grace;
A drum of life the Rājā gained;
  He feared not death to face.

And in his house was Sunwā reared,
  Well learned in gramarye;
Years fifteen had the damsel seen,
  And fair of face was she.

And all as they plucked the garden flowers,
  'Sister,' her maids 'gan say,
'Is there lacking of wealth in the Rājā's towers
  That he names not thy marriage day?'

Now Sunwā before the Queen is come,
  And, 'Hearken, Mother,' she said,
'My fellows go each to her husband's home,
  But me thou hast not wed.'

Uprose the Queen with thoughtful mien,
  And her way to her lord did take;
The feet of the sleeping king she pressed;
  She joined her hands and spake.

'Is Naipālī's race, O my husband, base,
  That thy child is unwedded yet?
The maiden is ripe of age by now;
  It is time that the day were set.'

The Rājā heard his lady's word,
  And passed to the outer door;
Barber, herald, priest, and bard,
  He called them forth all four.

Three lakhs of gold as gifts he told
  To plight his daughter's hand;
He bade them seek a bridegroom meet,
  And fare to every land.

'But go not down to Mahōbā town,
  Where the king Parmāl doth reign;'
So the messengers have the betrothal gifts
  And the king's son Bijyā ta'en.

To every rājā they proffer the gift,
  Through every land they roam;
But none was ready the pledge to lift,
  So came they bootless home.

Before Naipālī the messengers bent,
  When back the gifts they brought;
'To each rājā we went, but none would consent,'
  Then sat he heavy in thought.

Now certain days were gone and spent;
  From all the countries round
Came rājās, each with his armament,
  And pitched at the outmost bound.

Crimson banner, spear, and tent,
  To east and west and north:
Then king Naipālī for Bijyā sent,
  Bade carry the kettledrum forth.

'Place the drum at the outer bound;
  Proclaim it far and wide,
Who first shall cause the drum to sound,
  My daughter shall be his bride.'

But each chief bowed down with his offering,
  And did in the presence cry,
'Aid, O king, 'gainst thy foes we bring,
  But we may not mate so high.'

Now hear what lady Sunwā said,
  And thus her vow vowed she,
'In my father's house I will dwell unwed,
  Or Ālhā my lord shall be.'

Then straight she called for Hīrāman's cage,
  And nigh on her couch she placed;
'I have brought thee up from thy nestling age
  With fruits of the sweetest taste.

'Parrot, be thou my help to-day,
  For sore is now my strait;
Speed to Mahōbā town and say
  To Ālhā all my state.'

'Now write me a writing speedily,
  O Sunwā,' Hīrāman spake;
'And I to Mahōbā town will fly
  And thy message to Ālhā take.'

Kālpī paper she took in haste,
  And pen-case in hand beside;
The title with Ūdan's name she traced,
  Saying, 'Greeting from Ālhā's bride.

'Rānī Sunwā hath vowed a vow,
  She will none but Ālhā wed.
Ūdan, the bridal train bring thou
  The seven rounds to tread.

'If thou art Rājpūt leal and true,
  Thou wilt make me Ālhā's wife;
If thou fail a maiden's bidding to do,
  Thou hast wasted thy knightly life.

'Great be the shame on thy Rājpūt name,
  If help thou do not bring;
In my husband's brother my hope is strong;
  I have trusted thee, Uday Singh.'

The letter which Rānī Sunwā writ,
  On the neck of the parrot she tied;
I wis he tarried never a whit,
  But away to Mahōbā hied.

Day and night he took his flight
  Till he reached Mahōbā town;
In the sandal wood garden did he alight,
  And thither came Ūdan down.

When Ūdan spied the letter tied,
  'Brave bird, what dost thou there?
And who has sent thee forth,' he cried,
  'And unto what land dost fare?'

'Rānī Sunwā bade me go;
  From Naināgarh I fly;
Now, Thākur, Ālhā's palace show,
  And where is Ūdan Rāi?'

'Now hear my word,' he laughed, 'O bird,
What doth thy lady write?
Ālhā's younger brother am I,
And Uday Singh am hight.'

The letter he loosed from Hīrāman's neck,
And he read it speedily;
With the popinjay he took his way,
And blithe of heart was he.

Thronged was the court of the king Parmāl;
He held his royal state;
Rājās, princes, nobles, all,
Each in his order sate.

Slowly over the throne of gold
Did the heavy chaurīs wave;
Ālhā, Dhēwā, and Malkhān bold,
Held each in hand his glaive.

When Ūdan bowed amidst the hall,
The letter the Rājā read;
Letter by letter he read it all,
But never a word he said. 35

He hid the writing beneath his thigh;
His soul was astonied sore;
'What news hast here,' quoth the brave Malkhay,
'And why dost thou hide thy store?'

'Ask me no news, thou Malkhān brave,
For these I must not tell;
This writing know the princess gave
Who in Naināgarh doth dwell.

'East and west to every land
They sent her betrothal fee;
Was never a rājā would take it in hand,
And now it has come to me.

'But, Malkhān, send it back straightway,
As thou art lief and dear.'
'O father, heed what the world will say;
Of shame hast thou no fear?

'If hither to-day to Mahōbā gay
  They have brought the betrothal fee,
If thou send the pledge from thy home away,
  Thou hast broken thy Rājpūtī.'

'Now be thou ruled by me, my son;
  Bethink thee well and know,
Naipālī a drum of life hath won;
  Him none can overthrow.

'Take counsel yet,' the Rājā saith,
  'Give back the betrothal fee.'
'I will not reject, come life, come death,
  The pledge that is sent to me.

'Now, brother Ūdan, hear my word,
  Send an order the host around;
Let the Kshatrīs prepare, and each man yare,
  And bid the great drum sound.'

But the Chandēl rose and straight he goes
  Where the painted palace stands;
When he came to Malhnā, his chiefest queen,
  She stood and joined her hands.

'Now why is thy lofty look downcast?
  Why droops from thy lip the hair?
What blight hath over thy body passed?
  What weight on thy mind doth bear?'

Her the Chandēlā answered, 'Dame,
  The tale may not be told;
From Naināgarh the token came,
  And strong I wis that hold.

'They who to Sunwā's bridal go,
  Shall none return again;
Counsel I gave to Malkhān so,
  But all my words were vain.

'Charge thou the lads, if chance they heed,
  To sit them at peace in hall.'
Then Malhnā bade a messenger speed,
  And Malkhān and Ūdan call.

The messenger went and greeting paid,
  When he the youths did see;
'Ye are stayed for in the palace,' he said,
  'So, Thākurs, come with me.'

With that before the queen to bow
  Right swiftly moved the two;
She touched their feet, she touched her brow,
  'My sons, now tell me true.

'Why have ye beaten the battle-drum?
  And whither are boune to ride?'
'From Naināgarh are the tokens come;
  And we go for Ālhā's bride.'

'Now hearken, Malkhān, to me, my son,
  Be warned and hold thy hand;
The Naināgarh king is a mighty one;
  Before him none can stand.'

'Now to my home the pledge is come,
  Mother,' brave Malkhān saith,
'Faint of heart should I send it back,
  My life were worse than death.

'Men are made to die in the plain,
  'Tis an evil fate to die in one's bed;
If I at Naināgarh am slain,
  Far through the world my renown shall spread.

'For still whate'er betide shall Ālhā win his bride,
  And never be forgot that day;
So bid the women sing, till all Mahōbā ring,
  Songs of joy to speed us on our way.'

FYTTE II

Now forth in haste the twain have paced
  While strains of joy uprose;
Dhēwā their brother they soon did find,
  And all the tale disclose.

'We through thy skill quelled Mārō's pride,
  And our father's wrong did pay;
To Ālhā's bridal I must ride;
  Now name a favouring day.'

Then Dhēwā took his astrologer's book,
And line by line he read;
'Mine art forebodes a happy end
To all your plan,' he said.

He called his Pandit and cast the hour;
'Be ready the oil to apply,
And the arbour fair with speed prepare
And duly sanctify.

The rites of marriage soon perform,
Nor to marshal the host be long.'
So the news did come to the painted dome,
And the women began the song.

Then the twelve queens all of the king Parmāl
To the arbour came full fain;
Dēvī and Brahmā came withal;
Loud rose the joyous strain.

The space they plastered with cowdung clean,
With pearls they marked the square;
The vessels were all of the golden sheen,
And of sandal every chair.

Seven matrons the bridegroom's oil applied,
While the Pandit did texts recite;
Then Ālhā's nails they began to pare,
While the women chanted aright.

Then to the Queen the barber cried
And largess loud did crave;
Two hamlets rich by Mahōbā's side
Queen Malhnā freely gave.

Whatever the bridal messengers would,
As their fee Queen Malhnā gave;
They anointed his body with saffron good,
And bathed him with Gangā's wave.

They bound on his wrist a bracelet bright,
That men might the bridegroom see;
Into the litter he leaped full light,
And soon to the well came he.

When Dēvī stepped to the edge of the well,
  Queen Malhnā in haste begun,
'From Dēvī Ālhā's birth befell,
  But thence is he Malhnā's son.

'To perform his marriage here at the well
  Rest for my heart will win.'
So down thereat Queen Malhnā sate,
  And dangled her foot within.

The first round treading when Ālhā came,
  He caught her by the hand;
'I vow a grove in my mother's name,
  But draw up thy foot and stand.'

The seven rounds thus he vowed his vow;
  At length the queen upstept;
He touched her feet, he touched his brow,
  Then swift to the litter he leapt.

She stroked his back and blessed him then,
  'May there fall from thy head no hair;'
Fast ran round the twelve bearer men
  Till they came to the sandal square.

Up with the host came Uday Singh
  And bade a messenger go;
And, when he the master of horse did bring,
  Gave turban and plume also.

Bade saddle them steeds of all good breeds,
  Arab and Turkman and all;
Of all good colours gray and bay,
  In haste did Ūdan call.

Silken saddles and girths tight bound,
  Glancing of pearls in crest;
All the steeds in Mahōbā found
  Stood ready at his behest.

He then to the master of elephants passed,
  Gave bracelets of gold to wear;
Bade elephants vast of each good caste
  Like moving hills prepare.

Army-scattering, passion-mad,
  Slaughterous, huge and gray;
Each with howda and velvet pad
  Did Ūdan and Malkhān array.

Each with pinnacles all of gold,
  Ready to march straightway;
Troop on troop by the hundred told
  Gathered in line that day.

And next for the captain of guns they sent,
  The cannon he ordered well;
Then midst the army Ūdan went,
  And every chief 'gan tell—

'No servants here but brothers I know
  Each who mine honour defends;
For fiercely the battle will ebb and flow
  Round Naināgarh, my friends.

'Now he who loves his child the best,
  Let him go and take his pay;
And he whose wife is the darlingest,
  Let him down his weapons lay.

'But he who yearns for the battle-field,
  Let him take two swords to wear;
And he who loves the sword and shield,
  Let him with Ūdan fare.

'Birth as man doth seldom come,
  Though many a life there be;
And he who dies on his bed at home
  Hath wasted his Rājpūti.

He that is killed in the battle-field,
  His fame shall last for aye.'
When Ūdan's word the Kshatrīs heard,
  They did on their war array.

Some on horses, on elephants some,
  Some rode camels upon;
They saddled their steeds at the earliest drum,
  At the next did their armour don.

At the third drum-beat to stirrup they stept;
Now Rāsbēndul was there;
To ride him Ūdan lightly leapt,
And Malkhān Kabutrī his mare.

Harināgar did young Jagnaik bestride,
The horse of the Chandēl king;
Mīrā the Saiyid his mare did ride,
On Manurthā did Dhēwā spring.

They called for Pachsāwad the elephant good,
Whom the driver brought to stand;
And ready saddled Papīhā stood,
As Malkhān gave command.

And they Ālhā's steed Karilyā did lead,
Unmounted the litter beside;
Mannā Gūjar too of Mahōbā town
Would with the procession ride.

Alī, Alāmat, Daryā Khān,
Jān Bēg, Sultān, the son,
Tēgh Bahādur, Alī Bahādur,
Fearless of death each one.

Loudly shouting on Alī's name,
Fast did the Saiyids ride;
With Ālhā thousands of warriors came,
Nobles and chiefs of pride.

The army marched as the drum did sound;
The procession took its way;
Seven days they journeyed, so to the bound
Of Naināgarh came they.

To pitch the camp they gave command,
Eight kōs the city fro:
On the high land the tents did stand,
The market on the low.

Arms were piled and belts untied,
Saddles and howdas unbound;
Down to bathe the chieftains hied,
Whilst their meals were cooked around.

Ūdan left the tented height,
  The garden soon he found;
There did he smite the drum with might,
  That it gave a thunder sound.

To Naināgarh came a messenger,
  Where Naipālī held his court;
Bowing head and joining hands
  To the Rājā he made report.

'The drum that doth at thy borders lie
  Hath been struck by a bridal train.'
Then the Rājā bade his three sons hie
  And bring him word again.

Jōgā, Bhōgā, Bijyā,
  Right soon they left the dome;
They saw the red tents all outspread,
  So soon the height they clomb.

To Naināgarh in haste they sped,
  When they that sight did view;
Before the king they bowed their head
  And showed him all they knew.

FYTTE III

Now Ūdan bowed to the brave Malkhay,
  'Call, brother, thy Pandit straight;
And bid him decide on a fortunate tide
  To summon the Rājā's gate.'

They called for Chūrāman the Pandit,
  And brought him the tent within;
'Now tell us,' they cried, 'a fortunate tide
  That we to our end may win.'

His star-book page by page he read,
  And planets and signs did weigh;
'This selfsame hour is happy,' he said,
  'In your mission be no delay.'

'Now hear, Lord Malkhān,' Rupnā said,
  Mahōbā's herald he,
'I will not ride to lose my head;
  Lay not this charge on me.

'Right stark is the Rājā of Naināgarh;
  Durst no man thole his stroke.'
'Are thy wits astray, such words to say?'
  In thunder Ūdan broke.

'Whom brother I, not servant, call,
  Will he prove faint of heart?
Though to Ālhā this day no bride should fall,
  Yet its glory will ne'er depart.'

'Now hear, Lord Malkhān,' Rupnā cried,
  'Give shield and faulchion fair,
And Karilyā, Ālhā's steed, to ride;
  So I will thy missive bear.'

Then Malkhān the brave all weapons gave,
  Nor sword nor shield did spare;
The horse Karilyā Rupnā rode,
  And forth the missive bare.

He bowed and went; four gharīs[1] spent
  To Naināgarh he came;
'Whither and whence?' the porter asked,
  'Thy tale and country's name?'

'Rupnā, Mahōbā's herald, I,
  Of the city of king Parmāl;
Ālhā doth ride to claim his bride,
  So I summon the Rājā's hall.

'The hour for the rite is waning fast,
  Go bid the Rājā know.
Then, porter, see thou bring my fee;
  'Tis time that I should go.'

'And what dost thou claim as thy fee this day?
  That I to my lord may show.'
'Four gharīs, say, that swords must play,
  And the gate with a blood-stream flow.'

The porter fast to the Rājā hied,
  'A herald has reached the yett;[2]
Hither comes Ālhā seeking a bride,
  At our frontier his banner is set.

[1] A gharī is about twenty minutes. [2] Gate.

'The messenger stands and his fee demands
  That swords at the gate may play.
Ne'er was such messenger seen in our lands;
  His bearing I could not say.'

Jōgā and Bhōgā the Rājā sent,
  'Go see what means this din.'
To the outer gate the princes went,
  And Rupnā they brought within.

Filled was the hall of Naipālī there,
  The court of the king was met;
Stool by stool and chair by chair
  So close together were set.

Warriors huge they sat in a crowd,
  That targe did reach to targe;
Seven paces off the herald bowed,
  And down he cast his charge.

The Rājā raised his eyes and gazed,
  And thus to Rupnā spake,
'Now what thy name? and whence art come?
  And whither thy way dost take?'

'The messenger I of Mahōbā's king,
  And Rupnā is my name;
The bridal summons to thee I bring;
  Now give the fee I claim.'

The Rājā's ire blazed like fire,
  When the herald answered so;
'Set on,' he cried, 'and hew him down;
  From the door he must not go.'

A thousand warriors sat in the hall,
  With drawn sword on the knee;
But Pūran rose then first of all,
  And Patnā's lord was he.

He struck with his mace at Rupnā's face,
  But the herald 'scaped the blow;
He pierced with his spearpoint Pūran's head,
  That the blood o'er the shaft 'gan flow.

Then every warrior bared his glaive,
  They beset the doorway through;
Small hope had Rupnā his life to save,
  But his sword in his need he drew.

As the wolf the sheep, as the lion the deer,
  The Kshatrīs down he cast;
The summons he raised on the point of his spear,
  And so to the portal passed.

He struck his steed with whip and spur,
  Did over the threshold bound;
Then rose a cry in Naināgarh,
  'Ho Kshatrīs, hem him round.'

There was swordplay held in the winding lanes,
  There was clashing of steel begun,
And the gallant grey bore crimson stains
  Ere the skirt of the town was won.

Now the king Naipālī sat thoughtful there,
  To Jōgā and Bhōgā spake,
'Mighty in arms are Mahōbā's men
  And of weapons the mastery take.

'If their messenger hewed unhelped from my door
  His way midst a thousand swords,
What manner of men, I am doubting sore,
  Must be that messenger's lords!'

'Now, father of ours, at ease be thou,'
  Jōgā and Bhōgā cried,
'The men who are come from Mahōbā now,
  Not one of them back shall ride.

'We will smite the heads from every one,
  For the trench of the city to hold;'
So both through the camp to the drummer are gone,
  And bangles have given of gold.

'By beat of drum through the host proclaim
  That the Kshatrīs be ready anon;'
Soon through the lines the summons came,
  'Ho, don your armour on.'

'Call the Baghēl, call the Chandēl,
  Every Thākur, Janwār, Pamār,
Sūrajbansī, Chandarbansī,
  Raghubansī and Rājkumār;

'The men of Hārā and Būndī call,
  Bais, Sōmbansī and Gahilwār,
Rāthōrs, Guhlōts, and Saksēnās, all
  Whose portion are swords and the battle scar.

'Summon the Tōmars of Tumar fort,
  Mainpurī Chauhāns and chiefs of Mārwār,
Nikumbh and Gaur, the Bhadāwar power,
  Jādav and crafty Parihār.

'Each royal clan of Rājasthān,
  Thirty and six on the roll they are;
Habshī savage who feeds on man,
  And fierce Durrānī who comes from far.'

Jōgā and Bhōgā to camp they came,
  To the drummer gave bangles of gold to wear.
They bade him through all the host proclaim
  That the Kshatrīs hold themselves watchful and yare.

At the first drum-beat each saddled his steed,
  And donned his arms when it sounded again;
At the third drum-beat they were ready at need,
  In nālkī or pālkī[1] or elephant wain.

Some on horses, on elephants some;
  And the eight-metalled pieces on camels they bound;
But the thunder-voiced cannon on waggons did come,
  With powder-bags filled and with balls piled around.

There was creaking of wheels as the fire-throats moved,
  So gallantly Jōgā and Bhōgā did ride;
The red flags did flaunt, and the bards loud did chaunt,
  And cheerly Mahauts to their elephants cried.

[1] Two kinds of litters.

FYTTE IV

Now Rupnā the while before Ālhā stood,
So soon as the camp he won;
When Malkhān marked him bathed in blood,
He questioned what was done.

'I may not tell of that Rājā fell,
His sword bites keen and sore;
Scarce had he heard Mahōbā's name,
He bade them bar the door.

'Full gharīs four the swords were plied
And blood flowed forth in strife;
But that Bhavānī proved my guide,
I had not scaped with life.

'What sleep, O lords, your eyelids charms?
Unready sit ye here
While Naināgarh hath flown to arms;
E'en now their van is near.'

Forth Ūdan gazed—with marching men
'Twas dark on every side;
In haste he turned to Malkhān then,
And, 'marshal the host,' he cried. 5

Through all the camp a cry doth run;
They harness themselves with speed;
One with saddle, with saddle-cloth one,
Each girthed in haste his steed.

Malkhān sprang there on Kabutrī his mare,
On Rāsbēndul did Ūdan bound;
All the army he ordered to march,
So loud the drum did sound.

As far bold Ūdan spurred in van,
Jōgā and Bhōgā spake,
'Say, strangers, whence your course began,
And whither your way ye take.'

'In Mahōbā town dwells king Parmāl;
O princes, thence I came;
Ālhā's brother am I withal,
And Uday Singh my name.

'Now have we sped our brother to wed,
  And the bride must be Sunwā fair;
'Tis time the seven rounds to tread,
  So all things meet prepare.'

The eyes of the princes flashed fiery red,
  So wrathful waxed the twain;
'Now why these swelling words hast said?
  What folly hath thee o'erta'en?

'The Banāphar caste is contemned of all,
  Most mean on the Rājpūt roll;
But, since ye avenged your father's fall,
  Ye have waxen proud of soul.

'Back to Mahōbā we rede ye ride,
  Nor lose your lives for nought.'
Thereon laughed Ūdan out and cried,
  'Now springalds hear my thought.

'Their sphere may quit both moon and sun,
  Yea down to earth may fleet;
But for Ūdan return is none
  Till this marriage be complete.'

Then cried they in ire, 'The cannon fire,
  And blow these braggarts away.'
They loaded the powder, they rammed the shot,
  They did not make delay.

There is lighting of match and priming of pan,
  And the smoke spreads over the skies;
While here a horse, and there a man,
  And next an elephant lies.

The hooves of the horse to dust were sent,
  The camel staggered and fell,
Warriors limb from limb were rent
  By rocket and ball and shell.

Elephants screaming, missiles shrilling,
  A great turmoil was born;
Till cannon I wot waxed overhot
  And the archers' hands were torn.

When the tight bows slack as water grew,
Their artillery down they flung;
Then spears full fast they both did cast,
Till the red blood bubbling sprung.

There was many a blade in Wilāyat made
And Bardwān broadsword plied;
Ah! pity the plight of the widowed wives,
So many a warrior died.

The veteran strong and the smooth of face,
They sank there side by side;
Some wept for a child's or a parent's case,
And some for a new-made bride.

And some for water were craving sore,
As in pools of blood they lay;
Oh, water than gold was valued more,
But none could be bought that day.

Friend from foe might no man know,
Yet 'Kill' was ever the cry;
Of all the host with Jōgā marched,
One fifth on the ground did lie.

The men of Mahōbā cut them down,
Their onset none could stand;
Back through ravine to 'scape unseen
Fled many a broken band.

But Jōgā did to Bhōgā call,
When he saw his warriors fly;
'Go, haste and show the Rājā all:
Then speedily did he hie.

The council was met and the seats close set,
He bowed, and thus he said,
'The sons of Dēvī, O sire, have come,
And a heavy slaughter made.

'Of all the host with me did ride,
One fifth lie on the sward;
Five thousand eke on Mahōbā's side,
They wielded a gallant sword.

My sister now is grown our foe,
  And the land is captived thus:
If her litter doth to Mahōbā go,
  Who water will drink with us?'

Out and spake Naipālī then,
  And an angry man was he,
'Let no such word from thy mouth be heard,
  Or thou breakest thy Rājpūtī.

'All the men that Mahōbā sent,
  I charge ye have them killed.'
With that to his inner palace he went,
  To the house with treasure filled.

The drum of life he brought thereout,
  And soon he gave his son;
'Go, let that sound on the border ground,
  So hast thou the battle won.

'For all the wounded their bodies will shake,
  And rise up free from pain;
And all the dead to life will wake
  And start the fight again.'

Right gladly Bhōgā the drum did take,
  And soon he reached the ground;
The dead did shake their bodies and wake,
  When they heard the life-drum sound.

The Naināgarh armies together drew;
  They rallied and shouted, 'Slay;'
There was not a wind in heaven that blew,
  As the swords closed round that day.

As the fruit from the mango bough men smite,
  Sound the strokes of the fierce attack;
Wounded with moaning rise to fight,
  Yea bodies the head that lack.

Corpse on corpse in the crimson lake
  With shields for turtles lay,
Firelock scattered for long black snake,
  And turban for lotus gay.

Ūdan to Malkhān musing came;
  'A marvel strange,' quoth he,
'Those whom my hands have slain, the same
  Are fighting anew with me.

'How live again these warriors slain?
  O Malkhān, think this o'er;
Call back our men from the battle plain,
  And seek the camp once more.'

The livelong day was in fighting spent,
  Yet the swordplay was not done;
Back the host of Mahōbā went,
  And in gloom their tents they won.

Now Ūdan left the camp alone,
  And southward far did ride;
Then turned his steed, and came with speed
  On the city's further side.

All the women of Nainā town
  Ran up to their roofs to see;
Sunwā marked him then, and down
  From the seven storied tower came she.

Down to the lattice grate with speed
  Stepped Sunwā, stair by stair;
Ūdan was riding his goodly steed,
  And a purple turban ware.

'Now save thee, brother,' quoth Sunwā fair,
  'Say how the matter stands.'
'Now, sister, hear and the truth declare,'
  Quoth he, and joined his hands.

'Why hast thou sent the letter to us
  To come to thine aid in haste?
To quench our candle in darkness thus,
  And turn our house to waste?

'Dead warriors fight me face to face,
  They live in fight who fell;
What gives the slain their life again?
  Fair sister, pray thee tell.'

Him Lady Sunwā answered soon,
'Now hear me, Dasrāj' son;
A drum of life hath the king, the boon
Of mighty Indra won.

'Whenever a Kshatrī falls to ground,
The drum he bids them smite;
When the ear of the dead is reached by the sound,
He lives again to fight.

'Fancy not fondly a Mārō here,
As where thou didst thy father wreak;
In vain wilt thou fight 'gainst my father's might,
Yet hear me the secret speak.

'At morning rise—in a flowerseller's guise—
To Dēvī's temple come;
Thither go I my vows to pay,
And with me I take the drum.

'If the drum thou bear from the sandal square,
Thou hast won good hap in all.'
So Ūdan away on his road is gone,
And she to her painted hall.

Back to the camp then Ūdan went,
And slowly he lighted down;
He bowed himself in Malkhān's tent,
'The morrow success shall crown.

'Sunwā has shown me the secret way.'
So passed the night in rest,
Till cocks did crow ere dawn of day,
And small birds chirped in nest.

Then Ūdan donned his guise with speed,
And a basket of flowers bare;
Behind the temple he bound his steed,
And he sat waiting there.

FYTTE V

Now how it fared with Sunwā, hear;
To the painted hall came she;
When the mother saw her daughter dear,
She took her upon her knee.

'What wouldst thou, dearest daughter mine?
For I trust in thy word alway.'
'Let me go to worship at Dēvī's shrine,
For this is the promised day.

'And get me the drum of life also,
For singing and beating the drum;
With baskets and music I vowed to go
When my bridegroom's train should come.'

'The drum thy father will never give,
And what hast thou then to say?'
'If he give not the drum, I must not live,
But will stab my heart this day.'

Queen Keśarī went and awoke the king
On his couch of the jewelled sheen;
'Sure needs it must be some urgent thing,
That thou breakest my rest, O Queen.'

The Rānī joined her hands and spake,
'Now hear, my lord, thy wife;
Our daughter hath vowed a procession to make,
So lend her the drum of life.'

'The drum is not to be given, O Queen,
Make no such vain request;'
'If thou the boon refuse, eftsoon
Thy child will have stabbed her breast.

'Let but for one gharī the drum be beat,
So she both her vows will pay.'
To that the Rājā gave consent,
So bare she the drum away.

Then the princess called for her maidens all,
And loud the joy-songs swelled;
She struck on the drum, and in hand withal
A necklace of cloves she held.

To the temple come, she laid the drum
Without on the sandal square;
She gave Ūdan a sign as she passed to the shrine,
And he rose and away it bare.

He mounted his steed and he rode with speed
  And the drum by Malkhān placed;
'Now, brother,' he cried, 'no more delay—
  Let the host be arrayed in haste.'

To the drummer a pledge of the betel they cast,
  And he made the kettledrum sound;
Then did Ūdan spring on Rāsbēndul fast,
  On Manurthā did Dhēwā bound;

And Jagnaik eke on Harnāgar came,
  Which the moon-sprung monarch bore;
And Rupnā on fleet Papīhā, the same
  Was Dasrāj' steed of yore.

And Mannā the Gūjar mounted his horse,
  And many a warrior more;
At the kettledrum's sound the Mahōbā force
  Were ready the camp before.

Prancing, dancing, caracoling,
  Champing the bit with pride,
Ambling, gambolling, sideways rolling,
  Fret and curvet, on they hied.

Riders shout and horses neigh,
  Paw and chafe and rear and vault;
Toward the town they took their way,
  Three kōs off they made a halt.

To Nainägarh a messenger sped,
  And bowed where the court was set;
'Rājā, the foe is at thine head,
  What sleep art sleeping yet?'

On that he called for the princes three,
  And for Pūran, Patnā's lord,
'Let none of the men of Mahōbā flee,'
  He cried, 'unsmitten of sword.'

The drum was heard in Nainägarh;
  To arms the warriors sprang;
Fast in front did the princes spur;
  Then rose a mighty clang.

With beat of drum the host did come
  Where the enemy stood prepared;
'What Kshatrīs here have assailed my land,
  Or to cross my boundary dared?'

Forth bounded Ūdan hastily,
  To Jōgā and Bhōgā fared;
'A Kshatrī, Mahōbā-born, am I,
  Who to cross your boundary dared.

'For Ālhā's bridal hither I ride;
  Prepare the rounds to tread.'
Then Jōgā waxed wode with wrath and pride,
  And his eyes were as torches red.

'Speak thus again and thy death is near,
  I will smite each Mahōbā head.'
'Yet, Jōgā and Bhōgā, mine answer hear,'
  To the twain bold Ūdan said.

'Give me a wound for every hair;
  Hew bone from bone on the field;
The corpse of the slain would rise again
  And still the broadsword wield.

'Hacked be the flesh from every limb;
  My body be all beshred;
One step on the field I will not yield,
  Till Ālhā be throughly wed.'

'In Mahōbā,' cried Bhōgā, 'the touchstone lies,
  Turns iron and steel to gold;
O my men, of the spoil of their camp make prize,
  And all shall be yours to hold.'

Their swords the Naināgarh heroes drew,
  Right glad in the fray to mell;
Cannonballs, arrows, and bullets flew,
  Swords clashed and champions fell.

Footman with footman, knight with knight,
  Close locked in stour they met;
Tusk to tusk did the elephants fight,
  Howda gainst howda set.

Faulchion clanged and scimitar clashed;
  Ūdan came spurring his steed,
'Art sleeping,' he cried, as by Rupnā he dashed,
  'Be wary, brother, and heed.'

And to Mīrā the Saiyid he called, 'On the right,
  Uncle, be thou mine aid.
This Naināgarh is a place of might:
  Be wakeful, Jagnaik,' he said.

So on one side charged the Saiyid then,
  Jagnaik on the other side;
Here Mannā Gūjar led his men,
  And there did Ūdan ride.

Where Malkhān charged across the plain
  And dashed amid the foe,
It was as the blast of the hurricane
  That lays the forest low.

To every howda Rāsbēndul leapt,
  And his rider with tough wood spear
Howdas twenty and two he swept,
  Till he drew to Jōgā near.

'Now play we, Jōgā, by turns the game,
  As the girls at the well-side draw.'
'Ye Dasrāj' sons, from a far land came,
  So strike thou first by law.'

'The Chandēlā a charge upon me has laid,
  I cannot strike first in play;
Strike first, or in paradise,' Ūdan said,
  'Thou wilt mourn for thy wasted day.'

Then Jōgā took his bow in hand,
  And slowly an arrow drew;
The shaft was strong with a triple prong,
  And he fitted it deftly and true.

With shoulder and arms the bow he drew,
  And thrice the string did cry;
At Ūdan's breast he aimed full true,
  So let he the arrow fly.

From left to right Rāsbēndul sprung,
  So Ūdan 'scaped the blow.
A mighty javelin next he flung,—
  Its weight was a man[1] or moe.

But high in air Rāsbēndul leapt,
  So whistling beneath it passed;
'Say, cherished thy mother a fig-tree? or kept
  Thy father a Sunday fast?

'Enough hath been done to complete thy fame;
  Now back to Mahōbā go.'
'It is not the rule of the Kshatrī name
  Their backs in the field to show.

'Thy third stroke try, O Baghēl Rāi,
  If thou wouldst not in heaven repent.'
Then Jōgā spurred his steed so nigh,
  That neck by neck was bent.

He drew and brandished aloft his blade,
  Then at Ūdan's head he straik;
His rhinoceros targe on the left displayed
  Three doughty blows did break.

Unhurt, he poised his spear with speed,
  And round his horse did wheel;
Then lighted the blow upon Jōgā's steed,
  Seven paces back did reel.

With that came Bhōgā spurring in,
  And fast to Ūdan hied;
'By flight thy life thou shalt not win,
  Thy death is near,' he cried.

When Malkhān saw his brother's need,
  He spurred to Bhōgā's side,
'Now sit thou warily on thy steed,
  Thy death is near,' he cried.

In haste then Bhōgā drew his sword,
  And struck at Malkhān brave;
But Maniyā Dēo, Mahōbā's ward,
  In battle did Malkhān save.

[1] i. e. a maund, or 80 lb.

Then his massy mace did Malkhān raise,
  And a blow at Bhōgā deal;
The club, as it fell, the horse did graze,
  And made him backward reel.

'Hold, strike not Bhōgā,' Ūdan said,
  'Lest all our hopes thou break;
Who else would sow rice when the rounds we tread,
  Or the gifts of marriage take?'

Then Malkhān his mare Kabutrī spurred;
  Amidst the throng he burst,
The ranks of Bhōgā were troubled and stirred,
  Then every side dispersed.

Of all the force who with Bhōgā rode,
  Two-fifths on the sward there lay;
The plain with blood as a river flowed,
  And the gore was trodden to clay.

Bhōgā saw that the field was lost,
  None stayed his foot a space;
Hither and thither fled the host,
  Whilst Ūdan urged the chace.

FYTTE VI

Bhōgā rode to the palace gate,
  He bowed to the king and spoke;
'The Mahōbā men are swordsmiths great,
  We may not thole their stroke.'

The Rājā rose and did in haste
  To his treasure house repair;
His secret coffer he soon unbraced;
  No drum of life was there.

His body was troubled and sore distraught,
  His senses were dizzied all;
Again his palace chamber he sought,
  And straight to his sons 'gan call.

'The drum of life is stolen and gone,
  The Banāphar has ta'en it away;'
To the goddess's temple he hastened anon,
  I wis he made no delay.

Ten thousand mans on the altar he burnt,
  And began a penance severe;
The penance he wrought was so terror fraught
  That the gods rose up in fear.

There came a voice from heaven that tide—
  'What troubles the Rājā's mind?'
'O Mother,' with joining hands he cried,
  'Be thine ear to my prayer inclined.

'The Banāphar caste is the basest caste,
  They by theft have my wealth undone;
Twelve years I passed in penance and fast,
  Ere from Indra that boon I won.'

To all the gods then Indra spake,
  'This Ālhā, Dēvī's son,
A charmèd life doth he partake,
  And hath Śāradā's favour won.

'Bring forth, O gods, to the boundaries,
  And break the drum of life;
Nor this nor that shall hold the prize;
  So will we end the strife.'

So the gods brought the drum from out the tent,
  And dashed it to pieces all;
Back to his palace Naipālī went,
  And for paper and pen did call.

First did he write the heading aright,
  Then greeted his brother well,
A doughty knight, Harinandan hight,
  Who in Sundarban did dwell.

'From Mahōbā are come the Mahōbā men;
  Banāphars, a caste most base they are;
If they accomplish this marriage, then
  No man will drink from our water-jar.

'A mark of disgrace will cloud thy face,
  And nought but death our life will be;
Come from thine island our foes to chase;
  They are mighty and death they laugh to see.'

The letter he wrote and the messenger sped,
  Till he to Harinandan did come;
Line by line Harinandan read,
  Then he bade them sound the drum.

The army heard, and the camp was stirred,
  And he sprang to the howda high;
Five days they journeyed to Naināgarh;
  Then he camped at the boundary.

To hold a dance where he pitched his tent,
  The barges he bade them plank;
Now it chanced that Ālhā for bathing went,
  And he stood on the river bank.

Twelve pairs of dancing girls there danced,
  With boys in women's guise;
When Ālhā to see the sight advanced,
  Harinandan turned his eyes.

'Say, whence art come, and what thy name,
  And why on the bank dost stand?'
'From Mahōbā's city', quoth he, 'I came,
  And that is king Parmāl's land.

'Ruler of all his house am I,
  And Ālhā am I hight;
And hither fair Sunwā to wed I hie;
  Even now is the marriage dight.'

'Art thou the son of such a king—
  And standest to see this show—
Who the touchstone owns, that precious thing,
  As all the world doth know?

'Come thou aboard, Banāphar lord,
  And see this dancing rare.'
Up Ālhā stepped at the Rājā's word,
  And he gave him a seemly chair.

But the Rājā did it in subtilty,
  Had the ropes of the barge untied;
And the boatmen in silence their poles did ply
  Till they reached the further side.

Ālhā he cast into prison strong,
  And in Sundarban held him bound.
Thought Ūdan, 'Ālhā tarries long.'
  No rest his spirit found.

Meanwhile came Rupnā speeding in,
  And did to Malkhān bow;
'Ho brother,' did Ūdan straight begin,
  'Where leftest Ālhā now?'

He joined his hands, 'I dare not say.
  On board a barge he stept.
The Banāphar Rāi has been carried away.'
  Astonied up he leapt.

'Ho Dhēwā, brother, the fortune cast;
  And see thou cast it right;
Brave Dhēwā, what mischance hath past,
  That Ālhā is lost to sight?'

He marked the star-signs one by one,
  He cast the fortune right;
'It is Harinandan of Sundarban,
  Who hath stolen Ālhā from sight.'

'Now, brother, the secret means display.'
  'As a merchant of horses go;
Ālhā will meet thee then straightway,
  And back shalt thou win him so.'

He hath taken Karilyā, Ālhā's steed,
  And Bēndulā eke, his own;
He hath saddled and girthed them ready at need,
  Strings double of precious stone;

Neck chains triple of silver bright,
  And silver stirrups, I ween,
Frontlets were dight and bands drawn tight,
  And cruppers of jewelled sheen.

The court he reached in a merchant's guise,
  All on the fifth fair day;
So, when on Ūdan he cast his eyes,
  The porter began to say—

'Stranger, to me thy state declare,
  Whence come and whither wouldst go?'
'A merchant of horses, from Kābul I fare,
  Go, this to the Rājā show.'

The porter straight to the palace hied,
  And before the Rājā told,
'Never have I such horses eyed;
  I cannot their praise unfold.'

Back Harinandan the messenger sent
  And bade him the horses bring;
Quickly back to the gate he went,
  'Thou art summoned before the king.'

Ūdan straight the horses led,
  And soon to the king he came;
As he bowed in the presence, the Rājā said,
  'What price for these steeds dost claim?'

'Now, hear me, Rājā,' Ūdan replied,
  'First mark their paces well;
Send for thy men the steeds to ride,
  And then I the price will tell.'

Then the king did call for his Kshatrīs all,
  And bade the horses ride:
Said, 'put them through their paces in view,
  And deftly before me guide.'

Covered with shame was each who came;
  Back went they dazed and blind;
'Neither steed would our guidance heed;
  They flew as flies the wind.'

'Ten horses,' quoth Ūdan, 'from Kābul I brought,
  And in Jhunnāgarh one I sold;
Country to country a buyer I sought,
  But none the value told.

'So journeying down, to Mahōbā town
  And the king Parmāl I brought;
Two of the stock on my hands he left,
  And seven good colts he bought.

'Now, having heard of the Rājā's fame,
  In the war field excellent,
With the two that remained to thy gate I came,
  My tribute to present.

'But the men of Mahōbā are horsemen good,
  And well my steeds can guide;
If one of that land doth before thee stand,
  Go call him forth to ride.'

'The Banāphar is bound in my house,' he said,
  'Go, summon him hither straight.'
Forth in haste was Ālhā led,
  And stood at the palace gate.

'Now ride this horse in the sandal square,
  And so will I set thee free.'
The feet of the earth he worshipped there,
  And then to the sun bowed he.

Up he leaped and in selle did sit,
  Then out bold Ūdan spake,
'Make the horses fly and this island quit,
  So our way to the camp we take.'

Ālhā sat on Karilyā fain,
  And on Bēndulā Uday Singh;
They cried amain and they loosed the rein,
  And forth the steeds did spring.

Day and night their way they went,
  Until the camp they found;
Then before brave Malkhān bent,
  And slowly stept to ground.

FYTTE VII

To brave Malkhay spake Ūdan Rāi,
  Said, 'Brother, hear my rede.
The seven rounds it is time to tread,
  Get ready the camp with speed.'

The Kshatrīs all did their weapons prepare,
  Through the camp the order rang,
Kabutrī the mare brave Malkhān bare,
  On Harnāgar Jagnaik sprang.

Mannā did on his arms that tide,
  On Manurthā did Dhēwā bound,
On strong Pachsāwad did Ālhā ride,
  As the war drum 'gan to sound.

The huge wheels creaked to the oxen's tread,
  The ochre-stained guns that bore;
Mighty standards, banners of red
  Went flaunting on before.

'Soon fades,' cried Ūdan, 'the forest flower;
  The Sāwan[1] month soon ends;
Soon comes the mother's travail hour:
  Soon life is spent, my friends.

'There are homes in heaven stand ready for all,
  To-morrow—to-day if not;
And their names, who in Naināgarh manfully fall,
  In Mahōbā shall ne'er be forgot.'

Forth set the army cheered in mind;
  First footmen marched three kōs;
Three kōs then tusk on tusk did grind,
  The elephants marched so close.

The war-flutes shrilled, the trumpets blared,
  The bards sang songs of glee;
To the sound of the conch the Rājpūts fared,
  A valiant sight to see.

They halted three miles from the city gate;
  A messenger spied and ran,
Where king Naipālī in council sate,
  He bowed and his tale began.

'The Mahōbā host have the border crost,'
  Then loud the king 'gan say,
'Go, Bijyā, Jōgā, and Bhōgā,
  Sound drum and the troops array.

'Let none of the foe escape our hand;
  Smite each Mahōbā head.'
Then every man girt on his brand,
  Through the camp as the summons spread.

[1] July–August.

And Jōgā, Bhōgā, and Bijyā,
  On horses rode the three;
But Pūran, lord of Patnā,
  His elephant mounted he.

And cannon of weight of the metals eight
  Were loaded on wains good store;
So for a watch the army marched
  Till they came their foe before.

Then Jōgā and Bhōgā in thunder cried,
  'Ho, sons of Mahōbā's king,
The land is ours whereon ye ride,
  So silence your drum-beating.'

'Now, princes, hear,' quoth Ūdan bold,
  'Nor counsel from me refuse;
In Naināgarh a bridal hold,
  Let your sister her husband choose.

'Living or dead, till I see her wed,
  I turn not back, I trow.'
'This marriage can never be,' they said,
  'So in peace to Mahōbā go.'

'If the bride in her litter with me fare,
  Then will I to Mahōbā turn.'
Angry men were the princes then,
  And their eyes with fire did burn.

'Of the men of Mahōbā let 'scape not one:
  Take heed, ye warriors all.'
Then linstocks were set to every gun,
  And smoke spread up like a pall.

The cannon balls fired from either part
  Ploughed furrows across the plain;
Thick fell bullet, arrow, and dart,
  Like drops in the time of rain.

The shoes of the soldiers slipped in gore,
  And the horse-hooves in crimson mud;
With blood the howdas were running o'er,
  And the horsemen dripped with blood.

Friend from foe might no man know,
  So loud they shouted 'Slay;'
Charging forth did Ūdan go,
  So brave he rode his way.

O'er trench by trench did Bēndulā bound,
  And Ūdan cried amain,
'Such an hour, O friends, will never be found,
  Nor such season come back again.

'Though Ālhā's marriage should ne'er be won,
  Yet in fame shall abide this deed;
And home if I go when the wedding is done,
  Ye shall none of you miss your meed.

'Mine honour, O friends, is in your hands;
  From the battle let no man fly.'
With that the Kshatrīs closed in their bands,
  And their swords all around did ply.

The rush of Mahōbā swept the field;
  Each way the fainthearts sped;
The long-robe-wearers cast down shield,
  The bridegrooms of battle fled.

When Jōgā saw his followers break,
  'Ho Dasrāj' son,' he cried,
'Why turn thy hand on a servant band,
  'When we should the game decide?

'Till one be slain and one remain,
  Be the fight 'twixt thee and me.'
Then Ūdan heard his words full fain,
  So face to face came he.

'Strike, Jōgā, first, or in paradise
  Thou wilt sit and lament thy fate.'
Then Jōgā took his bow in a trice,
  Its bolt was a pound in weight.

He aimed with care and the bolt let fly,
  But it went on the left side past;
So when to five paces came he nigh,
  He took up his spear to cast.

He struck at Ūdan a stroke full stark;
  To the right did his courser bound;
The spear of Jōgā missed its mark,
  And whistling fell to ground.

Then drew he his sword and brandished it high,
  But Ūdan his shield sustained;
Jōgā's sword did to pieces fly,
  And only the hilt remained.

Then wist he well that death was near:
  'It hath elephants hewed, this sword;
It hath lopped the legs of horses sheer,
  But now it hath failed its lord.'

Ūdan on that his courser wheeled,
  Then straight in face came round;
He thrust him down with a blow of his shield,
  Then fast his arms he bound.

Up Bhōgā did speed on his prancing steed,
  But Malkhān charged between;
'With which of the twain is Rām displeased,
  Must now in our turn be seen.'

Then Bhōgā drew his sword in a trice,
  Over Malkhān he brandished it;
With all his strength he struck him thrice,
  On his body it nothing bit.

So Malkhān caught him unaware,
  And his arms he pinioned fast;
Cried Bijyā, 'Malkhān, ride with care,
  Thy death is near at last.'

But Dhēwā with him to contend
  Rode forth, and, 'Now,' cried he,
'Fight on and take thy fill, my friend,
  'Tis turn for thee and me.'

Then Bijyā drew his falchion bright,
  Over Dhēwā brandished it;
Four strokes of sword he struck with might,
  Yet wounded him ne'er a whit.

Him Dhēwā off his guard did take,
And bound him with iron chain;
And it was Pūran then that spake,
When he saw the three were ta'en.

'I will give your flesh to the kites and crows;
Ye shall not mine arm outrun.'
When Jagnaik heard that, up he rose,
The Chandēl's sister's son.

The elephant-driver he first did smite,
And dashed him down from his place;
Pūran was dazed at his driver's plight,
But he grasped his massy mace.

On Jagnaik a bitter stroke he laid;
Him God preserved that tide;
So his horse to rear young Jagnaik made,
The elephant's head beside.

On the howda he struck with his sword full hard,
And the canopy wholly brake;
By a feint he caught him off his guard,
And so in chains did take.

Swords were plied till eventide,
All day the game went on;
The armies of Ālhā backward hied,
So they to their tents are gone.

FYTTE VIII

When Māhil beheld the prisoners four,
He called for Lillī his mare;
He galloped on her to Naināgarh,
And the council was sitting there.

Thrice he louted low to the king,
Who placed him a sandal chair;
'Rājā, what news from the camp dost bring?
And how do the armies fare?'

'I dare not tell the tale,' he said,
'Howbeit the king require;
Ālhā and Ūdan, Mahōbā-bred,
At Mārō they wroke their sire.

'Now have they bound thy three sons fast,
  And Pūran the fourth also;
The Banāphar caste is a low-born caste,
  As I will to the Rājā show.

'Their fathers of Rājpūt blood were they,
  But their mothers of cowherd race:
Dasrāj and Bachrāj all on a day
  Went forth the deer to chase.

'A cowherd's two daughters, as chance befel,
  Devī and Brahmā hight,
Wending to market their curds to sell,
  In the woodland crossed their sight.

'There two wild bulls of the buffaloes fought,
  They barred that path unwide;
A bull by the horns each maiden caught,
  And thrust him back aside.

'"The sons of these girls", stout Dasrāj cried,
  "Will be swordsmiths stark, God wot,"
So Dasrāj took him Dēvī as bride,
  With Bachrāj was Brahmā's lot.

'So Malkhān and Sulkhān this one bare,
  That Ālhā and Ūdan withal;
As their mothers forest-maidens were,
  Banāphar men them call.

'If Sunwā with this Ālhā wed,
  'Twill our Rājpūtì pollute;
Then, O Baghēl Rāi, with my word comply,
  For my counsel brings thee boot.

'Go, bring thou Ālhā thine housê within;
  Let flattering words be said;
Gather around them all thy kin;
  Then smite thou every head.'

When the Rājā heard false Māhilā's word,
  He did him in haste array;
For the messengers four of the bridal called,
  And took to the camp his way.

From his palace with speed Naipālī went,
And, when to the camp he came,
'Now where', quoth he, 'is Ālhā's tent?
Show me, I pray, the same.'

The tent was all of the kīmkhāb[1] good,
Which Rupnā the herald showed;
Before the door the macemen stood,
And the bodyguard cleared the road.

The Rājā to Ālhā bowed full low,
As he stepped within the room:
'Now happy, Mahōbā-born, art thou,
And happy is Dēvī's womb.

'And happy the lot that my child has won,
Who Banāphar Rāi shall wed:
The fortunate time is ere rise of sun,
So come thou the rounds to tread.'

Through all the camp, when Malkhān heard,
He bade the drum to sound;
'Nay hear, Banāphar Rāi, the word,'
Quoth he, 'that I propound.

'What need of a host arrayed have ye?
Be only the bridegroom dight.
Let my sons free, each one of the three,
And the rounds shall be trodden aright.'

Quoth Ūdan, 'To us in our tents doth seem,
Thou, Rājā, framest a plot.'
But Naipālī made oath by the Ganges stream;
Then ready in haste they got.

Dhēwā, Malkhay, and Ūdan Rāi,
They all were boune to ride;
Jagnaik, Rupnā, and Mannā,
And Mīrā the Saiyid beside.

Ālhā then in his litter sate,
Which the messengers four did precede;
With kinsmen eight he reached the gate,
And the princes three were freed.

[1] Gold embroidery.

The princes hied to the painted hall,
  And the arbour with thatch did roof;
But the king did his mightiest warriors call,
  And hid them in closets aloof.

Down from his courser light sprang each,
  To the groom the bridle cast;
As soon as the litter the arbour did reach,
  The gates were behind made fast.

With the bridegroom's gifts was bedecked the bride;
  Joy songs sang all her maids;
Bridegroom and bride in one knot were tied,
  While the Pandit read the Vēds.

As the first round began the pair,
  Jōgā his falchion drew;
He struck at Ālhā, but Ūdan there
  On the right his shield up-threw.

And when they took the second round,
  Then Bhōgā drew his glaive;
But Ālhā's body felt no wound,
  For him did Malkhān save.

And when the third time round they came,
  Young Bijyā drew his blade;
But as at Ālhā he took aim,
  Stout Dhēwā sprang to aid.

But when the fourth time round they passed,
  The king to his chamber went;
A mighty spell Naipālī cast
  And over the arbour sent.

He struck the princes blind and dumb;
  'Now Ālhā is lost,' thought she;
'My father,' she said, 'is my foe become,
  And a widow forlorn makes me.'

A paper of Bīr Mahamdī she took,
  And scattered the powder in air;
Spell 'gainst spell encountered fell,
  So the seventh round trod the pair.

Then Sunwā fair did to Ūdan say,
  'Now, brother, hear my rede;
Bring straightway the litter I pray,
  And bear it forth with speed.'

So Rupnā brought it without delay
  Beside the door to stand;
But the princes three to bar the way
  Called forth their secret band.

They cried, 'The men of Mahōbā smite,
  Let none of them homeward go.'
Beside the gate then rose the fight,
  And blood began to flow.

The Mahōbā champions twelve were wroth;
  Right furiously they fought.
Jōgā and Bhōgā they seized them both,
  And through the gateway brought.

So, when they forced their passage through,
  Right onward sped the band;
Behind did all the host pursue
  Till they came to the border land.

And the army of Harinandan too
  Marched round to bar the road;
Twelve kōs their swords their path did hew,
  And blood like a river flowed.

Ūdan the litter-pole grasped he,
  And took the Mahōbā way;
Three long kōs right furiously
  Stout Dhēwā's sword made play;

Two kōs brave Malkhān slew his foes,
  All round the wounded lay;
Ālhā bore the mace's blows
  And tholed the rearward fray.

Up came Naipālī the king at last,
  And reached Pachsāwad strong;
O'er Ālhā the spell of silence cast
  And bare him a captive along.

'Now let no hand on the lad be laid,
  Or all is undone,' quoth he;
'Jōgā and Bhōgā are prisoners made,
  And this shall our hostage be.'

FYTTE IX

All at Prāg Rāj[1] the tents were pight;
  The banners of red were set;
Ūdan searched the camp outright,
  At length with Malkhān met.

'Ālhā is not the camp within,
  And how shall he be to find?
Call Dhēwā wise to mark the skies.'
  Then soon he the case divined.

'He to Nainagarh is a captive led;
  Go, brother, and set him free.'
As thus he said, bold Ūdan sped,
  And to Sunwā fair spake he.

'On Ganges tide hath thy father sworn;
  Yet for us a snare designed;
Ālhā now hath he captive borne,
  And what should be done to find?'

'Now hear me, brother,' quoth Sunwā fair,
  'Nor of my counsel doubt;
I must with thee to the town repair
  And seek my Ālhā out.

'So fleet Karilyā with thee lead,
  And on Rāsbēndul ride.'
And he has taken either steed,
  And eke his brother's bride.

In haste they journeyed all the night;
  Ere dawn they reached the town;
At a flower-seller's house that Puhpā hight,
  'Twas there they lighted down.

[1] The confluence of the Ganges and the Jumna, near the present Allahabad. Here is the famous 'Achhaibar' or 'Tree of Ages', referred to in verse 24.

Then straightway as they summoned her,
  She stood before the bride;
'Let no man know it in Naināgarh,
  But us in thy cottage hide.

'Where is Nūn Ālhā laid? declare.'
  'O daughter, that will I;
In the crystal hall is thy husband, there
  Thou wilt find the Banāphar Rāi.'

O she hath put on a milkmaid's guise,
  Takes with her her dairy ware;
To the palace of crystal where Ālhā lies
  Doth with curd-pan on head repair.

Beneath his window she cried her ware,
  As she passed the palace through;
When Ālhā beheld a maid so fair,
  Right merry of mood he grew.

He opened the sandal lattice well,
  'Come hither, fair maid,' quoth he;
'Thy pan of curds I pray thee sell,
  And what dost thou ask as fee?'

'The daughter of Mōhan am I, Sir knight,
  Chittaur my native land;
All in hope to gain thy sight
  As a milkmaid here I stand.

'Now will my father set thee free,
  When word to him I bring;
But send a token of truth by me.'
  So Ālhā gave his ring.

[Back Sunwā went as morning broke,
  To Puhpā's house went she;
'Up, Ūdan, up,' the princess spake,
  'And set thy brother free.[1]

'In the palace of crystal Ālhā lies,
  With thy horses for sale advance.'
So the horses twain hath Ūdan ta'en,
  At the gate he made them prance.

[1] This and the seven following verses have been put between square brackets by the translator. The passage is little more than a repetition of the story of Ālhā's escape from Harinandan in the Sundarban.

And when they told the news, straightway
To the door stepped forth the king;
'Now where were bred these horses, say,
Which thou to my hall dost bring?'

'A Kābul merchant, I heard thy fame,
So bring them to thy gate.'
'The price of either courser name
That I may buy them straight.'

'First to the gate thy Kshatrīs call,
And bid them mount and ride.'
But, when they came, the Kshatrīs all
Back with excuses hied.

'Horses are these of the flying breed;
They are not for us to guide.'
'A man of Mahōbā could ride my steed,
O Rājā,' Ūdan cried.

'If such within thy palace bide,
Him let the Rājā call.'
'Come forth, Nūn Ālhā, these coursers ride,
And show me their paces all.'

Ūdan signed for Ālhā to see,
And each his steed bestrode;
Eftsoons they cast their bridles free
And took the Mahōbā road.]

Fair Sunwā eke had left the town,
To Prāg did safely fleet;
And Ālhā and Ūdan to bathe went down
Where the sacred rivers meet.

The tree of ages they glorified,
And Bharadwāj' holy feet;
Benī-Mādhav and all the gods beside
They honoured with worship meet.

They summoned the Gangā's priestly sons,
And with kine them gratified;
They gave sacrifice due and offerings too;
So forward the host did ride.

The Banāphar's army eight marches marched,
Till they reached Mahōbā's soil;
The tents are pight and the arms undight,
And they rest by the sea from toil.

So Rupnā the herald was sent before;
He reached the palace gate;
And Malhnā the Queen and Dēvī, I ween,
And Brahmā stood there to wait.

They gaze along the distant way;
'When come our sons?' they cry;
If they view a traveller afar, they say,
'Can this be Ūdan Rāi?'

When Rupnā then at the gate they viewed,
Queen Malhnā halsed him well;
'Ūdan, Ālhā, Malkhān, Dhēwā,
Where hast thou left them? tell.

'And what at Naināgarh was wrought?
Show clearly what befell.'
'O, Mother Malhnā, ask me nought,
For sooth I may not tell.

'Naināgarh is a mighty place,
A kingdom seated high;
There are princes three of the royal race,
They do not fear to die.

'A drum of life in their halls is stored;
At their fear the armies quake;
And, but our Bhavānī stood our ward,
This marriage we ne'er could make.

'Now have we bound their champions fast,
And have trodden the seven rounds;
Eight days in the strife of swords were past,
Till with blood-flow streamed their bounds.

'The bridal litter of Sunwā we bring,
And beside the sea set down;
Songs of joy let the women sing,
Send word through all the town.'

The Pandit has chosen a happy tide
  The Banāphar's litter to greet;
Then word that Ālhā has brought his bride
  Was spread through every street.

Of the betel-leaf sellers nine hundred there
  And the four and eighty trades;
Twelve hundred the daughters of Brāhmans were,
  Sixteen hundred were Rājpūt maids.

These met in the painted dome all told,
  Where Malhnā the queen did sit;
She took in her hand a censer of gold,
  And the lamps all round she lit.

She bore it unto the gate anon;
  To Ūdan a runner hied;
'Make haste to send the litter on,
  For this is the happy tide.'

The bearers twelve took up their load,
  They ran with a merry hum;
And Ālhā's elephant down the road
  And up to the gate did come.

They brought a stair of the sandal fair
  And against the howda set;
Slowly Ālhā alighted there
  Where the welcoming band was met.

First he touched queen Malhnā's feet;
  Then raised to his brow his hand;
Even so did Dēvī and Brahmā greet;
  Then joining his palms did stand.

Her hands o'er his head his mother spread,
  'Long live thou safe from harms;'
Queen Malhnā painted the sign on his brow,
  And worshipped the might of his arms.

She waved the censer the litter above,
  Fulfilled the rite as due;
The litter-curtains she back did move,
  And Sunwā forth she drew.

She gave the nine-lakh chain from her neck,
  When she looked on the maiden's face;
And she the bracelets her wrist did deck
  At the Rānī's feet did place.

Songs of joy the women did sing;
  So passed they within the hall:
And word of this to the court they bring,
  Where sat the king Parmāl.

Ālhā, Ūdan, Dhēwā, Malkhàn,
  And the Saiyid together went;
And when the five at the court did arrive,
  They stood with heads down bent.

The king embraced them each and laughed,
  'Hail, Dēvī's sons—well done—
That from Naināgarh through your warrior craft
  Ye return with the maiden won.'

Then the kettledrummer he bade them call,
  And a note of triumph swell;
The changes were sounded before the hall
  With clarion and with shell.

And the Rājā called for the captain of guns,
  And plume and turban gave;
The thunder all Mahōbā stirred,
  For hundreds of cannon did rave.

So through every land were tidings spread,
  How Ālhā his bride has won;
And how they at Naināgarh have sped.
  My tale is told and done.

CANTO V

THE MARRIAGE OF MALKHĀN

ABSTRACT

THE opening invocation relates how seven virgins went to Nīmsar-Misrik,[1] where they performed penance and prayed for husbands. Their prayer was granted, and Gaurī obtained Śiva, Sītā was married to Rāma, Mandōdarī to Rāvaṇa, Rādhā to Krishna, Gajmōtin to Malkhān, Kusum Dē to Lākhan, and Phulwā to Ūdan.[2]

Rājā Gajrāj, the Bisēn, is king of the Bisēn country, the chief fortresses of which are Pathrīgaṛh and Jhunnāgaṛh.[3] He has in his house the sorceress Sēmā Bhagtin, a fire-breathing horse, whose breath destroys armies, and a daughter named Gajmōtin. When she is sixteen years of age she is taunted by her companions with being yet unmarried and complains to her mother, Champā Rānī, who persuades the Rājā to send out the betrothal invitation. He sends it in charge of his son Surjā, with a present of three lākhs in value, telling him to take it to every Rājā except to Parmāl of Mahōbā. Surjā goes to Delhi, and then to Kanauj, but is rejected at each place on the ground that no one can contend with Gajrāj and that to send a son there to be married was to send him to death. He then goes to Uraī (Māhil's stronghold). He is there met by Ūdan out hunting, who forces him to bring the invitation to Mahōbā, where Parmāl very unwillingly accepts it for Malkhān. Ūdan compels him to do this, declaring that he has no fear of the Bisēn, for 'I have conquered Datiā and Orissa and my horse's hoofs have resounded at the Sētbandh (Adam's Bridge). My flag was planted across the river at Attock. I have conquered Kumaon and Pēshāwar. Mūltān and Būndī tremble before me. In Mēwāt women bolt their doors and frighten children with my name.' The usual ceremonies are per-

[1] Probably Nimkhar and Misrikh in the Sītāpur District of Oudh. Here there is a great fair held, at which pilgrims congregate, beginning their journey at Nimkhar and finishing it at the great tank (*sar*) of Misrikh.

[2] Malkhān's marriage is the theme of the present canto, Kusum Dē's of Canto XI, and Phulwā's of Canto VII.

[3] These places have not been identified. Jhunnāgaṛh cannot be the Jūnāgaṛh in Kāṭhiāwār. At the present day, the Bisēn Rājpūts are most powerful in the East of the United Provinces and in Oudh. Jhunnāgaṛh is often mentioned in the poem, and was the capital and residence of the king. Pathrīgaṛh seems to have been a frontier fortress.

formed, and Surjā returns to Bisēn in seven days, Ūdan promising to come for the marriage in the light half of the month of Māgh (January–February).

As soon as Māhil hears of this he hastens on his mare Lillī to Bisēn, and urges Gajrāj to refuse to ratify the betrothal; but the latter is persuaded by Surjā that it is better to wait till the bridegroom comes, and then to cut his head off. In the meantime Ūdan gets the army ready, invites Rūpan, Rājā of Siraunj, Madangōpāl of Pataunj, Bīr Sāhi of Baurīgaṛh, Naipālī of Naināgaṛh (Ālhā's father-in-law), Prithīrāj of Delhi, Jaychand of Kanauj, and Māhil the Parihār to join the wedding party. After the usual ceremonies at the well, &c., they start, Khunkhun Kōrī, Madan Gaṛariā, and Mannā Gūjar of Mahōbā being mentioned among the leaders of the army. When they reach Pathrīgaṛh in Bisēn they send Rūpnā Bārī, the herald, on ahead, when exactly the same events occur as at Ālhā's marriage. Rūpnā presents the 'aipan-bārī'[1] and brings it out again, cutting his way through ten thousand men. After this, by Māhil's advice, Gajrāj pretends friendship. He gives the Mahōbā party a rocky site for their camp, where no wooden tent-pegs could be driven into the ground; but by Ālhā's forethought they had brought fourteen cart-loads of iron pegs, with which they make their tents fast. Gajrāj next sends them nine hundred vessels of poisoned sherbet. As Ūdan begins to drink he sneezes. Alarmed by the omen they give some first to a dog, who presently dies. Then all the sherbet is thrown away and those who brought it are beaten.

Gajrāj next visits the camp, and represents to Ālhā that he is most anxious for the marriage, but that it is a custom of his family that the bridegroom should come alone, and nothing of iron, not even a knife, with him. They suspect treachery, but when he has sworn on Ganges water to act fairly, they send off Malkhān in a palankeen. As soon as he is inside the fortress of Jhunnāgaṛh, the gates are shut and a thousand knights fall upon him, but he defends himself with the palankeen-pole, and kills eight hundred. Then the Rājā explains that this is all a joke and the custom of his house, and that another custom is that the bridegroom must perform his seven circuits round the wedding post with his arms bound behind his back. Malkhān submits to this. He is bound to the sandal-wood wedding post, and beaten with bamboo rods till his clothes are torn to pieces and he is covered with blood. Phuliyā Mālin sees this, and tells Gajmōtin, who comes to the spot and asks who it is that they are beating. 'It is a defaulter who has not paid his revenue for twelve years,' say they. 'No,' she cries, 'I see the bracelet on his arm and all the tokens of marriage. This is the boy who has come to wed me and you are disgracing him.' Hearing this, Malkhān is filled with shame. He shakes himself free of his bonds, and, rooting up the sandal-wood post for a weapon, attacks his assailants. The Rājā then interferes

[1] This is a jar decorated with *aipan* (a paste of rice and turmeric) and filled with water (*bārī*), which is sent as a ceremonial token on such occasions.

and again explains that it is all a joke and a custom of his family. Malkhān submits to be bound again, and is this time cast into a pit. Phuliyā finds this out and tells Gajmōtin, who visits him at night with food and a silken cord to escape by. She removes the cover of the pit, but he refuses to accept any aid from her except that she may send news of him to Ālhā. So she writes a letter and sends it by Phuliyā. The Mālin is met by Māhil, who tells her he is Ālhā, takes the letter (which she has hidden in her hair) and threatens to take her life if she tells any one about Malkhān. She, however, meets Ūdan and tells him. He finds out the deception of Māhil and takes the letter from him with a very mild reproach. The army is equipped, and sets out from Pathrīgaṛh for Jhunnāgaṛh. It is met by Gajrāj's army under his son Surjā and Mān Singh, Rājā of Jagnik. These are defeated, whereupon Sēmā Bhagtin, the sorceress, comes forth and casts the spell of silence over the Mahōbā army, turning them all to stone. Ḍhēwā alone escapes and returns to the tents to tell Ālhā, who sends him to fetch Indal (son of Ālhā and Sunwā) from Mahōbā.[1] When Ḍhēwā arrives with the message, Indal goes to the temple of Śāradā Dēvī, tells her his trouble, and threatens to kill himself if she will not help him. The goddess promises aid, and goes straight to heaven to the god Indra, from whom she asks for *amṛita* (or water of life). He obtains it for her from Vāsuki, the snake-god. She returns and gives it to Indal, saying she will accompany him. Sunwā too goes with him, and the goddess sprinkles the water over the stone army which straightway again comes to life. They attack the Jhunnāgaṛh army, and Ūdan takes Gajrāj's two sons Surjā and Kāntāmal prisoners. The Rājā then comes out himself, riding his fire-breathing horse, and bringing Sēmā with him. She rains fire on the army, but Sunwā rains water to quench it; she raises a storm, but Sunwā quells it; then they both become kites, and fight in the air, ultimately falling together to the ground. Indal gallops up and catches Sēmā. He refuses to kill her as she is a woman, but cuts off her hair, so that all her witchcraft is destroyed. Next the fire-breathing horse advances, but, on Sunwā's hint, Indal cuts off its tail, by which it loses all its power. The elephant Pachsāwaḍ strikes Gajrāj off his horse and Ālhā takes him prisoner. He then declares that he gives up all opposition and will have the wedding performed honestly.

But Māhil still suggests new plots, and Gajrāj now says that it is the custom of his family that only the bridegroom and his special friends should come to the palace in Jhunnāgaṛh. Accordingly the five Banāphars (Ālhā, Ūdan, Malkhān, Sulkhān, and Ḍhēwā) come with Brahmā, son of Parmāl, Lākhan (nephew of Jaychand of Kanauj),

[1] These people became fighting men at an early age. Ūdan was twelve years of age when he captured Māṛō. As Indal is now of fighting age, at least twelve years must have elapsed since the fighting described in Canto IV, in which Ālhā won Sunwā. It will be remembered that in that canto she is described as a skilled magician.

Jōgā and Bhōgā (of Nainägaṛh, brothers of Sunwā), Chandan, son of Prithīrāj, Jagnaik (sister's son of Parmāl), and Mōhan (son of Bīr Sāhi of Baurīgaṛh), twelve in all. When the bridegroom and the bride, with clothes knotted together, are performing the first circuit round the wedding post, Surjā strikes a blow at Malkhān, but Ūdan wards it off; in the second circuit, Kāntāmal's blow is warded off by Jagnaik; in the third they are set upon by a thousand knights, whom they repulse, killing nine hundred. The post and roof of the wedding arbour are broken in the conflict, but they set up spears for a post, and thatch it with shields. In this way they finish the seven circuits and carry through the marriage. After this comes the 'rice-eating' ceremony, and again the Rājā, by Māhil's advice, plots against them. After swearing on Ganges water, he gets the twelve to come without arms, and attacks them while eating. They beat off the assailants with waterpots and stools, and then merrily finish the meal, sitting on dead bodies in place of the stools broken in the fight. At last the Rājā gives in. Gajmōtin is beautifully attired and sent off in her palankeen, and they all return to Mahōbā, where they are received with great rejoicings.

CANTO VI

THE MARRIAGE OF BRAHMĀ

ABSTRACT

THE subject of this canto is the marriage of Parmāl's son, Brahmā, to Bēlā, the daughter of Prithīrāj. The marriage was never consummated, for, unlike the cases of Ālhā and Malkhān, after it had been duly solemnized, it was arranged that the bride should remain in her parents' house for a full year before she was formally taken away by her husband. As we shall see in later cantos, this last ceremony never took place.

The introductory invocation takes us back to the mythic days of the great Mahābhārata war, which took place in a former age, known as the Dwāpara Yuga, and preceding the present age, or Kali Yuga. In those days the gods mingled with men, and we are here told how Śiva once visited the famous five Pāṇḍava brothers, the heroes of the war, and how one of them accidentally shot at him with an arrow. Thereupon Śiva cursed their common wife, Draupadī, to be born again in this world as Bēlā, the daughter of Prithīrāj, and to be the cause of many battles.

So, in the course of time, it happened, and to accompany Draupadī, her husband Arjuna, the most heroic of the five Pāṇḍavas, was also born again as Brahmā, Parmāl's son. On the other hand, Karṇa, the implacable foe of the Pāṇḍavas, was born again as Tāhar, Prithīrāj's son and Bēlā's brother; and the Brāhmaṇ Drōṇa, one of the leading generals against the Pāṇḍavas, was reborn as Chauṇṛā, the Brāhmaṇ general of Prithīrāj. With this preface we come to the real story of the canto.[1]

Prithīrāj Chauhān, king of Delhi, and his queen, Agmā, have a daughter named Bēlā, and she, being twelve years of age, is taunted by her companions on the ground that, although it is high time she were married, she has not yet found a husband. Her father is accordingly persuaded by Agmā to send out an invitation. He offers a present of three lākhs in value, and writes his conditions. 'There shall be fighting at the doorway and valiant sword-play round the wedding post, and when the bridegroom comes to the after-marriage feast, his head will I cut off.' This letter he gives to his son Tāhar and to Chauṇṛā the Brāhmaṇ, and tells them to take it to all Rājās.

[1] We shall see in Canto XIX that Mīrā Tālhan was an incarnation of Bhīmasēna, and Lākhan (Jaychand's nephew) of Nakula, also two of the Paṇḍava brothers.

But go ye not to Mahōbā, for there dwell the Banāphars, men of meanest caste.' Tāhar, on his horse Dalganjan, and Chaunṛā, on his one-tusker elephant, go forth to Jhunnāgaṛh,[1] then to Baurīgaṛh,[2] then to Narwar,[3] then to Bundī,[4] then to Uraī,[5] and, by Māhil's advice, to Kanauj, but everywhere the conditions attached compel the Rājās to refuse the marriage. Returning from Kanauj to Uraī, Tāhar meets Malkhān out hunting, who asks him his business, and proposes Brahmā (or Brahmānand), son of Parmāl, as bridegroom for Bēlā. Tāhar will not consent to this, so Malkhān makes him and Chaunṛā prisoners, and conveys them to Sirsā.[6] He leaves them there in charge of Sulkhān, his brother, and goes himself to Mahōbā, where he forces Parmāl and (with Dēbī's[7] co-operation) Malhnā to give an unwilling consent. Then Tāhar is introduced, and they make him dismount at a place where seven plates of iron are artfully sunk in the ground. He drives his spear through the plates, and challenges Brahmā to draw it out, but Ūdan steps in and draws it up 'like a radish'. The betrothal invitation is then accepted (in spite of the bad omen of a sneeze), and Tāhar returns to Delhi.

Māhil, on hearing of this, rushes off to Delhi on his mare Lillī, and tries in vain to get Prithīrāj to refuse to ratify the engagement. He then returns home, and goes to his sister Malhnā (Parmāl's queen) with a forged letter from Prithīrāj in which was written, 'Bring thou Brahmā alone, and I will have performed the seven circuits; but if any Banāphar come, his head will I cut off.' Persuaded by Māhil, and without consulting any one else, she sends her son off with him. Ūdan hears of this, and after sharply reproaching Malhnā, sends word to Malkhān to intercept Māhil. This is done and Māhil is hung up by the arms to the gate of Sirsā.

Meanwhile, all the Rājās summoned to the marriage arrive, and the army starts. They come to Sirsā, where Ālhā has Māhil released and forced to accompany them in a palankeen, all his followers being turned back. In seven days they reach Delhi. Chūṛāmaṇ, the Paṇḍit, proclaims the time auspicious, and Rūpnā Bārī is sent on to Prithīrāj's throne-room, where sit 2,000 valiant knights, and 3,000 lancers headed by Dēbī, a Marāṭhā of the south. 'Angad of Gwālior City was there, and Randhīr of Lahore. Dhāndhū, the son of Prithī's brother, Khāṇḍē Rāi, was seated there with his naked sword upon his knee. Bhūrā, Mughul of Kābul, was there—he who was not afraid to die. Rahmat and Sahmat of Jinsī, of the terrible

[1] See the preceding canto.

[2] Where Chandrābal, Parmāl's daughter, was married to Indrasēn, son of Bīr Sāhi, the Jādōṇ (Canto VIII).

[3] Where Ūdan married Phulwā (Canto VII).

[4] Where Lākhan married Kusum Dē (Canto XI).

[5] The fief of Māhil, the traitor.

[6] A frontier fortress on the road from Mahōbā to Delhi. It was Malkhān's fief, and, as long as it was held, it protected Mahōbā from invasion from the West. Its fall is described in Canto XIII.

[7] Dēbī here, as in Canto XXII, is called Machulā.

two-edged swords. Bīr Bhugantā, the hero of Jagnik (he was chief of all the heroes), and eke the seven sons of Prithīrāj—Sūraj, Chandan, Sardan, Mardan, Gōpī, Mōtī, and Tāhar.' The same scene occurs as before, and Rūpnā, cutting his way out, returns to Parmāl's camp. Prithī (by Māhil's advice) sends a quantity of poisoned sherbet into the camp; but (as at Pathrīgaṛh) it is detected by the omen of a sneeze. Then Māhil (who comes and goes between the camp and Delhi) suggests another trick. Prithī sets up a golden vessel on a pole at the gate, and by it he sets two elephants whom he has made mad with liquor. He then sends his son Sūraj out to conduct the Mahōbā party in in a friendly way. When they reach the gate they are told that it is the custom of the house that they must first fell these elephants, which are let loose on them. Malkhān seizes one by the tusk and Ūdan takes the other by the trunk, and they knock them both down. Then they are told they must take the golden vessel from the pole, and when Jagnaik advances to do this, Kamlāpat opposes him on an elephant, but is cut down from shoulder to waist. Then Rahmat and Sahmat attack him, but are cut down by Mannā Gūjar and Ḍhēwā. This is followed by a general engagement, and after 150,000 Delhi men have been killed, Ūdan knocks the vessel off with his spear, and the ceremonies of 'the door' are performed. Next Rājā Parmāl is sent for to perform the *samdhōrā* [1] rites, but when he comes Prithīrāj tells him that it is the custom of his family that he must first fix a betel-leaf on his (Prithī's) breast. When Parmāl sees Prithī with his chest a good yard wide and his eyes flaming like torches, he is so frightened that he gets into his palankeen and flies back to camp. Then 'as an elder brother is the same as a father',[2] Ālhā is sent for, and he first puts curd on the Rājā's breast, and then sticks on a betel-leaf. They embrace each other and the door-rites are performed.

Next comes the *chaṛhāō*, or offering of presents to the bride; but when Bēlā sees the pearls sent her by Parmāl, she throws them away, crying that they are poor ornaments of modern times. She must have jewels of the Dwāpara Yuga (or the age when she existed as Draupadī). Ālhā goes to Śāradā Dēvī's temple and worships. As he is about to cut off his own head as a sacrifice, she appears and he tells her what he wants. She goes to Indra, who orders Vāsuki to produce Draupadī's buried treasure, which he, as snake-god, had been guarding all these centuries. Vāsuki does so, and Dēvī gives them to Ālhā. He sends them to Bēlā, who is delighted with them.

Preparations for the marriage ceremony are then begun. Chandan is sent to say that it is the custom of the house that only the nearest friends of the bridegroom should accompany him. After Chandan

[1] The two fathers-in-law are respectively 'Samdhī' to each other. The *Samdhōrā* is the formal mutual recognition of the relationship. Between the two there is generally a mutual exchange of presents, and of cloaks and garlands.

[2] Though not actually brothers, Ālhā and Ūdan were brought up with Brahmā and treated as such.

has sworn on Ganges water not to deal treacherously, Brahmā sets out, accompanied only by Ālhā, Ūdan, Malkhān, Ḍhēwā, Jagnaik, Mannā Gūjar, Jōgā and Bhōgā of Naināgarh, Bīr Sāhi Jādōn of Baurīgaṛh and Mōhan (his son). Then Prithī conceals 4,000 knights in ambush. When the bridegroom and the bride perform the first circuit round the wedding post, Sūraj strikes a blow which Jagnaik wards off. At the second, Chandan was stopped by Ḍhēwā; and so through all the seven circuits, each of Prithī's seven sons striking an ineffective blow in turn. The concealed knights then attack them, but are beaten off. The seven sons of Prithī are bound, and Sūraj is forced to sow the rice and to give the 'brother's gift'. Then Chauṇṛā comes in and after he has persuaded them to unloose the seven brothers, the bridegroom is invited into the women's apartments to eat the wedding breakfast. Ūdan insists on accompanying him as 'best man'. When they sit down to eat, Chauṇṛā, who has got in dressed as a woman, stabs Ūdan in the side. All the women expostulate and lament the treachery. Bēlā is fetched and she cuts her little finger, puts her blood into the wound, and it heals at once.

The Mahōbā party then prepare to return. Prithīrāj tells them it is a custom in his house never to send the bride to her husband's home immediately after the wedding, but that he will let her go in a year. So they return to Mahōbā, where they are received with great rejoicings.

Canto VII

THE MARRIAGE OF ŪDAN

ABSTRACT

The short opening invocation states that Rāvaṇa was born to carry off Sītā, Rāma to kill Rāvaṇa, Hanumān to burn Laṅkā, and Krishṇa to destroy Kaṁsa.

At Māhil's suggestion, Parmāl calls for volunteers to go to Kābul to buy horses for him. Ūdan offers to go. He starts with Ḍhēwā and fourteen mules laden with gold coins. On reaching Narwar[1] in seven days' time, Ūdan learns from the women drawing water that the Rājā's name is Narpat, and that his daughter, Phulwā, is exceedingly beautiful. He and Ḍhēwā then picket their horses in a garden of grape-vines and dates belonging to Phulwā, giving 1,000 gold coins to the gardener, and, afterwards, the same to his wife, Hiriyā Mālin, to let them stay. She recognizes him, and tells him that she was born at Naināgaṛh[2] and that Sunwā (Ālhā's wife) was like a sister to her. She therefore asks them to stop in her house. This they do, and remain there five months, during which period no opportunity occurs of seeing Phulwā.

The Mālin every day weaves and takes to Phulwā a wreath of flowers. One day Ūdan sends Hiriyā to the bazaar to buy horses' food, and offers to weave the wreath himself; but, instead of a double chain, which she used to make, he weaves a fourfold chain mixed with pearls. He tells Hiriyā that, if Phulwā notices it, she is to reply that her sister's daughter from Mahōbā has woven it. Phulwā does notice it, and divines that it was woven by a man, but tells Hiriyā to bring her niece. Ūdan then has his nose pierced and a nose-ring put in, dresses like a woman, and accompanies Hiriyā to the palace. Phulwā is sitting on a bed, and Ūdan refuses to sit on a stool, or at the foot of the bed, or anywhere but at the head, on the ground that his Rājpūthood would be destroyed if he sat below a woman; but this is excused on the ground that he is Chandrāvali's[3] Mālin and always was so treated by her. He explains the hardness of his muscles by saying that he was accustomed to run after the buffaloes and to water the garden at home.

[1] Name of a well-known and ancient town, now in the Gwālior State.
[2] As told in Canto IV, Sunwā came from Naināgaṛh.
[3] Or Chandrābal, Parmāl's daughter, married to Bīr Sāhi of Baurīgaṛh. See the next canto.

Hiriyā is then sent away, and Phulwā and Ūdan pass the night in playing cards and dice. As she is fanning herself, she blows away the cloth on his chest and discloses the hilt of his sword. She then explains to him that she is Bijaisin (see Canto III, Fytte xii) and reminds him how at Māṛō he had promised to marry her, and how she had told him at the time of her death that she would be born again at Narwar. She also tells him that Narwar is a mighty place, possessing an enchanted wooden horse, an arrow that never misses, and a *sēl*, or javelin, that always kills; but he promises to bind her brother Makrand, and to get the marriage performed.

In the morning he goes back with Hiriyā. Ḍhēwā begins to laugh at his nose-ring, but his curiosity is excited by Ūdan's account of Phulwā's beauty, and he wishes to see her too. In order to do this they disguise themselves as Jōgīs, and go and sing and drum before the Rājā. When he wants to feed them, they declare that they have a vow only to eat food cooked by a virgin, not a Brāhmaṇ. The Rājā then directs that Phulwā should cook it. She brings it to him, but Ūdan then reflects that it is contrary to his Rājpūthood to eat food cooked by a virgin, and as he takes the first mouthful, pretends to fall down senseless. There is great consternation. Ḍhēwā declares that there are Churails (evil spirits) in the place who have entered into Ūdan, but Phulwā takes him by the hand and tells him to play no such tricks, lest her brother should hear of it. Then they go out, and as they have now expended the fourteen mule-loads of gold and cannot buy horses, they return to Mahōbā, where again Ūdan pretends to be possessed.

All the doctors and magicians are sent for in vain, and Ālhā is in great distress, when Sunwā (his wife) hears of it, and suspects the reason. She has Ūdan brought to her and he confesses to her that he has acted this fraud through love of Phulwā, and persuades her to espouse his cause. She goes to Ālhā and tells him the secret, and when he protests that he has no heart to fight with Narwar, she reproaches him so keenly with cowardice that he gives in. The Rājās of Jhunnāgaṛh, Baurīgaṛh, and Naināgaṛh are all invited, the army equipped, and the 'well' and other ceremonies performed, as in the case of Ālhā (Canto IV). They reach Narwar in eight days, and Rūpnā Bārī is, as usual, sent on with the *aipan bārī*. The usual contest ensues, and Rūpnā wounds Bījai Singh, Rājā of Bijahaṭ, and cuts his way forth. The Narwar army under Makrand then comes out and is worsted, Makrand's horse being wounded in single combat with Malkhān. He then returns to Narwar, and comes back bringing Hiriyā Mālin, and riding on the enchanted wooden horse. Hiriyā sends forth the unerring arrow and the *sēl* so terribly among the Mahōbā men that the army is routed, and then she spreads the spell of silence over them. Ūdan puts off his bridegroom crown and dress and arms himself. He attacks Makrand, but is overcome by the spell and taken prisoner.

Ālhā then sends Ḍhēwā back to Mahōbā to fetch Indal. Indal, on hearing the news, goes to Dēvī's temple and obtains her help. Dēvī goes off to Indra, gets the *amṛita* (water of life) from him and is told by him that she must steal the enchanted horse and weapons of Narwar. Sunwā blesses her son and binds the spell of Bīr Mahamdī on his arms. They go off together to Narwar, where Dēvī restores the army to life with the *amṛita*, steals the weapons from the Narwar palace, and kicks the horse, by which all its virtue is lost. Hiriyā's spells avail nothing against Indal, who is protected by his mother's counter-spell, and he cuts off her hair and so destroys her power to do harm. He vanquishes Makrand in single combat, and Malkhān binds his arms. When Narpat hears this he goes barefooted and bareheaded, with a leaf of grass in his mouth, to Ālhā, and promises to let the marriage go on and to release Ūdan and all his prisoners. He invites the ten Mahōbā heroes to accompany the bridegroom. As usual, during the marriage circuits, Makrand, and afterwards a body of knights, attack the ten and are repulsed. As the whole place is disordered, the ten make a new wedding post with a spear, and roof the arbour with their shields. The wedding ceremony is then completed. The same treachery is practised at the wedding breakfast, at which the ten are without arms, but successfully defend themselves with pots and stools. Then Narpat at last gives in, and Phulwā is sent away with Ūdan and the Mahōbā party, who return home and are received with rejoicings.

CANTO VIII

THE RETURN OF CHANDRĀ BEL

THIS canto was only partly translated by Mr. Waterfield, and I have added an abstract of the rest. In the original, the canto is named 'The Battle of the *Chauthī* of Chandrābal'. The word *chauthī* means 'fourth day', and here allusion is made to the custom under which, on the fourth day after going to her husband's house, the bride pays a visit to her parents. In the case of Chandrābal's marriage to Indrasēn, the son of Bīr Sāhi, the Jādōn (or Yādava) of Baurīgaṛh, this visit had been delayed for twelve years. The full name of the girl was Chandrāvali, which the bards have contracted Chandrābal. Mr. Waterfield has changed this to 'Chandrā bel'.

The month of Sāwan (July–August) had several festivals in Mahōbā, culminating near the end of the month in the festival of the Bhujariās, concerning which we shall hear much in Canto XIV.

All this apparently occurred after Brahmā's marriage to Prithīrāj's daughter Bēlā, as described in Canto VI. It will be noted that, in spite of the fierce fighting that took place on that occasion, Prithīrāj is now on quite friendly terms with Parmāl. He readily helps Ūdan on his way with advice and presents, and also sends troops under his own son, and under his own general, to help Ālhā and Malkhān in the march to Baurīgaṛh.

THE depths of Ocean Rāma sought, the fourteen treasures thence he brought;
Hanumān sought through Lankā's isle and news of Sītā found;
The woodland of Braj was sought all through ere the glory of Yadu Kansa slew;
Ālhā sought through every land and stoutest champions bound.

FYTTE I

When Tīj brought near its festal hour,
And the sweet month Sāwan fell,[1]
Queen Malhnā wept in her seven-storied tower,
As she thought upon Chandrā bel.

[1] On the *tīj* (i.e. 3rd day) of the bright fortnight of the month of Sāwan (July–August) a festival is held at Mahōbā.

'No one has led her back, she said,
  To visit her mother's home;
Twelve years have sped since my child was wed,
  And yet no news has come.

'In Mahōbā is none who such might hath won
  As my daughter home to lead;
For dread is the Jādōṉ of Baurīgaṛh,
  Doth on rapine and slaughter feed.'

Dark Ūdan stood in the palace near;
  He watched King Parmāl's sleep;
The Queen's lamenting reached his ear,
  So sorely did she weep.

He rose in haste, to the tower he went,
  He joined his hands and said,
'Now why is thy mien so saddened, O Queen?
  And why these tears dost shed?

'And who is the Baurīgaṛh Jādōṉ? tell,
  And whom do they Bīrsāh call?
And who is the husband of Chandrā bel?
  I pray thee show me all.'

Queen Malhnā feigned, her thought to hide,
  'When the sweet month Sāwan came,
Glad girls sung songs of the Sāwan-tide,
  Each naming her brother's name.

'And I wept because for me, the Queen,
  No daughter's carol swelled.'
But Ūdan drew his dagger keen
  And against his breast it held.

'Now by the Chandēl's self I swear,
  I will stab my heart and die;
O mother, tell who is Chandrā bel,
  Nor mock me with feigned reply.'

'Thine own sister was Chandrā bel,
  In Baurīgaṛh wed was she;
And none doth so brave in Mahōbā dwell,
  Can fetch my daughter to me.'

'Never till now have I chanced to hear
  These tidings,' Ūdan said;
'Thou wert but an infant, Ūdan dear,
  What time my child was wed.'

'To Baurīgaṛh I will ride in haste
  To bring my sister home;
And Baurī shall be but a dusty waste
  If he will not let her come.'

As Ūdan came the King before,
  He spake with joining hand,
'Give me, I pray thee, gold good store,
  I am bound for the Baurī land.

'In the Sāwan month of this very year
  Will I Chandrā bel homeward bring;'
'Now I charge thee, young Uday Singh, give ear,'
  So answered the Chandēl king.

'I have no longing for Chandrā bel,
  Nor care for her coming back;
In a work which regards thee not if thou mell,
  Thou soon thy life wilt lack.'

'I may not be ruled, O King, by thee;
  Whatever rede thou give,
Baurīgaṛh I must surely see,
  Be it mine to die or live.'

The Rājā rose displeased of mood,
  To his lady's bower went he;
And Malhnā joined her hands and stood
  When she her lord did see.

He chode his Queen, 'To Ūdan why
  The tale of Baurī show?
Now he my rede will nothing heed,
  But straight to Baurī go.'

'Now hear, my lord, thy lady's word,
  Nor think my counsel vain;
All the world is greedy of wealth,
  And who is there loves not gain?

'Gold if thou send to Baurīgaṛh,
  He will give her leave full fain.'
With that the Rājā parted from her,
  And came to his hall again.

Chariots eighty, litters three score,
  Five thousand good steeds from stalls,
Twenty-two tuskers that howdas bore,
  And twenty priceless shawls;

Twelve talents of gold in coin he told,
  And turban and plume did add;
Seven lakhs was the present for Baurīgaṛh,
  Young Ūdan to carry he bade.

'And go thou down by Dihlī town,
  Greet Prithī with greeting due;
What counsel soever King Prithī may give,
  Take heed thou his bidding do.'

And fifty-two jars the Queen to boot
  Made ready and painted fair;
Filled some with sweetmeats, and some with fruit,
  With pearls and corals rare.

Coins of silver and coins of gold,
  Caskets of goldsmith's ware;
Cloth in Egypt or Māldah sold,
  All did the Queen prepare.

She gave in charge each precious thing
  To the bridal messengers four;
And Ūdan on Bēndulā's back did spring,
  Stood saddled without the door.

From Mahōbā wall he marched full fast,
  He took the Baurī way;
Until the border line he passed,
  His course he would not stay.

Now Māhil came riding from proud Urai,
  He reached Mahōbā fair;
On the Chandēl's court he cast his eye,
  No Uday Singh was there.

Māhil in haste to the palace sped,
  And did from each inquire,
'Whither is gone the youngest?' he said,
  But from none did he gain his desire.

None would give him an answer of sooth,
  Till an oilman's daughter he met;
Mahōbā wed, but in Ūrai bred,
  And from her did an answer get.

'To Baurīgaṛh went Uday Singh,'
  To Māhil the truth did she say;
'Chandrā bel to her home to bring,
  Ūdan has taken his way.'

Then Māhil mounted on Lillī his mare,
  I wis he made no stay;
Fast he rode to Dihlī, where
  King Prithī's lordship lay.

And Ūdan eke was arrived thereat,
  And his tents in the grove were pight;
Where on his throne King Prithī sat,
  There Māhil down did light.

When Prithī the King did Māhil espy,
  Bade set him a lofty chair;
'Come in, come in, thou lord of Urai,
  And all thy news declare.'

'How shall I tell what should not be told,
  Or the marvellous tale begin?
The Chandēl I wot has laid a plot;
  The plunder of Dilhī to win.

'For Chandrā bel he feigns to have sent,
  Bids Ūdan before to spy:
In the grove already is pitched his tent,
  And to-morrow comes brave Malkhay.

'He will set thy Dihlī all aflame,
  And the spoil he will carry away.'
'O, Māhil Parhār,' did Prithī exclaim,
  'Such words thou shouldst not say.

'After long days thou comest, O Māhil Parhār;
'Now thou speakest what no way can be;
No quarrels twixt me and the Chandēl are,
And why sets he brave Malkhān on me?

'Ūdan for Baurī is marching true;
Speak not falsely, O Māhil Parhār.'
Māhil thereon abashed withdrew,
And to Baurī has ridden afar.

Wrapt in thought sat Prithī the King,
To Sūraj his son did say,
'Haste to the grove and Ūdan bring.'
Then went he without delay.

He greeted him fair, 'Come Ūdan with me,
The Rājā calls thee straight.'
On Bēndulā Ūdan came riding free,
And so he reached the gate.

He stood and fitting homage paid
Three paces from Prithī's throne;
At the feet of the King his turban he laid,
Hands joined and face bent prone.

The Rājā caught him by the hand,
And clasped him to his heart;
'Now tell me, Ūdan, to what land,'
Quoth Prithī, 'bound thou art.'

'To Baurīgaṛh have I set my face,
Home to bring Chandrā bel.'
'Baurīgaṛh is a right strong place,
Where the Jādōn chief doth dwell.

'There, Ūdan, wilt thou sure be slain,
So back to Mahōbā go.'
'Thou brave Chauhān,' quoth he again,
'I pray thee speak not so.

'Only if with me my sister I lead,
May I to Mahōbā fare.'
'Ūdan will not counsel heed,'
Then Prithī was well aware.

Thereon for a turban and plume he sent,
  Not a lakh of silver would buy,
Said, 'this to the Jādōn chief present,
  That he may not the leave deny.'

So leave of Prithī took Ūdan bold,
  And came to his camp anon;
But when to Queen Agmā the news was told,
  That hither came Dasrāj' son,

She bade a messenger Ūdan call,
  Then straight from the palace went he;
'They have summoned thee, lord, to the painted hall,
  So come thou along with me.'

Then forth rode Ūdan with all his train,
  To the gate his way he took;
From every house came the women, fain
  Upon Uday Singh to look.

When they beheld how fair the youth,
  Then with one voice they spake,
'Queen Agmā, counsel thou Ūdan sooth
  The Mahōbā way to take.'

Ūdan from Bēndulā lighted down,
  He touched Queen Agmā's feet;
'Now, Ūdan, go back to Mahōbā town,
  So give I thee counsel meet.'

'Never till Chandrā bel with me fare,
  Will I take the Mahōbā way;
And who is the champion in Baurī there,
  That durst her departure stay?'

'Ūdan my counsel will not brook,'
  Then well was the Queen aware;
Thereon a robe of price she took,
  To Ūdan gave it there.

'For the mother-in-law of Chandrā bel,
  Give her this gift from me;'
To touch her feet then Ūdan fell,
  And so to horse came he.

In haste to the camp did Ūdan spur,
For the march bade sound the drum;
Twelve days he journeyed toward Baurīgaṛh,
So did to the border come.

So far is Mr. Waterfield's translation. The rest of the story is as follows:—Ūdan pitches his camp a couple of miles from Baurīgaṛh, and informs Bīr Sāhi by letter that he has come to conduct Chandrābal on her *chauthī* visit to her parents. Bīr Sāhi is pleased by the letter, and sends his son Jōrāwar to invite Ūdan to the court. He then dresses a hundred knights exactly like himself, sits among them, and waits to see to whom Ūdan will make his bow. Ūdan arrives, and at once bows to Bīr Sāhi, presenting to him the letter sent by Parmāl. Bīr Sāhi receives him with all courtesy and invites him into the female apartments, where he gives to the Queen (Sundarī by name) the presents sent for her from Mahōbā and from Delhi.

In the meantime Māhil arrives, and (with solemn oaths) persuades Bīr Sāhi that Ūdan's visit is merely a trap to get Chandrābal to Mahōbā, where they wish to dishonour him by making her a slave. Bīr Sāhi accordingly directs his seven sons to mix poison in Ūdan's food. They do so and invite Ūdan to come and eat. Indrasēn (Chandrābal's husband, and one of the seven) explains that it is the Baurīgaṛh custom to leave behind the sword which he is wearing, as there is no cause for fear. Ūdan at first refuses, alleging the custom of his own house, but is overpersuaded, and leaves his sword in the tent.

As he sits down to eat, Chandrābal from a window informs him by signs that the food is poisoned, so he takes Indrasēn's dish instead of his own, saying it is the custom of his country to change dishes with a brother-in-law. At this the seven get angry, and attack Ūdan with their waterpots. Ūdan defends himself with his pot and with a stool, so that all are wounded. Then the other knights attack him and he defends himself in the same way. Chandrābal offers him, through the window, her husband's (Indrasēn's) sword, but he refuses to take it, as to kill any one with it would pollute his Rājpūthood. They all set upon him, beat him to his knees, bind his arms, and throw him into a pit, over which they put a heavy cover. Puhpā Mālin tells Chandrābal of this. The latter goes down at midnight with a silken rope which she lets down into the pit after removing the cover. He refuses to come out by her help, but asks her to send news of his plight to Mahōbā. He refuses also to eat food which she offers him, as it is against Rājpūt custom to eat food in such a place. She replaces the cover of the pit, goes back to her apartment, writes a letter, and gives it to Hīrāman, her parrot, with instructions to take it to Mahōbā.

On the way the parrot halts, hungry after three days of flying, in a garden at Narwar. Māhil catches sight of it and of the letter hanging to its neck, and informs the Rājā (Narpat, Ūdan's father-in-law). Makrand (Narpat's son) catches the parrot and gives it to the Queen, but keeps the letter himself. In the meanwhile Māhil has gone away to his home at Uraī. At midnight the parrot tells the Queen the state of affairs. She gets the letter from Makrand, fastens it again to the neck of the bird, and sets it free. The parrot flies in three days to Mahōbā and gives the letter to Malhnā, who, after reading it, sends for Malkhān.

Malkhān collects the army and sets out for Baurīgaṛh with Ālhā, Ḍhēwā, and Brahmā. In five days they arrive at Delhi. Prithīrāj sends an army to help Malkhān under the command of Surjā, on his horse Sabjā, and Chaunṛā, on his one-tusker elephant.

The joint army reaches Baurīgaṛh in twelve days. The four (Ālhā, Malkhān, Ḍhēwā, and Brahmā) disguise themselves as Jōgīs, enter the fort, and dance and sing in the bazaar. Kēsarī, a maid-servant, sees them and tells the Queen. The Queen invites them to stay in the palace, but they refuse in the usual formula. Chandrābal sends for them, and they disclose themselves to her. She tells them where the pit is in which Ūdan is confined. They return to camp and set the 'sappers and miners' to work digging a mine. In a single day they dig into the pit and release Ūdan, who joins them in camp.

The armies then march on Baurīgaṛh. The Baurīgaṛh forces, headed by Jōrāwar and Sūrajmal (two of Bīr Sāhi's sons), advance to meet them. After arguments, the forces join battle, and the Baurīgaṛh army is routed. Malkhān defeats Sūrajmal and Jōrāwar each in single combat and takes them both prisoners.

Indrasēn (on his horse Surkhā) and the remaining four sons of Bīr Sāhi then march at the head of another army. The battle is joined. Ūdan takes Mōhan (another son) prisoner, and Ḍhēwā takes Jagman. Chaunṛā's troops defeat their army. Finally Malkhān takes Indrasēn prisoner, and then captures Bīr Sāhi's two remaining sons.

Bīr Sāhi then himself comes forth on his elephant Bhūrā at the head of another army, which in its turn is routed. Ālhā takes Bīr Sāhi prisoner.

The Mahōbā force then enters Baurīgaṛh and Ālhā suggests to Brahmā that he should set the city on fire. Bīr Sāhi asks who Brahmā is, and, on being told that it was Parmāl's son come to escort his sister on her visit to Mahōbā, he makes profuse apologies, and explains that he has been misled by Māhil's lies. Thereupon Ālhā releases Bīr Sāhi and his seven sons. Chandrābal is willingly put into a palankeen and sent off, escorted by the army, to Mahōbā, where she is received with great rejoicings.

CANTO IX

THE CARRYING OFF OF INDAL

ABSTRACT

THE Invocation is addressed to the Ganges, who was brought by Bhagīratha from heaven to Hardwār, and who, though she cleansed all the world from sin, did not cleanse Bhagīratha himself, whose bones are lying in a well at Sōrōṉ. But she will return at the end of the present, or Kali, age, and will pardon both him and all his family.

Ūdan resolves to go with Ḍhēwā to Biṭhūr[1] in order to bathe at the Dasahrā festival. Ālhā dissuades him, saying he is sure to pick a quarrel with some rājā there, but when he finds that Ūdan is resolved to go, he advises him to take Māhil with him. Indal, the son of Ālhā and Sunwā, is very anxious to go with his uncle, and threatens to stab himself if refused; but Ālhā positively forbids him, saying that magicians from Kāmrū (Assam) will be there. Ūdan, however, takes Indal with him in spite of his father's orders. They reach Biṭhūr in five days, and when they get there Lākhan, Jaychand's nephew, sends to forbid them beating the drum. There is very nearly a fight over this; but at Ḍhēwā's persuasion Ūdan goes to Lākhan and, presenting a gift, makes friends. Lākhan withdraws his order, and allows the Mahōbā drum to be beaten.

Meanwhile Chittar-rēkhā, daughter of Rājā Abhinandan of Balkh-Bukhārā has come (in twenty-one days' march) to Biṭhūr with her brother Hansāmal, a maid named Kēsarī Naṭin, and a magic cage of gold made in Bengal. She and Kēsarī disguise themselves as Carnatic women, and dance in the Mahōbā camp, but Ḍhēwā suspects there is some treachery, and turns them out. Then he, with Ūdan and Indal, go on the river for a row. Chittar-rēkhā throws her spells over them, makes Ūdan and Ḍhēwā blind and helpless, turns Indal into a parrot and puts him into the cage, and at once goes back to her home.

When Ūdan and Ḍhēwā come to themselves they think Indal has fallen overboard and been drowned, and they search for his body with nets. Then they decide that he has been carried off by magic, and return home resolving to search for him everywhere. Māhil goes on ahead and tells Ālhā that Ūdan has killed his son. Ālhā will not believe it. He says that Ūdan loves Indal better than he himself does, and has

[1] On the Ganges, near Cawnpore. In the Mutiny it was the headquarters of the Nānā Sāhib. It was in Jaychand's territory.

always fed him before he took his own food, but when Māhil swears on the Ganges he is convinced. He will not speak to Ḍhēwā, and when Ūdan comes to him with his head bare, his hands bound with cloth, and a leaf of grass in his mouth, he binds him to a post, and falls to beating him with bamboos. Dēbī (Ūdan's mother) comes to remonstrate in vain. Sunwā (Ālhā's wife and Indal's mother) intercedes, reminding him how Ūdan had saved him from his prison in Sundarban (Canto IV), but he knocks out of her hand the pot of water she brings for Ūdan, and beats her and drives her out. Phulwā (Ūdan's wife) comes and laments that she will be left a widow, with her ornaments taken away from her, but Ālhā undertakes to support her and to take care of her himself. Ūdan shows, by uprooting the post to which he is bound, that he could resist if he chose, but he reflects that it is contrary to his profession as a Rājpūt to resist his elder brother. When Ālhā is tired of beating him he calls for executioners and tells them to take Ūdan into the forest and kill him and bring back his eyes and liver. Sunwā and Phulwā bribe them and they let Ūdan go on condition that he does not return to Mahōbā. They kill a deer, and bring the eyes and liver to Parmāl. This is the first news the Rājā hears of the tragedy. He reproaches Ālhā, recounting all Ūdan's exploits. Ālhā cries out that a stone has fallen on his understanding, and that he will not look upon the face of man again. He covers his eyes with a bandage, has a trench dug, and falls into it face downwards.

Meanwhile Ūdan has gone to Sirsā,[1] where Malkhān has the gates shut against him. As he stands there lamenting his misfortunes, Ḍhēwā—who had gone to the forest to recover his body and had tracked him all the way—comes up and swears never to leave him. They resolve to go to Narwar (the home of Phulwā, Ūdan's wife, Canto VII), and, by a false story of an attack by Prithīrāj on Mahōbā, get access to Makrand (Phulwā's brother), who at once promises to help them. The three—Makrand, Ūdan, and Ḍhēwā—resolve to search for Indal everywhere disguised as Jōgīs, going first to Jhunnāgaṛh (the home of Malkhān's wife, Gajmōtin, Canto V). Kusmā, wife of Makrand, gives each a magic powder to put into his mouth, when no spell can harm him. When they get to Jhunnāgaṛh the women fall in love with them, and use charms, but in vain, to make them return their love. Ūdan goes to a temple of Dēvī, and she tells him where Indal is. Then they disclose themselves to the Queen. She sends Kāntāmal (her and Gajrāj's son) with them, and gives them four more magic powders, by the aid of which they cross the fordless and boatless river at Attock.[2]

In twenty days they reach Balkh-Bukhārā. Tārā, a maidservant of Abhinandan, takes tidings of them to the Queen, Champā by name, who sends for them, and summons her daughter to see the dance. Ūdan pretends to be faint with hunger, so Chittar-rēkhā

[1] A fortress on the Mahōbā frontier, guarding the country from incursions from the West. It was Malkhān's fief.

[2] On the Indus. They reach it in seven days from Jhunnāgaṛh.

takes him to her room, where she has sweetmeats. Then she says to Indal—whom she keeps as a parrot by day, but changes into a man by night—that hitherto she has thought him more beautiful than any one, but now she thinks the Jōgīs are more handsome. He tells her to veil her face, for it is no Jōgī, but Ūdan. Ūdan asks her to give up Indal. She says she cannot do that, but if he will call a Paṇḍit and get them married at once she will accompany them. Ūdan says they cannot marry secretly, or without bloodshed, but he swears on the Ganges to bring Indal back to marry her. She gives him the cage and a charm which he is to cast over the parrot when he is out of the Balkh-Bukhārā territory. He does this, and they set forth on their return journey, halting at Maurang-gaṛh,[1] and Sirsā. At Sirsā, Malkhān explains that he had shut his gates on him because he believed the story that Indal had been killed. Ūdan declares that he will not return to Mahōbā, but will wait at Maurang-gaṛh and accompany Indal's wedding procession. He writes a letter to tell Sunwā all the story, and Malkhān takes Indal to Mahōbā.

They find Ālhā with his eyes still bandaged, and Malkhān reproaches him about Ūdan. He offers to stab himself, but Parmāl intervenes with the argument that Prithīrāj will come and sack the place when he hears it is void of defenders. Then they tell Alhā the truth, but he is greatly dispirited through fear of Balkh-Bukhārā and its nine hundred thousand soldiers. He declares he cannot go there and make war on Abhinandan. At last Sunwā's bitter reproaches stir him up, and he sends out invitations and prepares his army. They pass by Maurang-gaṛh, where Makrand joins them (but Ūdan remains behind), and reach Balkh-Bukhārā in twenty-two days. Rūpnā Bārī presents the *aipan bārī* under the usual circumstances. After two days' fighting the Mahōbā army is defeated and retreats. Then Ālhā sends off Rūpnā to fetch Ūdan. When he comes he and Alhā are reconciled, and Alhā swears that he will burn every house in Uraī to punish Māhil for his treachery. The battle is renewed, and Ūdan, Malkhān, and Ḍhēwā take the seven sons of Abhinandan (Hansāmal, Sukkhā, Mōhan, and four others) prisoners in single combat, after his army had been put to rout by Kāntāmal on the east, Makrand on the west, Ḍhēwā on the south, and Malkhān on the north. Abhinandan then comes out and gets the better of Chaunṛā of Delhi, who has accompanied the Mahōbā army, but Alhā takes him prisoner. He then gives in, his sons are released, the marriage is performed, Chittar-rēkhā is sent off with the army, and they all return to Mahōbā.

[1] Apparently the same as Narwar.

Canto X

ĀLHĀ'S BANISHMENT

ABSTRACT

WITH this Canto begins the story of Ālhā's adventures, under the protection of Jaychand, at Kanauj, after his banishment from Mahōbā through Māhil's machinations.

The opening invocation dwells on the accidents of Fate. King Nala was reduced from riches to misery in a single day; in a single day a demon carried off Rāmachandra's wife Sītā; and so, when his fated time came, Alhā fell.

Māhil visits Prithīrāj at Delhi, and warns him that Malkhān has built a fort at Sirsā which bars the way to Mahōbā. Prithīrāj asks for his advice. Māhil tells him that the champions of Mahōbā (Alhā, Ūdan, &c.) can never be conquered so long as Parmāl has control of the five famous flying horses, Harnāgar, Bēndulā, Hansāmani,[1] Papīhā, and the mare Kabutrī. He advises Prithī to demand them from Parmāl. Prithī accordingly sends a letter to Parmāl demanding the horses. The latter, in his cowardice, decides to comply, and sends to Daspurwā for Ālhā and Ūdan. He reads the letter to them, and tells them to make over their two horses to him. They refuse, and counsel him to resist. Parmāl argues that Prithīrāj, possessing the magic arrow, is invincible, but Ūdan rises in a fury, and, with little respect for the king, details his many victories over warriors as great as Prithīrāj. Parmāl, therefore, need have no fear. He and Ālhā flatly refuse to deliver up their beloved steeds.

In rage at this uncompromising speech Parmāl pronounces against them a sentence of banishment from Mahōbā. The decree is uttered with every accompaniment of ignominy, and with the threefold curse:

> If from this day ye eat in Mahōbā, may cows' flesh be your food.
> If ye drink water here, may it be to you as cows' blood.
> If your wife be in your bed, may she be to you as your mother.

Alhā and Ūdan return to Daspurwā and collect their troops. They consult as to whither they should go. Ūdan has defeated all the neighbouring kings, so that they are his enemies, and it is useless to apply to them. Finally, they decide to seek refuge with Jaychand of Kanauj, whom they had never attacked, and who was the enemy of Prithīrāj. They consult their cousin Ḍhēwā, and he tells them that now is the propitious hour for setting forth.

There follows an interview with Dēbī, Alhā and Ūdan's mother.

[1] Apparently the same as the horse elsewhere called Karilyā. It was Ālhā's steed. Ūdan's was Rāsbēndul or Bēndulā.

She at first urges patience, but, when she hears of Parmāl's threefold curse, she agrees to accompany them; and Ālhā, Ūdan, their mother, with Ḍhēwā and Indal, Ālhā's son, and the three wives, all set forth on the journey to Kanauj, taking with them their troops, their magic horses, and Alhā's special elephant Pachsāwaḍ.

They first visit Mahōbā, where there is an affecting parting with Malhnā, Parmāl's chief queen, who has treated them as if they were her own children. She endeavours to dissuade them, but to no purpose, although she points out that, with their departure, Mahōbā's foremost champions will be gone, and that no one will be left to defend it from Prithīrāj. They set forth from Mahōbā amidst universal lamentations.

In the meantime Malkhān, at Sirsā, hears the news. He hurries to intercept the cortège, and urges Ālhā and Ūdan to come with him to Sirsā, where they will be safe from Parmāl. They refuse, and Malkhān returns to Sirsā, the only defender now left for Mahōbā.

It is the month of Bhādōn (August–September), in the latter part of the rainy season, and the journey is full of difficulty. Sometimes they are drenched with rain, and at other times the army nearly dies of thirst. They cross the river Bētwā, the boundary of Mahōbā, and, after three days' journey, they reach the Jumna, which they cross at Kālpī Ghāṭ, thence marching to Parhul. There they halt for two days, and then march slowly for four days to Siarī Maū, where they pitch their tents, and rest for three months. It should be noted that Siarī Maū is represented as a ride of four *gharīs*, or one hour and twenty minutes, from Kanauj.

Then Ālhā, on Pachsāwaḍ, with a magnificent retinue, visits Kanauj, where he interviews King Jaychand. The latter receives him kindly, but when he hears of the sentence of banishment, he denies refuge. Ālhā returns disheartened to the camp.

After another month Ūdan mounts his horse, Bēndulā, and rides to Kanauj. There he prays for success at various holy shrines, and goes straight into the bazaar and plunders the shops. The inhabitants run to Jaychand and complain. In a rage he orders cannon to be got ready, and directs Lākhan and the gunners to blow Ūdan to pieces. Just then Mīrā Saiyad (i.e. Mīrā Tālhan) counsels Jaychand to show patience and prudence. He recounts Ūdan's mighty deeds, and winds up with a narrative of how, unaided, he had once felled a mighty elephant belonging to King Prithīrāj of Delhi (Canto VI).

Astonished at this exploit, Jaychand summons Ālhā and Ūdan before him from Siarī Maū, and in the meantime sets two great elephants before his gate, rendering them more furious by giving them an intoxicating potion. On the arrival of Alhā and Ūdan, Jaychand asks them if the story about the Delhi elephant is true. If so, let them fell the two elephants at his gate. Ūdan dismounts from his horse. He knocks one elephant down with a blow of his spear, and, catching the other by the tusk, whirls him round, and casts him to one side.

Jaychand, delighted at his prowess, gives Alhā and Ūdan the fief of Rijigiri. Thither they bring their family, and settle down in peace.

CANTO XI

THE MARRIAGE OF LĀKHAN

ABSTRACT

THIS Canto describes the marriage of Lākhan, son of Ratībhān, and nephew of Jaychand of Kanauj.

The opening invocation to Kṛishṇa describes how, when he played the flute, he drew towards him into the forest all the women of Bindrāban, and all things animal and vegetable.

When Kusum Dē (or Kusumā) becomes thirteen years of age, her father, Gangādhar, Rājā of Būndī,[1] begins to think that it is time for her to be married, and tells his sons Jawāhir and Mōtī to carry the betrothal invitation (*ṭīkā*) to every suitable Rājā who has an unmarried son, but on no account to go to Mahōbā, because Ālhā Banāphar, who lives there, is of mean caste. They go to Prithīrāj of Delhi, Bīr Sāhi of Baurīgaṛh, Gajrāj of Jhunnāgaṛh (Bisēn), but all refused to intermarry with Būndī, on the ground of the valour of its men, its natural strength, and its magic spells, which precluded all hope of a successful contest. After trying several other places unnamed, they come to Kanauj. Jaychand, too, is disposed to refuse, but yields to Ūdan's taunts and exhortations. While the betrothal rites are going on some one sneezes and the Rājā is even then disposed to turn back at this unlucky omen: but Ūdan cries out, 'Let those care for omens who load bullocks for traffic. What have knights to do with such things—knights who on the battle-field eat iron? If a drop of Lākhan's sweat chance to fall, there blood shall flow in streams; with sword-blows will I turn the dust to mud, and thus will I have the seven circuits performed.' So the rites are completed, and the two brothers return to Būndī and tell their father they have got a capital match for their sister, since Lākhan is the descendant of four 'chakravartī Rājās' (Emperors), one of whom was Ajaipāl, who ruled from sunrise to sunset. Moreover, Kanauj is a city with fifty-two bazaars, with shrines of Gōvardhanī, Sandohinī, and Phūlmatī. Here is the sacred spot where Sītā cooked her food, and the river Kālindī[2] flowing beneath the fort. At all this the Rājā is much pleased.

In the month of Phāgun (February–March) Jaychand collects his

[1] A well-known state and town in Rājputānā, about 250 miles west of Mahōbā, and a little more than that to the south-west of Kanauj.

[2] i.e. the Jumna. But this is a mistake. Kanauj is on the Ganges, not the Jumna.

forces and his friends for the marriage procession. These are Gangā Pamār of Kuṛhar, mother's brother to Lākhan; Parsū, Rājā of Parhul; Rūpan, Rājā of Siraunj; Mīrā (Tālhan) Saiyid of Benares; Dhanuā Tēlī, of Rijigiri, on his mare Bilundin; Lalā Tamōlī, of Ratkālā, on his horse Sabjā; and eleven hundred thousand soldiers, led by the Banāphars. In eighteen days they reach Būndī territory and encamp ten miles from the city. Bēnī Brāhmaṇ proclaims an auspicious time, and Rūpnā Bārī is sent on with the *aipan bārī*, when the usual scene occurs, as described before. He cuts his way out, killing twenty-two of his opponents, and returns to Jaychand. On this Gangādhar is discouraged, and declares that he will be a disgraced person if this marriage takes place under the auspices of the Banāphars, who are a mean clan, but that Rūpnā's success shows how little he (Gangādhar) could resist his masters. He proposes to entice Lākhan by a trick and sends his sons to the camp. They find Jaychand in a tent of kincob (gold brocade) with walls of velvet. They invite Lākhan to come alone to the marriage ceremonies, that being, they say, the custom of the family. Ūdan stipulates that he should go with him as *Sahbōlā*, or Best Man. He also dresses up twelve of his best knights as *nēgīs*, or bearers of presents, to accompany the palankeen. They leave their weapons at the gate, having made Jawāhir swear an oath that he will not deal treacherously. As they are set down to eat food, concealed knights attack them. After a gallant resistance, in which Ūdan's and Lākhan's only weapons are the frames of the beds placed there, the knights wound and capture them and cast them into a pit. The Rājā has a guard placed over it, and has the pit filled with black salt to choke them.

That night a Mālin (flower-girl) goes into the palace and tells Kusumā all that has happened. Kusumā says, 'the Raja has many pits. Tell me, in which of them are they confined?' The Mālin replies, 'in that at the right of the glass palace'. Kusumā goes at midnight, bribes the guards, and offers Lākhan food, and a silken rope to escape by. He refuses both, and tells her, if she loves him, to take the news to Ālhā.

She sends the Mālin to tell Ālhā. The Kanauj army is got ready and advances against the Būndī army led by Jawāhir. They join battle, and the Būndī army is driven back to its entrenchments by a combined attack of Mīrā Saiyid of Benares crying 'Alī! Alī!' and Dhanuā Tēlī of Rijigiri, but nothing decisive results, and Kanauj loses 300,000 men to 150,000 of Būndī. Ālhā goes to a temple of Dēvī in the Jhārkhaṇḍ forest and worships there. The goddess tells him that he must get help from Sirsā. Malkhān and also Brahmā (Parmāl's son) must come. Ālhā writes a letter which his messenger carries in nine days to Mahōbā. Brahmā and Malkhān both refuse to go, but after an hour the latter gets up and goes to consult his wife Gajmōtin, who entreats him to help Ūdan in return for the help Ūdan had given him at his marriage with her, when he (Malkhān) was cast into a pit (see Canto V). Malkhān agrees to follow her advice, collects his forces, takes Khunkhun Kōrī, Madan Garariā, and Mannā Gūjar with him, and persuades Brahmā, with Queen Malhnā's blessing, to accompany him. They reach Būndī in fourteen days, and there meet the Kanauj army under Ālhā and Jaychand moving disheartened away with a loss of 500,000 killed, and carrying the wounded in litters.

The two armies are nearly attacking each other when they recognize that they are friends. They combine to form a plan. Malkhān makes a circuit of twenty-eight miles and arrives at the other side of Būndī. Ḍhēwā attacks in front, and when the Būndī forces come out he retreats before them, and draws them away from the city. Malkhān meanwhile forces his way in, slays the garrison, and reaches the pit. Ūdan and Lākhan, one by the help of the Mahōbā gods, Śiva of the blue throat, Maniyā, and Śāradā, and the other by the help of the Kanauj gods and ancient heroes, Phūlmatī, Ajaipāl, and Bēn Chakravartī, come out and their wounds are sewn up and anointed. Malkhān's army then advances, and the Būndī force is enclosed and routed with a loss of 500,000 men. Mōtī and Jawāhir are overcome and taken prisoners in single combat by Brahmā and Malkhān, and Gangādhar is defeated by Ālhā.

Gangādhar then promises to perform the marriage ceremony. The prisoners are all released, and Lākhan is again invited to the marriage post with Ālhā, Ḍhēwā, Brahmā, Malkhān, and the Saiyid. Kusumā is called in and the rites begun. In the middle they are attacked by concealed soldiers, but they beat them off and finish the rites, as usual spears being substituted for the broken post, and the ruined arbour being roofed with shields. Rājā Gangādhar then, by his wife's advice, gives up opposition. The remaining ceremonies are completed, and he promises to send the bride home to her husband in a year. The Kanauj army then returns to Kanauj, and Malkhān and Brahmā to Mahōbā.

CANTO XII

THE GĀNJAR WAR

ABSTRACT

THE Invocation merely praises Rāma-chandra and Śiva, together with the three hundred and thirty millions of other gods.

Jaychand issues a challenge calling for volunteers to collect tribute from Gānjar.[1] Ūdan takes it up, and sets out on Bēndulā with an army headed by Lākhan on his she-elephant named Bhūrī, accompanied by Alhā on the elephant Pachsāwad, Ḍhēwā on the horse Manurthā, Indal on Hansāman, Jōgā (of Naināgaṛh) on the Mahōbā horse Papīhā, Bhōgā (of Naināgaṛh) on Sabjā. The army reaches Gōrakhpur in thirty-six days and halts ten miles from the town of Biriā. After three days Ūdan writes to Hir Singh, the Rājā, complaining that they had not paid tribute for twelve years, and demanding immediate payment. The letter is received by Hir Singh and Bir Singh, who, becoming alarmed on reading it, collect the army, which they lead against Ūdan. Ūdan again demands payment of the arrears of tribute, and Bir Singh retorts that once before Jaychand himself had invaded his territory, and had gone back without recovering a farthing. What fear, therefore, had he of Ūdan? The armies join battle, and Bir Singh's troops are routed. Ūdan himself takes Hir Singh and Bir Singh prisoners, and occupies Biriā.

Ūdan next invades the territory of Sātan, Rājā of Paṭṭī,[2] pitching his camp eight miles from that town. On hearing of his arrival, Sātan collects his army, and, riding on his elephant Bhūrā, goes out to meet him. Ūdan demands twelve years' tribute due from Sātan. The latter refuses, also saying that Jaychand had fought with him for twelve years and had been defeated. The armies join battle. After a severe combat the Kanauj forces retreat six miles, Ūdan's flying horse being struck with Sātan's mace and running away with its rider. Ālhā and Indal come to the rescue. Sātan is dismounted from his elephant and takes to horse. Jōgā and Bhōgā attack him, and he kills them both and wounds the horse Papīhā. Indal then

[1] The meaning of this word is obscure. The poem certainly uses it as the name of a tract of country, practically equivalent to all India east of Gōrakhpur. Several of the countries named herein are beyond my power of identification.

[2] Not identified. It may be Paṭṭī in the Partābgaṛh district.

attacks Sātan and takes him prisoner. Paṭṭī is occupied, and the contents of the treasury plundered.

Ūdan then marches for forty days to Kāmrū (Assam), of which the capital was Kamlā. The Rājā, Kamlāpat, goes out with an army to meet him. Ūdan demands arrears of tribute, which Kamlāpat refuses, and jeers at Ūdan. The latter says: 'I have conquered Datiā, Orissa, and the Sētbandh (Adam's Bridge); my flags have crossed the river at Attock, and I have conquered Kashmīr and Mūltān. The people of Delhi tell of my prowess, and because of me the city of Būndī shivers. Jhunnā and Pannā have I brought low, and the city of Jaipur have I plundered.' The armies join, and Kamlāpat hurls his spells[1] against Ūdan's army, but Dēvī Śāradā makes them all of no effect. Finally, in single combat, Ūdan takes Kamlāpat prisoner, occupies Kāmrū and Kāmākhyā,[2] loots the treasury, and marches off towards Bengal.

When Gurūkhā, Rājā of Bengal, hears of Ūdan's approach, he collects his army and marches to meet him at the frontier. As before, Ūdan demands twelve years' tribute and is refused in the same terms. The armies join and that of Bengal is routed. Ūdan takes Gurūkhā prisoner in single combat, and carries off the entire treasure of Bengal.

Ūdan then invades the territory of Cuttack, where he makes prisoner the two brothers Murlī and Manōhar, and loots their treasury. Then he attacks Jagman, Rājā of Jinsī,[3] takes him prisoner and loots his treasury. Similarly he takes prisoner and plunders Chintā Ṭhākur of Rusnī,[3] Sūraj of Gōrakhpur, Pūran of Paṭnā, and Hansāman of Kāśī (Benares). Thus in three months and thirteen days he takes twelve Rājās prisoner, and beats the drum of victory in their territories. Then he reports to Lākhan that he has collected all the arrears of tribute to the last farthing, and has imprisoned those who refused to pay. Lākhan thereupon exchanges turbans with Ūdan, and swears on the Ganges to accompany him when he should return to Mahōbā. Thus in one month and six days the army returned to Kanauj. 'So much is the tale of the fighting in Gānjar.'

[1] Assam is famous for its sorcerers.

[2] Kāmākhyā is really a name of Durgā, as the guardian goddess of Assam. The bard has made the word the name of a place.

[3] Not identified.

CANTO XIII

THE SIRSĀ WAR

WITH this Canto the story returns temporarily to Mahōbā territory, and enters the shadow of the tragedy which ultimately overwhelmed Parmāl and the Banāphars.

Prithīrāj of Delhi had for long been on terms of peace with Parmāl, and, indeed, is represented as actively helping Ūdan in the matter of the return of Chandrā Bel (Canto VIII). So, too, in the war with Abhinandan of Balkh-Bukhārā (Canto IX), we find his general, Chaunṟā, leading troops in alliance with the Banāphars. The fighting on the occasion of the marriage of Brahmā with his daughter Bēlā (Canto VI) was only an episode of normal occurrence, and, as in other cases, resulted in no permanent ill will.

On the other hand, there were the jealousy and continual acts of hostility between Prithīrāj of Delhi and Jaychand of Kanauj. Jaychand claimed and exercised suzerainty over a large part of India. In Canto XII we have seen a tradition that it extended even over Bihār, Assam, and Bengal. The poem expressly says that he exercised it over Parmāl of Mahōbā, and the reason for his hesitation in giving refuge to Ālhā and Ūdan was the fact that they had been banished by his vassal. So also we find Jambay, King of Māṛō (Canto II), forbidding his son Karinghā to go to Jājmaū, because he (Jambay) had for some years been refusing to pay tribute to Jaychand. But Prithīrāj was aiming himself at a rival suzerainty. When Jaychand called his vassal kings to attend Sanjōgin's choice of a suitor (Canto I) he summoned Prithīrāj amongst their number. Prithīrāj was deeply insulted at this summons. He refused to attend the assemblage, and asserted his independence by carrying off Sanjōgin by force of arms. He remained continually on the watch to extend his suzerainty at Jaychand's expense, and Parmāl, though on friendly terms, never felt safe against invasion from Delhi.

A strategical point, where a number of roads met, between Delhi and Mahōbā was the town of Sirsā.[1] Parmāl gave this to Malkhān as his fief. Malkhān with his brother, Sulkhān, and his mother, Birmhā (or Brahmā), moved there and built a strong fort. It will be remembered that when Ūdan was charged with murdering Indal (Canto IX) he came to Sirsā for refuge, but that Malkhān shut the gates against him. When Ālhā and Ūdan were banished by Parmāl

[1] It is now a village about two miles south-east of Dabōh in the Lahār Pargana of the State of Gwālior. Legends of the battle still exist in the locality.

(Canto X), Malkhān refused to accompany them, but remained, as his duty called, on guard at Sirsā. It was from Sirsā that he issued forth to help Ālhā and Lākhan in the war with Būndī (Canto XI), picking up Brahmā at Mahōbā on his way thither.

After Ālhā's banishment Mahōbā itself was left without defenders. Ḍhēwā and Mīrā Tālhan followed Ālhā and Ūdān into exile at Kanauj, and, excepting Parmāl's son Brahmā, the only competent general left to protect the kingdom was Malkhān at Sirsā. So long as that fortress could be held Mahōbā was safe from Delhi.

In this state of affairs history tells us[1] how Parmāl was guilty of an incredible piece of folly over which our bards are discreetly silent. In one of his raids Prithīrāj abducted the daughter of the prince of Samētā. Some of the wounded who had covered his retreat were assailed and put to death by Parmāl. Burning to avenge this insult, Prithīrāj declared war on Mahōbā, and just at this point, as the present canto tells us, Māhil, the traitor, came to him and told him how, owing to Ālhā's banishment, Mahōbā was denuded of its defenders, and all that was necessary to accomplish Prithīrāj's object was to capture Sirsā, where Malkhān was now alone and could hope for no support from the other Banāphars. The canto describes how Prithīrāj attacks Sirsā, and how, at first, it is brilliantly and successfully defended by Malkhān. There is some mystery about Malkhān's invulnerability and Māhil determines to solve it. We have seen that Malhnā, Parmāl's Queen, was his sister, and how she was on most affectionate terms with Birmhā, Malkhān's mother, whom she called her sister. Māhil therefore claims Birmhā as his sister and visits her, during the siege, at Sirsā. He questions her, and she lets out the secret that Malkhān, like Achilles, could not be killed till the lotus-mark on his foot was pierced. Māhil hastens with this information to Prithīrāj, measures are taken by the two conspirators, and Malkhān falls a victim to his mother's trust in Māhil and to Māhil's treachery. His body is recovered and Gajmōtin his wife, in spite of remonstrances, becomes *satī* with him on the funeral pyre. The site of the cremation was a place known as the 'Pachpērā' or the 'Five Trees', and we shall visit it subsequently, in Canto XIV.

WHO seeks for pearls on the woodland spray,
  Or the lotus on hill-top high?
Can youth be recalled that has passed away?
  Or loveliness fated to die?

Alas for the promise early fled,
  For the sun gone down ere night;
With Bachrāj' death is honour dead,
  With Malkhān truth took flight.

[1] Tod's 'Rājasthān' (ed. Crooke, vol. ii, p. 715).

When Prithī marched from Dihlī
  And down by Sirsā sat,
The streams ran stained, as saffron flows
  From out the dyer's vat.

The Queen of Malkhān saw her lord,
  When from the field he came,
Rejoicing in his garments dyed,
  As in the springtide[1] game.

Before the valiant hero's sword
  What countless foes did fly!
And, as his spirit fled, he still
  Upraised his battle-cry. 5

FYTTE I

Māhil has ridden by thorp and town
  Till he came to Dihlī's gate;
Before the court he lighted down
  Where Prithī sat in state.

'Now welcome, welcome, Rājā,
  What news from proud Urai?
How fares it with Mahōbā town?
  How fares the brave Malkhay?'

'Unguarded lies Mahōbā town:
  Banished is Ālhā brave:
If Sirsā fort be beaten down,
  Mahōbā naught can save.'

'Now beat on the drum, let my warriors come,
  Each brave Chauhān of the clan!'
At the first drum-beat they sprang to their feet
  And saddled his steed each man:

At the second drum-beat his armour bright
  Each took and his doughty sword:
At the third drum-beat each valiant knight
  Rode forth with Dihlī's lord. 10

Tāhar and Chandan, Prithī's sons,
  Pranced at their father's side;
And on the great one-tusker
  Did the Nāgar Chauṉrā ride.

[1] The Hōlī, which much resembles the carnival. A red powder is scattered or squirted on the dresses of passers-by.

They had not ridden in Sirsā land
  A mile but barely ten,
When Prithīrāj to Chauṇṛā spake,
  As he halted the Chauhān men.

'March forward, Chauṇṛā Brāhman,
  This honour thine shall be:
Smite down the walls of Sirsā fort
  Before thou return to me.'

To brave Malkhān a warder ran,
  'Take sword and spear in hand!
Prithī with all the Chauhān clan
  Comes riding through thy land.'

He called his warriors good at need:
  I wis he stood not still:
As he raised his foot to mount his steed
  He heard an omen[1] ill.

'Stand back, my son!' Queen Birmhā cried,
  'Tempt not the fight to-day.'
'Without doth Prithī vaunting ride
  And how can I delay?

'Thy blessing given, O mother sweet,
  Were an omen of greater worth.'
He stooped and touched his mother's feet:
  So rode brave Malkhān forth.

When Chauṇṛā saw brave Malkhān ride,
  With smiling face he spake,
'Cast down thy wall, 'tis Prithī bids,
  And peace and friendship make.'

'The walls I built shall I destroy!
  Let Prithī cast them down:
But walls may crack and gates burn black,
  Ere then, in Dihlī town.'

'Seize Malkhān, seize, my merry men all,
  And ours is Sirsā's spoil.'
Then matches did light and swords flashed bright,
  As they rushed to the soldier's toil.

[1] Sneezing is one of the most unpropitious omens.

There was right good play of swords that day,
  And many a wight did fall,
And shield on shield rang over the field
  That was ploughed by the iron ball.

At Malkhān's attack the Chauhāns gave back;
  Then the great one-tusker came:
Quoth Chauṉṛā, 'Why should our clansmen die,
  When we should play the game?

'Strike turn by turn, brave Malkhān,
  As the girls draw from the well!'
'Strike first then, lord of Baksar,
  Whose prowess all men tell.'

He poised his spear full craftily:
  He watched him off his guard;
But the mare Kabutrī sprang aside,
  And Chauṉṛā's blow was marred.

Then Malkhān leaped and the howda struck,
  That the canopy fell to the ground;
He dragged down Chauṉṛā from his seat,
  And fast his arms he bound.

Then straight to his tent with his prize he went,
  And decked him in woman's array;
With robe and shawl and jewels withal,
  Was never a bride so gay.

A letter he sent to Prithī's tent,
  'Chauṉṛā greets Prithī well;
I have done thy behest, and my sword found no rest
  Till the gates of Sirsā fell.

'When Malkhān fled, my course I sped
  Till I stormed Mahōbā's tower;
And thence king Parmāl's child I led,
  That sweet and lovely flower.

In a litter I send the prize I won,
  Of Chandēl land the pride;
From Sindh to Sāgar may seek thy son,
  Ere he gain a fairer bride.'

The litter-curtains king Prithī raised,
  Where Chauṇṛā chafed in bands;
And the Rājā gazed as a man amazed,
  While he loosed his champion's hands.

Then drums were beaten and tents were struck,
  And the red flags marched before;
And the bards made glad the warriors' hearts
  With songs of the fights of yore.

But, when they came to the four cross-roads,
  The king cried loud and free,
'What Kshatrī[1] bold hath built this hold
  And ta'en no leave of me?'

Out and spake Queen Birmhā's son,
  And louted down full low,
'A vassal I to the Chandēl Rāi[2]
  And to Dihlī's lord also.

'These walls I piled in a forest wild,
  And who shall give me blame?'
'Then cast them down or I burn thy town,
  And leave nor stone nor name.'

'O speak not thus, thou brave Chauhān,
  Hast thou forgot,' he cried,
'From magic spell and swords as well
  I bore away my bride?

'I dashed an elephant to the ground
  At Brahmā's[3] marriage gay:
Great Prithī's seven sons I bound,
  And where was the king that day?

'While yet a youth, I kept my truth
  And avenged my murdered sire:
Who razeth Sirsā's walls, good sooth,
  His lands shall pay with fire.'

When Prithī heard, he gave the word
  With anger rising high;
Then guns were fired and spears were stirred,
  And thick smoke filled the sky.

[1] The warrior caste. A title claimed by all Rājpūts. [2] Prince.

[3] The son of Parmāl, who married Prithī's daughter much against the wish of her family (Canto VI).

The bullets whistled, the arrows flew,
  The cannon-shot ploughed the ground;
And tusk with tusk and trunk with trunk
  The elephants fought around.

Full many a knight in valiant fight
  Has lost that day his life,
And the wounded did moan with bitter groan
  For mother or child or wife.

And the vulture from far knew the scent of war,
  And swooped to the dead man's side,
But his spirit above in joy and love
  Soared away with his fairy bride.

And the boundary flood ran red with blood,
  So deep were its waters dyed;
And Malkhān the brave with his upraised glaive
  Cheered the hearts of his men and cried—

'The Sāwan[1] month must soon be past,
  And the forest flower must fall:
The mother's travail must come at last,
  And death is due by all.

'Who dies at home, in the time to come
  His name is spoken never;
Who dies in the fight—with bard and knight—
  His fame shall live for ever!

'This day renown and warrior's crown
  Each Rājpūt's sword may gain!'
He leapt the entrenchment of Prithī's camp,
  And his merry men followed amain.

As the wolf the sheep, as the lion the kine,
  As the schoolboy drives the ball,
So Malkhān broke the Chauhān line
  With his Rājpūts following all.

As the blossoming mango tree is hewn,
  As the reapers the barley reap,
So goodly men in their path were strewn,
  And, ah! their wives may weep.

[1] July, the month of rain. I believe the meaning is the time of holiday from labour and journeying.

Sūrat the Hārā, Sūraj of Bānda,
  Angad of Gwāliàr,
Three kings that day did Malkhān slay,
  And terror he spread afar.

Comes Tāhar riding swiftly,
  And thus to Malkhān saith,
'Now guard thyself, brave Malkhān,
  For near at hand is death.'

But Malkhān charged like a lion wood,[1]
  And Tāhar turned and fled.
'This Malkhān is a swordsmith good,
  God wot!' King Prithī said.

'The Sirsā men no valour lack,
  And well their blades can ply.'
So Prithī rode to Dihlī back,
  And to Sirsā brave Malkhay.

FYTTE II

A slave on a day to Birmhā told—
  'O Mother, Māhil stands there!'
She took in her hands a censer[2] of gold
  And she stepped adown the stair.

The incense she shed round Māhil's head,
  And she greeted him fairly and well,
'Now welcome, brother, from proud Urai!
  Thy news to thy sister tell.'

'Sure, sister, thy son is a valiant one,
  That he turned the Chauhāns to flight!'
'Yes, he bears the sign of the grace divine,
  Which brings him safe from fight.

'If the lotus-mark on his sole be torn,
  That day my son must die;
But surely the Rājpūt is not born
  Who shall kill the brave Malkhay.'

[1] Mad.
[2] The usual ceremony described when a lady receives an honoured guest.

Right merry of heart was the false Māhìl,
'Now his life is in Prithī's hand.'
And little of rest he took until
He at Dihlī gate did stand.

'Now welcome, Rājā, seat thee nigh!'
Then stepped he lightly down;
'What news dost bring from proud Urai?
What from Mahōbā town?'

'The news I bring to Dihlī's king
Is the grant of our hearts' desire;
Mahōbā's spoil shall be ours anon,
And its houses burnt with fire.

'Queen Birmhā has told me all the charm
That guarded brave Malkhay:
If the mark on his foot should come to harm,
Then Sirsā's lord must die.

'Then listen my rede, and, King, take heed!
Before a blow thou strike,
Let pits and trenches be dug with speed,
Thickset with lance and spike.

'So hap what hap, 'tis a dainty trap
To set for Sirsā's knight;
And our luck shall be hard if he scape unscarred,
When next you meet in fight.'

His counsel he heard and spake the word;
So the army marched straightway:
At trench and drain they wrought amain
Through thrice a night and day.

A hundred pits stood open to view;
A hundred were roofed with grass;
With lance and javelin sharpened new,
That none betwixt might pass.

'Hear Prithī's word, Banāphar lord,'
He wrote to Malkhān brave,
'Thy walls down break and counsel take,
Or nought thy life can save.'

The herald is gone to Sirsā gate,
  Placed the scroll in the warder's hand,
'Go tell thy lord brave Malkhān,
  King Prithī has seized his land.'

The first word brave Malkhān heard,
  He laughed with angry glee;
The second word brave Malkhān heard,
  His sword and shield grasped he.

And he to the highest turret then
  His hasty way has ta'en;
And there he saw king Prithī's men
  Come marching o'er the plain.

To the gate he down did come and they beat on the great drum,
  And the Kshatrīs gathered around;
All the tribes of ancient race, from the sun and moon who trace,[1]
  Seized their arms at the warlike sound.

All the troops of Rajasthān, every famous warrior clan,
  All the sons of the kings of old,
Came the pure Sisōdhiyā blood, came the Būndī spearmen good,
  Came the Thākurs from the Tūmar hold.

Came the Rāthōrs in a crowd, came Baiswārā's chieftains proud,
  And the knights of Raghu's[2] princely line;
Warriors brave from Chandēl land, swordsmen stout from Baghēlkhand,
  Not a man but made him ready at the sign.

Brave Malkhān into the palace went
  And in Ganges water bathed;
For sandal paste for his forehead he sent,
  And in linen white was swathed.

[1] Every Rājpūt clan claims descent from one or the other.

[2] The ancestor of Rāma, who was the most renowned hero of the Solar line.

As a Rājpūt wont, in his broad waistband
  He pistol and sword did place;
And he fixed his dagger ready to hand,
  'Twas carved with a lion's face.

With a purple turban his head he wound,
  And his crown like the moonbeams shone;
Not Indra's[1] self o'er the sky encrowned
  With more glory is clothed upon.

The grains of rice has Queen Birmhā ta'en,
  As the mother of warriors will;
As on Malkhān's forehead[2] she fixed the grain,
  She heard an omen ill.

'Stand back, my son,' Queen Birmhā cried,
  'Tempt not the fight to-day!'
'O Mother, the foe without doth ride,
  And thou such words canst say!

'There are homes in heaven stand ready for all,
  To-morrow if not to-day;
And who for his country in fight shall fall,
  His name shall live for aye.' 25

All this the fair Gajmōtin heard,
  As she stood at the lattice grate;
'O husband, hear thy mother's word,
  Nor tempt to-day thy fate.'

'Now, cease thy prating, dame,' he cried,
  'Should she fear freits at all,
Who knows herself a warrior's bride,
  And a good steed in the stall?

'What thinks she of her bracelets,[3]
  Who dwells midst daily fights?
Sit thou at home in thy painted dome,
  Whilst I ride with my knights.

[1] The Hindu Jupiter.
[2] The sectarian mark impressed on the forehead by a parent or superior on all occasions of ceremony.
[3] A widow is not allowed to wear them.

'Should I sit still in Sirsā,
And Pithaurā at the door,
It were a shame to my father's name
Seven ages back and more.'

The brave Malkhay has ridden forth,
His warriors at his side;
Their hearts he stirred with a rousing word,
As through the gate he hied.

'Let him who loves his life to save
Cast sword and shield away;
But whoso loves the Rājpūt glaive,
Let him wear two to-day.

'Your bones are mingled with Chandēl salt,
That with Chandēl bread you eat;
But, if ye fall for the Chandēl land,
Ye well have paid your debt.'

But, when he reached the bounds, quoth he,
'Now greeting, Kshatrīs all;
What braves be ye that march so free
Beneath my Sirsā wall?'

Then forth the fiery Tāhar spurred
Three lengths before them all;
'Now hearken, Malkhān, to my word,
Cast down thy Sirsā wall!'

'The walls I built with mickle care
In dust I will not lay;
If Prithī bids me mar my work,
Tell Prithī, I say nay!'

'Now fire your guns at the lowbred hound,'
The hotspur Tāhar cried;
Then rose of cannon the warlike sound,
And swords were deftly plied.

Small hope had Malkhān his life to save,
But his blade he stoutly drew;
'Stand by me, friends, 'gainst the Chauhān brave,
And keep your honour true!'

As the lion the kine, as the wolf the sheep,
  As the schoolboy drives the ball,
So trench by trench did Malkhān leap
  With his Rājpūts following all.

'If I gave thee barley in winter,
  And oil in time of rain,
If Parmāl stinted thee not of milk
  In thy foalhood lightsome and vain,

'Kabutrī, my mare, my pigeon,[1]
  Mine honour save this day,
And let not thy foot take a backward step
  Whilst foes uphold the fray!'

Kabutrī arched her brown neck free,
  And they rushed on the Chauhān men;
But, where her master dealt with three,
  The mare she smote down ten.

For with teeth she tore and her heels she flang
  That she made a passage wide,
And, each howda she passed, in air she sprang,
  That her lord might reach the side.

Then those who felt a womanish fear
  Cast down both sword and shield,
And those who held their wives too dear
  Fled scattering from the field.

There were heroes found unhurt on the ground
  Beneath a heap of slain;
There were braves who stood, smeared with ashes[2] of wood,
  All naked over the plain.

'O bring not shame on the Rājpūt name
  By smiting a harmless band!
Pilgrims we are to holy Hardwār,[3]
  And as beggars we roam the land.'

'Malkhān,' king Prithī cried, 'well done!
  Well hast thou proved thy race!
Now try thy force against my son,
  And leave this meaner chase.'

[1] Kabutrī means a pigeon. [2] The guise of Jōgīs or Hindū devotees.
[3] The famous place of pilgrimage, where the Ganges leaves the Siwalik hills for the plain country.

O'er every trench did Kabutrī pass,
Nor lance nor pike did fear,
But she marked not the treacherous roof of grass,
And she fell on a hidden spear.

The lotus print that his foot did dint,
The cruel blade pierced through;
And, 'This is death,' brave Malkhān saith,
As he faint and fainter grew.

The mare made yet an effort stout,
Though she lay in evil stead;
She leaped with Malkhān bravely out
Before she fell down dead.

Now word is come to Sirsā straight
Of valiant Malkhān's wound;
Birmhā ran weeping to the gate,
And fell in deadly swound.

And word is come to Gajmōtin fair
How her noble husband fell;
Then she stepped down from the topmost stair
To hear the messenger tell.

'O, a pit was dug by craft, I trow,
The brave Malkhay to slay;
King Prithī has ploughed with an iron plough,
And the body is bearing away.'

O, she has arrayed her daintily
As a lady of high degree,
And has gone with Birmhā to Prithī's camp
Her husband's corpse to see.

'Think not, thou brave Chauhān,' she cried,
'The spirit of Malkhān fled!
There shall yet be fighting on Bētwā's[1] side,
And the fields with blood be red.

'And if upon Sirsā land thou ride
Till a hundred days shall fall,
A widow I'll make of every bride
Till one come to Dihlī wall.

[1] The great river of Bundēlkhaṇḍ. The battle prophesied did actually occur (Canto XVI).

'I am holy now with a Satī's[1] vow,
  And my curse like fire shall burn!'
Abashed was the king at her words I trow,
  And back to his land did turn.

Now the Rānī[2] has sent for sandal sweet
  To build the funeral pile;
It was raised, as fitting, where four roads meet,
  And drums were beaten the while.

And incense was swung and prayers were sung,
  And tales of the bards were told;
And she made her shrift with a golden gift
  And kine with their horns all gold.

She wound with pearls her jetty curls,
  And a priceless pearl[3] was she;
And she decked with care that beauty rare
  That was so bright of blee.

She placed a cocoa-nut in her hand,
  And betel upon her tongue,
And by the pile she took her stand,
  While still the prayers were sung.

Answered Ahmad, the Fakīr old,
  'Why lay thy sweet life down?
With those shouldst thou dwell that love thee well,
  And reign o'er Sirsā town.'

'Awake my husband, awake,' she said,
  'Or wait till thy love shall come!'
And still to every god they prayed,
  And still they beat the drum.

'O Satī,[4] listen an old man's rede,
  And pause in time,' quoth he;
'Why burn the living with the dead,
  Whom thou no more shalt see?'

[1] Literally a chaste woman, but well known, under the spelling 'suttee', to mean a wife who devotes herself to burn with her husband's body.

[2] Queen.

[3] Gajmōtin means a large pearl.

[4] Of course the Muhammadan Fakīr would see no merit in her self-sacrifice.

'Her husband's heart is the dearest part,
  O father, to wedded wife;
My husband is passed to another world,
  And how can I keep my life?

'If I die with the dead, my renown shall spread
  Among wives from day to day;
And my husband's name and my mother's fame
  Shall be sung by the bards for aye.

'Let the drums be beat and the incense sweet
  And the odours poured of price,
For my lord and I ere long shall meet
  In the bowers of paradise.'

Her parents' love she left that tide,
  And chose the funeral pile;
So, calling on Ālhā and Ūdan,[1] she died,
  And on her lips a smile.

All silent now lies Sirsā's wall,
  Not a mouse is heard to cry;
And crows build nests in the painted hall
  Since Prithī went wasting by.

But the Five Trees wave o'er a lonely grave
  That is held in honour there;
For beneath lie the ashes of Malkhān brave
  And of Gajmōtin fair.

[1] Her husband's kinsmen, to avenge him.

Canto XIV

THE BATTLE OF KĪRATSĀGAR

After the death of Malkhān and the sack of Sirsā, the way to Mahōbā now lay open to Prithīrāj.

Mahōbā is adorned by two fine lakes, the Kīratsāgar and the Madansāgar. The former is named after Kīrtivarmā, one of Parmāl's most famous ancestors. We have seen in Canto VIII how the latter half of the month of Sāwan (July–August) is, in Mahōbā, a festive period. It culminates on the last day of the month—the day of the full moon—on which is held the festival of the Sanīnō or of the 'Bhujariās'. A *bhujariā* is a small leaf basket in which are sown wheat, barley, &c. The grain springs up and in about ten days forms a little garden (like the 'Gardens of Adonis' of the West). On the full moon of Sāwan, the women of Mahōbā carry these *bhujariās* in procession to the Kīratsāgar, into which they throw them. The present Canto tells how this festival came on while Prithīrāj was investing Mahōbā, and what happened thereat.

ABSTRACT

The opening invocation is in praise of the holy places round Nīmsar-Misrik in Oudh, mentioned in the introductory verses to Canto V. It is stated that the River Gumtī was brought thither by the mythic saint Śaunaka.

In the month of Sāwan Prithīrāj attacks and surrounds Mahōbā, with an army of 700,000 men with contingents from Khurāsān and Gujarāt. His camps are pitched in the village of Kanmākhērā, at Madan Tāl, and the Bairāgī's Tāl, and his headquarters are at Chandan-bagiā (the Sandal Grove). The gates of Mahōbā are closed. No one can go out or come in, or, consequently, carry the *bhujariās* to the lake at the full moon of Sāwan. Malhnā prays to the goddess Dēvī to call Ūdan to her help, and Dēvī hastens to Rijigiri, informs Ūdan in his sleep of the state of affairs, and directs him to go to the help of Mahōbā. When he wakes, he tells this to Ḍhēwā and Lākhan,[1] and they get leave from Jaychand on the pretence of going hunting in the Gānjar. Alhā, hearing of the expedition, enjoins Ūdan on no account to go to Mahōbā. Ūdan promises accordingly, but has no intention of keeping his promise, and when he confides the secret to Sunwā she commends the plan.

[1] It will be remembered (Canto XII) that Lākhan had sworn to accompany Ūdan if ever he should return to Mahōbā.

Accompanied by Mīrā Tālhan they cross the Jumna and the Bētwā, and camping in the forest beyond, disguise themselves and their army as Jōgīs. First they go to Sirsā to inquire about Malkhān. They find the town in ruins, and a bird-catcher whom they meet tells them how Prithīrāj had had a pit dug, with spears fixed at the bottom, into which Malkhān fell, and died of a wound in his foot. He takes them to the place where Gajmōtin had become Satī, and there the ghost of Malkhān speaks to them, and tells them how Māhil had planned the contrivance of the pit, having learnt from Birmhā, his mother, that he was vulnerable only in the foot. Ūdan in wrath cries, 'To Mahōbā will I not go. It is but a short way off, yet Parmāl came not to your help. Let Prithī plunder it, not one step will I move.' The ghost of Gajmōtin then enjoins him to forget private feeling and to go and help Parmāl. To this he at length agrees.

They enter Mahōbā in the disguise of Jōgīs and (as in previous cases) get speech with Malhnā. She, not recognizing them, tells them of the trouble in which the city lies, and implores them, if they go to Kanauj, to carry the tidings to Ūdan, on whom she calls so pathetically that Lākhan whispers to Ūdan to disclose himself. He refuses, but promises to help Malhnā to prepare her festival, and to be a brother to Chandrābal. Māhil comes in as he is swearing to do this, and hastens off to tell Prithīrāj. Prithīrāj calls for Chauṇrā and Dhāndhū and orders them to hasten to the forest, where are still the headquarters of Ūdan's troops, all disguised as Jōgīs, and to tell them to move off at once. They refuse to march till fifteen days are over, and the full moon is past.

Māhil meanwhile conveys Prithīrāj's terms to Malhnā. He offers to march off if they give up the forts of Khajuhāgaṛh [1] and Gwālior, the five flying horses, the nine-lakh necklace, and Chandrābal [2] as the bride of his son Tāhar. Malhnā refuses this, and she and Chandrābal go to Brahmā, the son of Parmāl and Malhnā, who is married to Prithīrāj's daughter Bēlā, but he refuses to stir, telling them to look to the Jōgīs for help. On this Abhai,[3] Māhil's son, against his father's wishes, promises to protect her and to get the *bhujariā* rites performed. The troops are got ready, and Malhnā collects all the women of Mahōbā, dressed all in green and sitting in green litters. She gives each a powder of poison and a knife dipped in poison, and they all swear not to allow themselves to fall alive into the enemies' hands or to be carried off to Delhi. She herself takes with her gunpowder and flint and steel. They all set off in procession, fourteen hundred in number, each woman carrying her *bhujariā* in her litter, Chandrābal in the middle and Malhnā leading. Ranjit (Brahmā's younger brother) and Abhai accompany them on horse-

[1] Or Khajurāhō, the ancient seat of the Chandēls, who moved thence to Mahōbā about the year A. D. 900.

[2] This contradicts Canto VIII, where Chandrābal has long been married to Indrasēn, son of the Rājā of Baurīgaṛh.

[3] He is as loyal as his father was traitorous.

back. As they start some one sneezes and Ranjit's sword falls out of its scabbard, but he refuses to be daunted by the bad omen. 'Such are for shopkeepers, or for Brāhmaṇs or writers arranging a wedding, but not for knights.'

Prithīrāj sends Chaunṛā with orders to intercept the procession. He meets Abhai at the Gangā lake by whom he and his troops are routed. Then Prithī sends out his son Sūraj with Rājā Ṭankbai and four lākhs of men. Both Sūraj and Ṭankbai are killed by Abhai and Ranjit, and their forces are dispersed. Then Prithī sends his son Tāhar, with Sardan and Mardan, and three lakhs of men, and Tāhar kills Abhai and Ranjit in single combat. Brahmā hears of this, and, equipping his troops, comes to join in the battle, which the headless bodies of Abhai and Ranjit have kept going on till then, when Bhūrā Mughul waves a blue flag[1] over them and they fall down dead.

Brahmā kills Sardan and Mardan. When Prithī hears this, at Māhil's instigation, he enters the fight himself. Mahōbā is worsted, Brahmā is surrounded, and the litters are on the point of being captured, when Ūdan, Ḍhēwā, and Lākhan come into the field. Chaunṛā has reached Malhnā's litter, and demands from her the nine-lākh necklace. She refuses, saying that it is a disgrace to Prithī to make war on women. First, because he was Rājā of Delhi; second, because he was a Chauhān, and should remember Ūdan's gallantry at the marriage of Bēlā. She ends by crying aloud to Ūdan, if he is anywhere on earth or in heaven, to come to her aid. Just then Ūdan, having captured Dhāndhū, comes up, and Chaunṛā takes to flight. Meanwhile Tāhar has cut off Chandrābal's litter and carried it away to Pachpēṛā, where four roads join. Lākhan vanquishes Tāhar in single combat and they bring back the litter. Then they attack Prithī's headquarters in force, aided by the four rājās of Gānjar and the twelve princes of Banaudhā; together with Hir Singh and Bir Singh of Biriā, Murlī and Manōhar of Kalpī, Sātan of Paṭṭī, Gurūkhā of Bengal, Chintā Ṭhākur of Rusnī, Jagman of Jinsī, Mōhan of Hardīgaṛh, Rūpan of Siraunj, Madan Gōpāl of Pataunj, Chandan of Datiā, Pūran of Pūrā, Chintāman of Gōrakhpur, and Madhukar of Chitaur.[2] By them Prithī is driven from his entrenchments and retreats to the south bank of the Kīratsāgar, while the litters and the women, with Ūdan, come to the same lake on the north.

Chandrābal throws the leaf-basket of her *bhujariā* into the water. It floats to the other side, and Prithī at Māhil's suggestion sends Chaunṛā to take it up. On this she cries that if the enemy gets it, for her the festival will be ruined. Ūdan rescues it, and she goes up to him to fasten the plants in his turban, but he tells her that it is Lākhan who is the senior Jōgī and whom she ought to thank most. She gives Lākhan a plant, and he gives her in return a present of twenty-one elephants. Then she returns and gives a plant to Ūdan,

[1] Compare verse 29 of Fytte ii of Canto I.

[2] Most of these people are also mentioned in Canto XII, but there Murlī and Manōhar are located in Cuttack, and Pūran in Paṭnā.

who gives her in return the bracelet off his wrist. Then Malhnā and she recognize him by the bracelet, and Prithīrāj, hopeless of success until Ūdan returns to Kanauj, goes back to Delhi.

Hearing of Ūdan's arrival, Parmāl[1] comes out of Mahōbā to meet him. He embraces him and weeps over him, and offers to give him the philosopher's stone, and as guardian of Brahmā, the realm of Mahōbā, if he will return and live there, instead of going back to Kanauj. But Ūdan reminds him of his curses, and tells him that he can never come back to live there; though, for the sake of the salt he had eaten in Mahōbā, he has this time come to help. In reply to Malhnā's entreaties, he promises to come again and help them if needed. Then they thank Lākhan for his succour, and he and Ūdan, without entering Mahōbā, march back to Kanauj, and reach it in eight days.

[1] Parmāl now for the first time appears on the scene. He is throughout a contemptible coward. It is Malhnā, the Queen, who organizes the defence.

Canto XV

THE RETURN OF ĀLHĀ

As in the case of the Return of Chandra bel (Canto VIII), this canto was only partly translated by Mr. Waterfield, and I have added an abstract of the rest. After Ūdan's return from the Battle of Kīratsāgar, Mahōbā was again left defenceless, and Prithīrāj again attacked it. A truce was demanded by Parmāl, on the plea of the absence of Alhā and Ūdan. The present canto tells how a message was sent to Ālhā imploring his return, and how, after much hesitation, he consented. Another version of this episode is eloquently given by Tod in his Rājasthān.[1]

WHEN Rām was sent to banishment,
  King Dasrath pined and died;
How great the toil Rām underwent
  To seek his ravished bride!

The mighty bears, the monkeys great,
  To Sītā's aid they hied;
King Parmāl's state was ruined straight
  When Ālhā left his side.

FYTTE I

Māhil has ridden on Lillī his mare,
  At Dihlī he lighted down,
'Now welcome, Rājā, how dost fare?
  And how Mahōbā town?'

'Ālhā and Ūdan dwell in Kanauj,
  Alone doth the Chandēl bide;
Mahōbā's spoil with little toil,
  King Prithī, shall we divide.'

'Now beat on the drum, let my warriors come,
  All the braves of my Dihlī wide;
And Chandan, Gōpī, and Tāhar,
  My three sons, with me ride.'

[1] Vol. ii, p. 715 (ed. Crooke).

O, they rode on and onward yet,
  Till he pitched at the Kīrat pond;
And they girt Mahōbā at dead of night,
  That none might pass beyond.

'Ride forth, Māhìl, to Mahōbā Gate,
  And let these sleepers know,
King Prithī must have his ransome straight,
  If he in peace shall go.'

Queen Malhnā stood on the topmost tower,
  And looked out far and nigh;
And still the fires of Prithī's camp
  Made red the murky sky.

Queen Malhnā stood on the topmost tower,
  And looked o'er dale and down;
And there she saw her brother Māhìl
  Come riding to the town.

'What camp is this? why comes it here?
  Tell me, O brother,' she said;
'King Prithī is come for Mahōbā's spoil,
  So his ransome must straight be paid.

'Thou must Gwālior yield, both fort and field,
  And the strong Khajuhar hold,
And the touchstone which with its virtue rich
  Turns iron and steel to gold.

'Five colts of the wingèd breed as well,
  Which never did knight bestride;
And the litter of lovely Chandrā bel,
  Who shall be prince Tāhar's bride.'

'Go tell the King 'tis a valiant thing
  To war where he finds no men.
When Ūdan dwelt here why came he not
  To take our answer then?

'If the spoil of a woman in evil case
  Be worthy the Chauhān line,
Go bid him give me twelve days' grace,
  And then will I pay the fine.'

So Māhil went to Prithī's tent;
 'Thus doth Queen Malhnā say,
She asks but grace for twelve days' space
 And then the fine will pay.'

Now close beset was every yett,
 And none his food might cook;
Queen Malhnā called for her litter at night,
 And her way to Argal took.

She stood before prince Jagnaik's door
 Just at the break of day;
'Go tell King Parmāl's sister's son,
 Queen Malhnā comes this way.'

She halsed Jagnaik full tenderly,
 She told him all the state;
'King Prithī is come with a great menyie,[1]
 And is guarding every gate.

'He hath given us grace to the thirteenth day,
 And then will he spoil the town;
Call Ālhā and Ūdan back straightway,
 Or our honour is trampled down.'

'I cannot ride, I will not ride,
 I cannot bring Ālhā again;
When at your command from the Chandēl land
 They were driven in Bhādōn rain.

'Surely on me they would wreak that wrong,
 If they saw me at Rijgir there;
So put no trust in my aid, lady,
 For thy message I may not bear.'

Queen Malhnā wept. 'Mine honour is fled,'
 And her arms on high she threw;
'If Jagnaik would help me in this sore strait,
 Mine errand he would do.'

Jagnaik was moved at the Rānī's tears,
 And thus at length he cried,
'Let them saddle the horse Harnāgar,
 And I to Kanauj will ride.'

[1] Retinue.

When as they came to Mahōbā Gate,
  Māhil stood with Brahmā there.
'Now saddle the horse Harnāgar straight,
  Nor spurn thy mother's prayer.'

'What folly is this?' said the false Māhil,
  'That courser they demand,
For sake of whom the contest ill
  Made Ālhā flee the land.

'If him to Kanauj with Jagnaik thou send,
  The last of him thou hast seen.'
'O mother, my horse I cannot lend,'
  Quoth Brahmā to the Queen.

O, she hath taken a poisoned knife,
  And hath held it against her breast;
And hath vowed a vow to end her life,
  If he do not her behest.

He could not say his mother nay,
  He granted her every whit;
She called in that place for her Kālpī case,
  And thus with tears she writ.

'The Chauhān band ride over our land,
  Into every home they pierce;
And on Dēvī's hearth-stane have kine been slain,
  By Bhūrā the Mughul fierce.

'Ūdan's mango and Ālhā's fig
  King Prithī hath hewn them down;
And he will but stay till the thirteenth day
  Ere he sack Mahōbā town.

'If ye ride with speed when this letter ye read,
  Our honour may yet be our own;
If ye make delay, heap our ashes ye may,
  But the foe will have conquered and gone.'

Straight Māhil went to Prithī's tent,
  And he spake hasty words;
'The steed thou seekest with Jagnaik flees;
  So guard the forty fords.'

'Rise up, O Chauṉṛā Brāhman,
  Let not our booty flee;
Guard well with swords the forty fords,
  And bring Harnāgar to me.'

He mounted the great One-tusker,
  He guarded every ford;
And soon young Jagnaik he beheld
  Come riding over the sward.

'Now take thou heed, yield me thy steed,
  So safely onward fare.'
'Brother, my way lies to Kanauj,
  My steed I cannot spare.

'I have an errand to Ālhā,
  I must not now draw rein,
But I'll give to thee my horse so free,
  When I ride back again.'

Then Chauṉṛā took a good red bow,
  And placed an arrow nigh;
'Light down, light down, young Jagnaik,
  Before the arrow fly.'

Young Jagnaik spurred his good grey steed,
  He sprang in air full high,
He snatched the crown from Chauṉṛā's head,
  And laughing galloped by.

Abashed was Chauṉṛā, 'Leave the crown
  And ride in peace,' quoth he,
'If thou 'rt the Chandēl's sister's son,
  Thou art sister's son to me.'

'Mahōbā's spoil shall no man take,
  Whilst I can say them nay;
The crown I took goes to Ālhā now.'
  So Jagnaik rode away.

And aye he rode and aye he yode,
  Till he came to Kurhar town.
It was noonday height in the month of Jaith,
  And slowly he lighted down.

Harnāgar he tied close at his side
  Neath a shady banyan tree;
The saddle he spread to make a bed
  And he slept full wearily.

Now Gangā Pamār held court hard by,
  And the gardener came and spake,
'I chanced to see 'neath the banyan tree
  A horse of a noble make.

'Sure such a steed of a gallant breed
  Is not in the Thākur's stall;
In his servant's eyes so rare a prize
  To my lord must rightly fall.'

Then Gangā went and the steed unloosed
  While Jagnaik slept full sound;
And he vowed from a gun he would blow each one,
  Who told how the booty was found.

The day was running its downward course,
  Jagnaik woke troubled in mind;
'Sure Chauṉrā has followed and stolen my horse,
  But how the thief to find?'

He followed back his courser's track,
  Till he passed by Kurhar well;
The maidens came there for the well water,
  And thus he heard one tell.

'Sure never a horse was seen in the land,
  Such as Gangā stole to-day.'
'And where', he asked the damsel band,
  'Doth Gangā dwell, I pray?'

'On the roof of a palace are turrets of gold,
  And Gangā Pamār dwells there.'
So Jagnaik is gone to Gangā's court,
  And he greeted the Thākur fair.

'Now welcome, youth, thy race and name?
  What aid from me dost lack?'
'Jagnaik Chandēl, from Mahōbā I came;
  I ride to bring Ālhā back.

'My steed that is stolen to me restore.'
  'What folly is this to tell?
Sir boy,' said the chief, 'dost think 'tis a thief
  In Kurhar town doth dwell?

'Of any breed in my stalls that feed,
  Take thou for thy road the best.'
'The horse for my need is my own grey steed,
  What other will serve my quest?'

'If Harnāgar thou bring not back in sooth,
  In my breast my dagger I strike.'
The Rājā was wroth at the words of the youth,
  And he bade them bind Jagnaik.

At midnight Gangā's queen came down,
  And Jagnaik told her all;
'Prithī has marched from Dihlī town,
  And girt Mahōbā wall.

'A letter Malhnā wrote with tears,
  And me to Kanauj has sent;
If Ālhā or Ūdan this outrage hears,
  Shall Kurhar with fire be brent.'

'Now rest thee, prince, withouten doubt,'
  So answered him the Queen.
On the morrow she brought Harnāgar out,
  And glad was Jagnaik, I ween.

The whip that was priceless with gems and gold
  The Rājā gave not yet.
'Now farewell, Thākur, in tale well told
  Shall Kurhar pay this debt.'

And aye he yode and aye he rode,
  Till on the fifth fair day,
He saw the towers of proud Kanauj
  Rise on his evening way.

As he rode in by the bakers' stalls,
  He greeted them frank and free.
'Now tell me where doth Ālhā fare,
  Whom I ride so far to see.'

'There is Ālhā the oilman here,' one said,
'And Ālhā the city Kōtwāl,
But Ālhā the third, in Mahōbā bred,
Did fighting in Gānjar fall.

'Ālhā and Ūdan have both been slain,
And Indal is wounded sore.'
With a heavy heart he turned his rein
And slowly rode on once more.

The boys came trooping home from school.
'Now where is Ālhā's abode?'
'Ālhā he left the court but now
And home to Rijgir rode.'

Jagnaik turned to the baker's stall,
And his sugar pans made to fly;
Up and scattered the bakers all,
And in Jaychand's court 'gan cry.

'A lad is here from Mahōbā come,
And is spoiling our wares all round.'
'Now rise up quickly, Lākhan, my son,
And bring him before me bound.'

Then Lākhan for Bhūrī the elephant sent,
Whereon he would always ride,
And Mīrā the Saiyid with him went,
And sixty horse beside.

They met Jagnaik in a narrow track.
'Now turn thy horse, Sir youth.'
'He is fierce to bite and he will not back,
So thou must make way in sooth.'

Then Lākhan grasped his good red bow,
And an angry man was he;
'Now drag him down ere he leave the town,
And bring his horse to me.'

'What Kshatrī here did a lioness rear
That can take from me my steed?
Jagnaik am I of the Chandēl land,
And my horse of the Chandēl breed.'

Then Lākhan laid his red bow down,
  And gave him welcome free;
'If thou art the Chandēl's sister's son,
  Thou art sister's son to me.

'But, brother dear, let not Ālhā hear
  That Lākhan aimed shaft at thee;
If Ālhā know I had bent my bow,
  A deadly doom I dree.'

'Be sure my words shall breed no bate,
  But where doth Ālhā dwell?'
'Ālhā at Rijgir holds his state,
  And Uday Singh as well.'

A greeting fair young Jagnaik sent,
  And to Rijgir rode full fast;
To Jaychand's court prince Lākhan went,
  And has told him all that passed.

FYTTE II

'O Rājā, shall I bar the gate,
  Or shall I open wide?
Here on the horse Harnāgar
  Doth young prince Jagnaik ride.'

'O porter, such a tale to tell!
  Thy wits are gone astray;
In sweet Mahōbā Jagnaik may dwell,
  Why should he ride this way?

'But if Jagnaik without did wait,
  As little I think it be,
He'd have leapt his courser over the gate,
  Or ere he was stayed by thee.'

Then loud the porter 'gan to call,
  As to the gate he drew,
'Now leap thy courser over the wall,
  If Ālhā thou wouldst view.'

Jagnaik has spurred Harnāgar hard,
  And over the wall flew he;
He lighted in Indal's wrestling yard,
  Who halsed him tenderly.

'How fares it with Mahōbā town,
  And doth King Parmāl well?'
'First take me in place to Ālhā's face,
  Then hear the tale I tell.'

So far is Mr. Waterfield's translation. The rest of the story is as follows:—Jagnaik demands to be taken to Alhā and delivers to him Queen Malhnā's letter. Food is prepared for Jagnaik, who tells Ālhā, Ūdan, Ḍhēwā, Indal, Dēbī (Ālhā and Ūdan's mother), and Sunwā (Alhā's wife) the tale of the fate of Sirsā and of the deaths of Malkhān and Gajmōtin. They are all greatly distressed, but, while Ūdan is ready to start, Alhā refuses to go to help Mahōbā. 'Ne'er will I go alive to Mahōbā, though a crow may thither carry my bones when I am dead. Parmāl is a cowardly traitor, who stirred no hand to save Malkhān, although so near. Why should I succour him?' Dēbī bitterly reproaches Alhā for his ingratitude. She charges him with forgetting Malhnā's loving care for him, and wishes that he was a daughter and not a son, so that she could marry him away to whom she will.[1] Ūdan again entreats Ālhā to come with him to Mahōbā, and Alhā now excuses himself on the ground that Jaychand will not give him leave. At Ūdan's challenge he rides off to Kanauj and asks permission to go to save Mahōbā. Jaychand at first angrily refuses, and puts him in confinement. Alhā sends Rūpnā Bārī to tell Ūdan. Ūdan rises in wrath, but Dēbī pacifies him and advises him to take Jagnaik, and to approach Jaychand humbly. They do so, and he accuses Ālhā and Ūdan of having misappropriated the spoils of the expedition to Gānjar (Canto XII). This is indignantly denied. Ūdan says, 'On the contrary, you owe me for my horse Papīhā, which was wounded, and for Jōgā and Bhōgā, who were killed on that expedition. Give me in exchange for Papīhā your she-elephant Bhuruhī, and for Jōgā and Bhōgā give me Lākhan.' Jaychand then explains that he is only joking, and gives him carts loaded with treasure and his whole army, but he cannot give Lākhan without the permission of Rānī Tilkā, his mother. Tilkā refers him to Kusmā (Lākhan's wife) and Kusmā entreats Lākhan to stay, but he pleads his promise to accompany Ūdan, and he leaves her after a long and affecting parting scene, in which she urges him, on the way, to extinguish the

[1] Tod's account of Dēbī's reproaches, taken from the Prithīrāj Rāsau, is far more eloquent. In his version Dēbī is called Dewaldai:

'Would that the gods had made me barren,' said Dewaldai, 'that I had never borne sons who thus abandon the paths of the Rājpūt, and refuse to succour their prince in danger!' Her heart bursting with grief, and her eyes raised to heaven, she continued: 'Was it for this, O universal lord, thou mad'st me feel a mother's pangs for these destroyers of Banāphar's fame? Unworthy offspring! the heart of the true Rājpūt dances with joy at the mere name of strife—but ye, degenerate, cannot be the sons of Jasraj [i.e. Dasrāj]—some carl must have stolen to my embrace, and from such ye must be sprung.'

beacon on the top of the fortress of Parsū and Singhā of Parhul. It is visible from Kanauj, and is a perpetual challenge.

The army marches headed by Ālhā, Ūdan, Dēbī (here called Diwal Dē), and Lākhan, accompanied by four rājās of Gānjar, the twelve princes of Banaudhā, Dhanuā Tēlī, Lalā Tamōlī, and Mīrā (Tālhan) Saiyid of Benares. Tilkā solemnly entrusts her son Lākhan to the others, and they all swear that where merely the sweat of Lākhan will fall, there also will fall a stream of (enemies') blood. They arrive at Parhul, where Alhā, at the request of Lākhan, writes to the rājā (Singhā, who is brother of Parsū) asking him to put out the beacon on the top of his fortress. There is a fight, in which Singhā is taken prisoner, and Lākhan with an arrow shoots out the light of the beacon on the seventh story. They then march on, after adding Singhā's army to their troops.

They next come to Kuṛhar, where Gangā Pamār had stolen Jagnaik's horse, Harnāgar. Jagnaik reminds them that, though he had got back the horse, he had not got back the whip. Lākhan explains that Gangā is his mother's brother, and offers to write a letter asking for the whip. Gangā receives the letter and is enraged. He comes out on his she-elephant Shērsinghinī with 300,000 cavalry. There is a battle in which they are defeated, and Alhā in single combat takes Gangā prisoner. When the news reaches Kuṛhar, Baunā comes out and delivers up the whip. Gangā is then released, and joins the army.

They advance, and after crossing the Jumna, Lākhan sacks Kālpī bazaar. Ūdan is angry at this, as the city belongs to him, and Lākhan explains that this was a reprisal for the attack on Kuṛhar, which belonged to his (Lākhan's) uncle. They nearly come to blows, but Ḍhēwā pacifies Ūdan, and the army marches on till it halts by the river Bētwā. From here Jagnaik is sent on to give Malhnā the news. At Mahōbā Naibā the maidservant tells Malhnā and Chandrābal of his arrival. Just then Māhil turns up. Jagnaik, in order to mislead him, tells Malhnā that Ūdan refuses to come. Naturally, there is consternation and Māhil advises yielding to Prithīrāj's terms, which are here repeated. One of these was that the Philosopher's Stone was to be given up. Jagnaik points out a closet in which he says the Philosopher's Stone is kept, and tells Māhil to go in and fetch it. Māhil goes in, and Jagnaik locks him in there and gives to Malhnā Ūdan's letter in which all the true facts are recorded. Malhnā embraces Jagnaik, and shows the letter to Parmāl, who is much encouraged, while Jagnaik returns to the Bētwā.

There are songs of rejoicing among the women folk, and Māhil, grasping the situation, persuades his sister Malhnā to release him from the closet. 'I must go to Ālhā and warn him, lest some traitor persuade Ūdan to return to Kanauj. If he does so and if Prithīrāj sack Mahōbā, I swear on my son's head that I will sack Delhi in revenge.' As soon as he is released he goes straight off to Prithīrāj and warns him that Alhā is on the Bētwā. Prithīrāj at once dispatches Chaunṛā to stop all the forty-two crossing places and sixteen minor fords on that river.

Canto XVI

THE BATTLE OF THE BĒTWĀ

In the preceding canto we have learnt how Alhā's army has arrived at the River Bētwā, and how Prithīrāj's general, Chauṇṛā, has blocked the forty-two crossings and sixteen minor fords across that river. In the present canto we are told how Lākhan forces a crossing of the river, and so relieves Mahōbā.

ABSTRACT

The Invocation simply says that the land of the Chandēl without Ūdan was empty, as is a garden without a bird, a court without a sovereign, a night without the moon, a lake without a lotus, a tree without its leaves, or a wife without her husband.

Ālhā calls for volunteers to lead a force across the Bētwā. Ūdan offers, but Ālhā points out that he has had his opportunity of winning glory in the Gānjar, and now it is right that Lākhan should have an opportunity of volunteering. Lākhan does so. He, with Mīrā Tālhan and Dhanuā go out to look for a practicable ford. In the meantime Suphnā, the master of the elephants, takes 900 of Lākhan's she-elephants to drink in the river. Oppressed by the heat of midday, they enter the river and cross to the other side, where they are captured by Chauṇṛā, Suphnā escaping to tell Lākhan. Lākhan, Mīrā, and Dhanuā collect troops, cross the river, recapture them, and capture 700 more belonging to Chauṇṛā. Chauṇṛā comes up, and after the usual preliminary talk between the two generals, Chauṇṛā throws down his shield and dares Lākhan to take it up. Dhanuā rides up to take it, and is opposed by Dhāndhū on his elephant Bhaurānand. There is a single combat in which Dhanuā is victorious and picks up the shield. Then Lākhan throws down his dagger with a like challenge. Bhūrā Mughul advances to take it up and is opposed by Mīrā (Tālhan) Saiyid. The latter wins, and returns the dagger to Lākhan. The armies then join in battle, and Chauṇṛā's forces are routed. He then challenges Lākhan to single combat. This is accepted, and Lākhan knocks Chauṇṛā off his one-tusker elephant. Lākhan says that as a knight he cannot fight with a foot-soldier, as Chauṇṛā has now become, and tells him to run off home.

News of the defeat reaches Prithīrāj, who sets out with his son Tāhar (on Dalganjan) and a new force. Prithīrāj wears trousers of Egyptian[1] cloth and a coat of flowered muslin. On his waist he carries twelve knives and two swords, on each side a pistol, and on his left a dagger with a lion's head on the handle. His turban is red, with a pearl aigrette, his chest is a full yard wide, and his eyes flash like a torch. Tāhar opposes Lākhan. The other leaders are:

Delhi.	Kanauj.
Dhāndhū.	Dhanuā.
Bhurā Mughul.	Mīrā (Tālhan) Saiyid.
Kālnēm.	Hir Singh } of Biriā.
Pūran of Paṭnā.	Bir Singh } of Biriā.
Dēbī Marāṭhā.	Gangā Ṭhākur of Kuṛhar.
Bans Gōpāl of Datiā.	Parsū } brothers, of Parhul.
Rahmat.	Singhā } brothers, of Parhul.
Sahmat.	Gurūkhā, of Bengal.
Angad of Gwālior.	Chintā Ṭhākur, of Rusnī.

Tāhar is at first driven back, but Prithīrāj joins in and the Kanauj forces retreat. Even Lākhan's she-elephant Bhuruhī tries to run away. Lākhan jumps down and gives her a draught of wine. She returns to the charge and attacks Prithīrāj himself. Prithīrāj proposes to Lākhan to join his side, offering to adopt him as a son and give him the Mahōbā Philosopher's Stone. Lākhan indignantly refuses, and says that he is taking this opportunity to avenge the rape of Sanjōgin (Canto I). Māhil suggests to Prithīrāj that he should take Lākhan prisoner, and with this object Prithīrāj raises his bow.

Here the story harks back to the Kanauj camp. Rūpnā hastens to Dēbī and tells her of the rout of the Kanauj army, and how Lākhan is alone and surrounded by the enemy. Dēbī urges Ālhā to go to the rescue, but he refuses, saying this fight is Lākhan's affair. Ūdan refuses to go without Ālhā's permission, but Dēbī indignantly reproaches them both, and at length Ūdan starts off on Bēndulā and meets the allied forces retreating from the river, while Ālhā is collecting his troops. Ūdan rallies the retreating army, and they again advance against Prithīrāj. He finds Lākhan standing in front of Prithīrāj, who has his red bow raised. He reproaches Prithīrāj for warring against Jaychand and Parmāl, who never invaded his territory. Has he no shame in thus warring against a lad like Lākhan and against him—Ūdan? Prithīrāj drops his bow, and retires. Ūdan then wipes the blood off Lākhan and sets him again

[1] The word in the original is *misuru*, which I take to be a corruption of *miṣrī*, Egyptian. But it may be for *mashrū'*, a cloth of silk and cotton mixed, worn chiefly by Muslims at prayer. There was nothing, however, to prevent Prithīrāj using it.

on his elephant. In the meantime Ālhā's army comes up, and battle is joined again. Lākhan kills Bans Gōpāl, and attacks Tāhar, whose horse runs away. The whole army of Prithīrāj is finally routed, and his camp sacked and burnt down.

The Kanauj army then marches on to Mahōbā and is received with great rejoicings. Lākhan is welcomed by Malhnā and Chandrābal. Ālhā and Ūdan are reconciled to Parmāl, and they promise to stay and protect Mahōbā.

CANTO XVII

THE CARRYING OFF OF ŪDAN

THIS Canto is wrongly placed, for Malkhān, who in Canto XIII was killed at Sirsā, appears here alive and well. It does not form part of the main story of the Cycle. It is simply an episode telling how Ūdan was transformed into a parrot by a wandering gipsy girl, and how he was restored by the stronger magic of Sunwā.

ABSTRACT

The Invocation calls for success on Sarasvatī, the goddess of wisdom, and on Gaṇēśa.

At Sunwā's (Ālhā's wife's) request, Ūdan sets out with Jagnaik and 125,000 men, to take her and Phulwā (his wife) to bathe at Biṭhūr at the Jēṭh Dasahrā,[1] which was specially lucky, as it fell on a Sunday. Ālhā gives him permission to go after warning him against getting into a quarrel with any of the other rājās. They reach Biṭhūr in seven days, and pitch their camp there.

Subhiā Biṛinī[2] of Jhunnāgaṛh (where Gajmōtin, Malkhān's wife, came from) also comes there with Sahuā, her brother. She takes several gipsy girls (*naṭnīs*) with her, and goes out to see the fair, through which she dances and sings. She comes up to Ūdan's camp and throws enchantment over him, but, recognizing that Sunwā is a more powerful enchantress than she, she gives up the idea. While she is yet in the camp she sees Sunwā put her ornaments (worth nine lākhs of rupees) into her jewel-box, and, without Sunwā knowing it, makes the box disappear by magic. She then departs. Ūdan then takes Sunwā and Phulwā out to bathe, and having done this, and having seen the fair, they march back to Mahōbā. When they reach the Jumna the jewel-box is for the first time missed. Sunwā is much distressed. Ūdan promises to find it, sends Jagnaik with Sunwā and Phulwā on to Mahōbā, and himself returns to Biṭhūr.

When he arrives there he finds that the fair is broken up, but Subhiā meets him and he tells her the reason of his return. She

[1] The Dasahrā of Jēṭh (May–June) is held on the tenth of the light half of the month. It celebrates the birthday of the Ganges, and whoever bathes in the Ganges on that day is said to be purified from ten sorts of sins. It is to be distinguished from the Dasahrā in honour of Dēvī, held in the autumn. For Biṭhūr, see Canto IX. The town is on the Ganges.

[2] A class of wandering gipsies. They live in reed tents.

offers to help him to find it if he will play a game of chaupar (a kind of backgammon) with her. While they are engaged in play, she turns Ūdan into a parrot, and hastens with him and with her brother Sahuā to Delhi, where she tells Prithīrāj that she has brought Ūdan captive. Prithīrāj refuses to have anything to do with her, and has her turned out of Delhi. She wanders about from rājā to rājā, ending with Gajrāj of Jhunnāgaṛh, and tells how she has caught Ūdan at Biṭhūr and encaged him, but they all refuse to deal with her; so finally she goes off and pitches her reed hut in the forest of Jhārkhaṇḍ, surrounding it with magic guards.

As time goes on and Ūdan does not turn up at Mahōbā, Sunwā becomes anxious, and starts out searching for him. She puts a magic pill into her mouth, and changes herself into a kite. She flies first to Biṭhūr, and then all over India from country to country, but fails to trace him. At length she comes to the Jhārkhaṇḍ[1] and there sees Subhiā's tents and a cage with a parrot in it. She watches Subhiā take the parrot out of the cage, change it into a man, spread out the chaupar-board and begin playing a game with him. They play till midnight, and then she proposes that Ūdan should become a Musalmān and marry her. He refuses, and in a rage she ties his arms with a silken rope and hanging him to a tamarind tree starts beating him with bamboo rods till the knots made holes in his back, calling upon him to utter the Muslim cry of 'Allāhu Akbar'. He refuses, and as dawn approaches she turns him into a parrot again, and replaces him in the cage.

Sunwā then issues the spell of silence, so that Subhiā and every one became senseless. She takes Ūdan out of the cage and turns him back into a man. She commends his conduct in refusing to change his religion, and offers to take him and (if he wish it) Subhiā to Mahōbā. He refuses, as he has been beaten on the back (where he has never been beaten before) by a woman. Let Sunwā tell Ālhā to come with an army, and he will return to Mahōbā when this woman has been conquered in fair fight. She accordingly changes him again into a parrot, replaces him in the cage, and hastens to Mahōbā.

On her return to Mahōbā she summons Malkhān by letter from Sirsā. He comes and she tells him what has happened, and asks him to persuade Ālhā to release Ūdan. He does so, the army is equipped and starts for the Jhārkhaṇḍ, accompanied by Ḍhēwā on Manurthā, Indal on Hansāman, and Malkhān on Kabutrī. Sunwā accompanies the army in the shape of a kite, and when it reaches the Jhunnāgaṛh frontier she flies on to the Jhārkhaṇḍ, takes the cage, changes Ūdan into a man, and delivers him to Ālhā.

The magic guards rouse Subhiā and warn her that she has been surrounded by the army of some rājā. She calls her brother Sahuā, and produces a magic army of five thousand Naṭs (wandering gipsies). Alhā's army destroys two hundred Naṭs with cannon fire. Subhiā

[1] See note to p. 129.

then uses the magic of Dacca in Bengal, and produces a huge army of gipsies which puts Alhā's troops to rout, till they are rallied by Malkhān. Then Subhiā sends forth magic fire which consumes Ālhā's camp and again disperses his troops, till Sunwā, with counter-magic, pours water on it and extinguishes it. The Mahōbā troops make a concerted attack on Subhiā's army—Malkhān on the east, Ūdan on the west, Ḍhēwā on the north, and Indal on the south. Subhiā's troops flee, and she uses many spells to retrieve the position, but each spell is countered by a stronger spell from Sunwā. She changes herself into a kite and attacks Sunwā (also a kite) with the spell of Bīr Mahamdī, but all to no effect. They fight together in the sky, but neither wounds the other, so they come to the ground, Sunwā on the top of Subhiā. Sunwā calls to Indal to kill Subhiā. He refuses to kill a woman, but cuts off her hair, which deprives her of all power. The army then marches home. As it passes Jhunnāgaṛh, Gajrāj comes out and congratulates Alhā and Ūdan. Then they reach Mahōbā and are received with great rejoicing.

Canto XVIII

THE HOME-BRINGING OF BĒLĀ. I

In Canto VI we were told the tale of Brahmā's marriage to Prithīrāj's daughter Bēlā, and how Prithīrāj promises to send her to her husband's house in a year's time. This and the following cantos narrate the sequel to the promise.

ABSTRACT

The Invocation states that just as Jāmbavat was to Rāma, and as the Pāṇḍavas were to Virāṭa, so Dēbī (or Diwal Dē), his mother, was the chief adviser to Ālhā. Mahōbā produces no sugar-cane (i.e. sweetness), but did produce betel (i.e. bravery) and rice (i.e. bodily strength) in abundance. There no knight will ever be born equal to Ālhā, and there Parmāl will never rule again.

Māhil approaches Parmāl in public court, and suggests that it is time to arrange for the home-bringing of Bēlā. Parmāl agrees, and calls for volunteers in the approved style, offering a *bīrā* (betel roll) to be taken up by the champion. Ūdan takes it up. Māhil suggests to Brahmā that Ūdan's mean caste will give rise to difficulties, and spurs him on to snatch the *bīrā* from Ūdan. He does so, and Ālhā and Ūdan, feeling themselves disgraced, retire in dudgeon to Daspurwā.

Brahmā collects his troops for the march to Delhi, but his mother, Malhnā, is fearful because he is going without Ālhā and Ūdan to protect him. Lākhan (Jaychand's nephew) is in Mahōbā. She sends for him, and he offers to go with Brahmā and to take care of him. Ūdan hears of this, tells Lākhan that he is his companion, not Brahmā's, and that if he goes with Brahmā, he will first have to fight with him (Ūdan). Mīrā Tālhan intervenes, and persuades Lākhan to withdraw from the expedition.

So Brahmā (on Harnāgar) sets out alone, except for Māhil (on Lillī) as his companion and the troops. They reach Delhi territory and encamp. Māhil rides ahead, and tells Prithīrāj of Brahmā's arrival and of what had occurred at Mahōbā. Prithīrāj instructs him to tell Brahmā that he will not get Bēlā without first having his fill of fighting. Māhil returns to camp and persuades Brahmā to send Prithīrāj a letter of challenge. Prithīrāj dispatches his son Sūraj[1] with orders to bring Brahmā in a prisoner. Sūraj comes out with an army and Brahmā arrays his troops. After mutual challenges the armies join in battle, and the Delhi troops are routed.

[1] Another text says Gōpī, not Sūraj.

Sūraj challenges Brahmā to single combat and is thrown off his horse. Then Ṭōḍar and Mardan, in order, attack Brahmā, and are each similarly defeated, all three being killed.

Māhil then visits Prithīrāj and explains that a hero like Brahmā can be defeated only by fraud, and proposes that Tāhar should go out in a litter, disguised as a woman, and pretend to be Bēlā. Tāhar refuses, saying such disguise of a Rājpūt is against Rājpūt rules of honour; but Chauṉṛā, the Brāhman, offers himself for the task. He dresses himself like a woman, arms himself with a poisoned dagger, and sets out in a gorgeous litter. Tāhar (on Dalganjan), and Dhāndhū (on an elephant) accompany him. They arrive at the Mahōbā camp, and Tāhar sends word that he has brought Bēlā in the litter. Brahmā rides out to meet him and is politely received, Tāhar embracing him, and explaining that as Prithīrāj was not able to contend any more he now sends Bēlā. Chauṉṛā, in his woman's dress, descends from the litter and strikes Brahmā in the heart with his dagger. At the same time Dhāndhū pierces him with a spear, and Tāhar shoots him in the head with an arrow. Jagnaik advances, puts Brahmā's senseless body into a litter, and brings him back to camp. Brahmā there slightly revives, and Chauṉṛā, Dhāndhū, and Tāhar return to Delhi.

The news of Brahmā's apparent death reaches the Delhi palace. Agmā is much distressed, Bēlā isolates herself in her own apartments.

News reaches Mahōbā that Brahmā is sore wounded and can live only a day or two. There are great lamentations. Ālhā and Ūdan meditate revenge.

CANTO XIX

THE HOME-BRINGING OF BĒLĀ. II

ABSTRACT

INVOCATION. Whose is the upper chamber where the beacon shineth, and whose the bed upon which the withered flowers lie? Whose is the queen that weepeth in the upper chamber, and whose is the husband that hath gone to a far countree?

'Tis in Parhul's[1] upper chamber that the beacon shineth, and on Phulwā's[2] bed the flowers withered lie. In the upper chamber weepeth Kusumā,[3] and Lākhan hath gone to a far countree.

Bēlā writes to Ūdan asking him to carry out her home-bringing. She charges him with being at heart a woman, and implores him if he is really a son of Dasrāj to unite her to her husband. Shame on him for staying at ease in Mahōbā and sending Brahmā to his death at Delhi.

With Ālhā's permission Ūdan and Lākhan collect an army and start forth. They put the troops into black uniform, and give them black flags, directing the soldiers to say that they are men of Gānjar. They make double marches and in five days camp fourteen miles from Delhi. Chaunṛā comes and asks them who they are. They say that they are Hīr Singh and Bir Singh of Gānjar and that they have come to seek employment under Bēlā. He advises them to serve under Prithīrāj and asks what pay they want. Their terms are 100,000 rupees a day. Chaunṛā goes back and consults Prithīrāj, who says he cannot afford the pay. Chaunṛā strongly recommends their immediate engagement. 'They are great fighters. Jaychand of Kanauj fought with them for twelve years but got no tribute from them. Engage them only for eight days, and use them to sack Mahōbā.' Prithīrāj agrees, and sets these 'Gānjar' troops to guard Bēlā's apartments, as he has great fears of an attack from Ūdan. He then orders the 'Gānjar' elephants and horses to be branded with the Delhi mark. Bhuruhī, Lākhan's elephant, objects, and Lākhan persuades Prithīrāj to postpone the branding for a day.

The 'Gānjar' guard, with Ūdan, Lākhan, Ḍhēwā, Mīrā Tālhan, and Dhanuā Tēlī, take over the ward of Bēlā's apartments. Ūdan

[1] See Canto XV, p. 252. Parsū, the Rājā, had accompanied the force that relieved Mahōbā.

[2] Ūdan's wife.

[3] Lākhan's wife.

and Lākhan set to playing dice, and Lākhan, as he throws, says, 'If Bēlā is true I win.' Bēlā hears this and sends a slave-girl, Rūpā, to ask who are the soldiers that are taking her name in vain. They send word to Bēlā that Ūdan is waiting to take her away on the home-bringing. Bēlā cannot believe it, and tells the girl to ask Ūdan what had happened when the marriage took place. Ūdan, on receiving this message, writes a letter giving her a full account of all that occurred in Delhi at Brahmā's marriage (Canto VI). The letter is delivered to Bēlā and she sends for Ūdan. He tells his history since he last saw her, and how Brahmā has been sorely wounded. 'He is tossing on his bed, and will die to-day or to-morrow.' Bēlā curses him for allowing this, and he explains how he had originally taken up the *bīrā*, but Brahmā had snatched it from him. He, Ūdan, is not to blame. Bēlā, who, as we know, was an incarnation of Draupadī, then proceeds to tell Ūdan all her previous lives:

In her first birth, she was a female fish and Brahmā a male fish.

In her second, she and he were a pair of snakes.

In her third, she and he were a pair of *chakwā* birds, always separated at night.

In her fourth, she and he were a pair of deer.

In her fifth, they were a pair of swans.

In her sixth she was Draupadī, the wife of Arjuna, but called the wife of five husbands.

In her seventh, she is Bēlā, imprisoned in Delhi by her father, who has killed her husband.

In all these births she has had the same fate, never to be really united with her beloved. She is fated to this unhappiness, and Ūdan had better leave her and go back to Mahōbā. Ūdan declares that he and Lākhan are capable of carrying her off successfully, and they will surely bring her to Brahmā. They call in Lākhan and Mīrā Tālhan. She tells them that when she was Draupadī, Mīrā was then Bhīmasēna, and Lākhan was Nakula—two of the five Pāṇḍava brothers. She recommends them to go back to Mahōbā, and taunts Lākhan with not having conquered Prithīrāj when he abducted Sanjōgin (Canto I). Lākhan gets angry, and says he will now carry off Bēlā just out of revenge against Prithī. Having satisfied herself that they all mean business, she says she will not go secretly, but that the customary presents must be offered on her departure, and her dowry formally demanded.

Ūdan leaves Lākhan on guard, and, in his own character, rides up on Rāsbēndul to Prithīrāj, as if coming from Mahōbā. He gives four bags of gold coins for the customary presents, says he has come to conduct Bēlā on the home-bringing to her husband's house, and demands the dowry. Māhil instigates Prithīrāj to invite Ūdan, who is alone, to alight from his horse, and then to cut his head off. Ūdan refuses. Prithīrāj remarks that he is wearing the bracelet of battle, and asks why. Ūdan replies that he has worn eight other such bracelets and conquered each time, and that Bēlā has now given him this, the ninth. At Māhil's instigation Prithīrāj throws down two of his earrings, and dares Ūdan to pick them up. Instead of getting down to do so, as they hoped, Ūdan picks them up on his spear point and rides off.

In the meantime Bēlā gets into her litter, and starts off under the protection of Lākhan and Mīrā Tālhan. She stops at Agmā's palace to bid her farewell and to collect her jewellery. Agmā implores her to stay, saying she can easily get her married to some one else. Bēlā retorts that Prithīrāj has many other daughters whom she (Agmā) can marry to Musalmān Mughuls if she likes. But she is to think of her (Bēlā) as a widow, and prophesies that in three months and seventeen days Delhi will be sacked, and every married woman there (including her seven sisters-in-law, and Agmā herself) will become widows.[1]

Bēlā (here also called Bilam Dē), protected by Lākhan, having collected her jewellery, goes on and stops at the temple of Dēvī, which she enters in order to worship the goddess. She gets hold of a flower-girl of Delhi, named Phulwā, and by her sends a message to Tāhar. 'Lākhan is carrying off my litter to Kanauj, in revenge for Prithīrāj's abduction of Sanjōgin. Shame on your manhood.' Tāhar rides out at once with a thousand soldiers, but Lākhan defeats him and he has to retreat. Lākhan then conducts Bēlā to the Mahōbā camp.

Arrived there, Ūdan, who has successfully escaped from before Prithīrāj, joins them, and when Bēlā asks him what dowry he has got for her, he shows Prithīrāj's two earrings, worth nine lakhs. He hands them to her, and she is delighted. The army moves forth on the return march to Mahōbā. Prithīrāj sends Chauṇṛā with 125,000 men in pursuit. There is the usual challenge and counter-challenge between Chauṇṛā and Lākhan, and then the armies join in battle, the Delhi army being repulsed. There is single combat between Lākhan and Chauṇṛā, each on his elephant. Lākhan spears the latter's elephant. It falls to the ground and Chauṇṛā runs away on foot.

Prithīrāj takes another army headed by himself (on the elephant Ādibhayankar), Tāhar (on Dalganjan), and Dhāndhū (on the elephant Bhaurānand). In the preliminary challenges Prithīrāj invites Lākhan to join his side, but he refuses to desert Ūdan. There is a terrible conflict between the armies. At length Lākhan puts the litter in care of Dhanuā Tēlī and leads a charge of his own troops which puts the Delhi army to flight. When Prithīrāj sees his troops fleeing he sends Dhāndhū on his elephant to capture the litter. Dhāndhū attacks Dhanuā and wounds him in the thigh with a spear, so that he falls from his horse, and the litter is captured. But Lākhan rescues Dhanuā, who binds up his wound, attacks Dhāndhū's elephant, smashes the howdah, and recovers the litter. Angad and

[1] An evident reference to the defeat and death of Prithīrāj, and the capture of Delhi in 1192 by Shahabu'd-dīn.

Bhūrā Mughal then recapture the litter, but Mīrā Tālhan puts them to flight and gets it back. Then Tāhar takes it from Mīrā, and in turn is defeated (and his horse wounded) by Lākhan. Finally, Prithīrāj himself attacks Lākhan, and is about to shoot him with his unerring arrow, when Ūdan rides up, and upbraids him for fighting with one who is not his equal in rank. Prithīrāj, ashamed, drops his bow, and his elephant is attacked by Lākhan's elephant, Bhuruhī, and runs away. So Lākhan safely carries off the litter and brings Bēlā to Brahmā.

CANTO XX

BĒLĀ'S VENGEANCE

BRAHMĀ, in Canto XVIII, has been treacherously attacked by Chauṇṛā, Tāhar, and Dhāndhū, and now lies sorely wounded. The present canto tells how Bēlā took vengeance on her brother Tāhar. This canto illustrates the fact to which attention has more than once been drawn, that a Rājpūt wife's loyalty is to her husband, not to her own people. Bēlā, from the time of her marriage with Brahmā (Canto VI), although she still remained in her father's house till Lākhan carried her off to Brahmā as described in the preceding canto, took sides throughout with Mahōbā, and was ever ready to intrigue against her father, Prithīrāj, and the rest of the Delhi people. Here she exacts a terrible vengeance against her own brother, whom she has no compunction in slaying.

ABSTRACT

The Invocation dwells on the certainty of the advent of the day of calamity. On the day of calamity Rāma lost his wife Sītā. On his day of calamity Brahmā, the Chandēl, met his fate.

On her arrival at the camp Bēlā goes to Brahmā, offers him wifely obeisance, and gives him air with a fan of flowers. She utters a great cry of 'Awake, awake, my beloved', and he returns to consciousness. He asks who the lady is, and she tells him. In wrath he tells her she is the daughter of a traitor foul, and orders her to be driven from the tent. She replies that it is not her fault. Her father is her enemy too, and she has come to tend his wounds. His answer is that if any one bring him the head of Tāhar he will live again. She asks for his horse Harnāgar, his armour, and his turban, and promises to kill Tāhar, if he will first send her off to Mahōbā to be formally received as daughter-in-law by Queen Malhnā. She is put into a litter and sets out in charge of Ālhā.

Māhil hears of this, and tells Prithīrāj, who sends out Chauṇṛā with an army to intercept the litter. Ūdan comes to the rescue and defeats Chauṇṛā. Then Prithīrāj himself (on the elephant Ādibhayankar) and Tāhar set out and attack the litter. Lākhan comes to the rescue, and the litter is captured and recaptured several times, till Prithīrāj retreats, and Ālhā and the litter pursue their course, through Purwā,[1] where she is welcomed by Sukhiā Barain, and they finally reach Mahōbā. She is first received by Sunwā (Ālhā's wife), then by

[1] The same as Daspurwā, the fief of Ālhā and Ūdan.

Dēbī or Diwal Dē (mother of Ālhā and Ūdan), who gives her the nine lakh necklace, and finally by Malhnā (Brahmā's mother). Bēlā lays her bridal bracelet at the feet of Malhnā and describes Brahmā's wounds, a dagger wound on the left, a spear wound on the right, and an arrow wound on the skull. Chandrābal takes her to Brahmā's house, where she laments that she will now have no use for it, as she will be a widow, and calls on it to fall upon her. As she says this the portico falls with a crash. She is then shown Brahmā's garden with its bungalow, and the lakes near the city where there is further lamentation. She persuades Ālhā to take her to Brahmā's bungalow on the Sāgar Tāl lake. There she tests him, first assuming a beautiful form, and attempting to seduce him, and then appearing as an ogress, and attempting to terrify him. He is unmoved by both apparitions, and she knows she can trust him.

She then gets leave from Malhnā, and, still under Ālhā's guard, she starts off in her litter to the scene of Gajmōtin's Satī at Sirsā. There she meets Gajmōtin's ghost, which tells her of Māhil's treachery and prophesies that in three months and seventeen days every married woman in Delhi and Mahōbā would become a widow. Bēlā assures Gajmōtin that she will soon join her, as she intends to become Satī as soon as she is a widow, and then goes on to the camp, where she visits Brahmā. He asks her if she has brought the head of Tāhar. She replies, 'Not yet. I had first to visit my mother-in-law at Mahōbā. Now I am going to Delhi to fetch it.'

She dresses herself as a man, puts on armour, mounts Harnāgar, and starts off with an army. Ūdan wishes to accompany her, but she will not have him. Arriving at the Delhi border, she writes a letter in Brahmā's name, stating that he has been restored to health by Bēlā. 'Half of Bēlā's dowry is still due. Let Tāhar bring it to me here, or else Delhi city will I burn down.' Prithīrāj on receiving the letter, dispatches Tāhar with Chauṉra and an army. As Tāhar puts his foot in the stirrup, a sneeze is heard, and Chauṉrā begs him not to start. Tāhar makes the usual reply about omens being fit for shopkeepers and not for knights. They reach the Mahōbā camp. Bēlā, disguised as Brahmā, demands the half of the dowry. Tāhar refuses, the battle is joined, and the Delhi troops are routed. Tāhar then challenges the false Brahmā to single combat. As they fight her sleeve is torn, and her woman's bangles become visible. Chauṉrā recognizes that she is Bēlā, and warns Tāhar; but it is too late. Bēlā attacks Tāhar and decapitates him. The news reaches Delhi, and there are great lamentations, but Bēlā takes up Tāhar's head, and rides to camp, where she presents it to Brahmā.

CANTO XXI

THE BATTLE OF THE SANDAL-GROVE

ABSTRACT

THE Invocation states that wisdom is lessened by association with thieves, and anger by good counsel; sin is lessened by virtuous acts, and disease by taking medicine; friendship is lessened by frequent requests, and water by the hot season; strength is lessened by association with women, and the fear of death by praising God.

Bēlā brings Tāhar's head in a charger to Brahmā and arouses him, 'Awake, my Lord, upon thy jewelled bed. Lo, I am here, thy wife. Tāhar's head have I brought. Open thine eyes and look upon it.' He opens his eyes and gazes on Bēlā. 'If thou desire royalty, Bēlā, become not a Satī with my corpse. If thy father's house be dear to thee, take thy way to Delhi. But if in thy body there be aught of faithfulness to thy troth, let thy body be consumed upon my pyre. Brahmā hath no longer to live, no efforts of thine can aught avail. Mine enemy hast thou shown to me, and now am I at peace.' With these words he breathes his last. Bēlā breaks into heartrending lamentations, and when the news arrives all Mahōbā is filled with weeping.

Bēlā sends for Ūdan. She announces her intention of becoming Satī and asks him to bring wood for the funeral pyre from her father's sandal-grove at Delhi. Ūdan urges her to remain alive, but to no purpose, and she threatens to curse[1] him if he does not bring the sandal-wood.

Ūdan (on Rāsbēndul) and Lākhan (on Bhuruhī) collect their troops and set out for Delhi. They halt at the sandal-grove ten miles away from the city. Next morning Ūdan calls for carpenters and they cut down the trees of the sandal-grove. Prithīrāj is informed and sends out an army under Chauṉṛā (on the one-tusker elephant) and Dhāndhū (on Bhaurānand). In the meantime Ūdan has had the wood loaded on carts and the camp struck. They have just started when Chauṉṛā comes up. After the usual challenges, Chauṉṛā attacks Ūdan, but is compelled to retreat, and the general engagement begins. Bijai Singh, Rājā of Bīkānēr, rushes upon the carts. Under Lākhan's orders, they are defended by Bir Singh, who, with his brother Hir Singh, is killed by Bijai. Then Gangā Singh attacks Bijai and with a single blow of his sword cuts his body into two pieces, cleaving through from left shoulder to chine. Then Hirāman of Charkhārī attacks Gangā with his spear, but is killed with a blow of Gangā's

[1] The curse of a woman about to become a Satī is supremely terrible.

mace. Finally the Delhi army is routed, Lākhan marches off from the grove with his carts, and reaches the camp. Ūdan, with Lākhan's permission, goes to Bēlā and tells her he has brought the sandal-wood.

Bēlā points out that the sandal-wood is damp and will not burn. She must also have some dry sandal-wood. Ūdan offers to get some from Kanauj, but she refuses, saying that there are twelve sandal-wood pillars over against the audience-chamber of Prithīrāj's palace in Delhi, and that he must bring those. Ūdan remonstrates. The attempt to get them would mean certain death to all concerned. She flies into a rage. Says he is too fond of his precious life. He has schemed to get Brahmā killed, in order that he may possess her and become king of Mahōbā. She again threatens to curse him if he does not fetch the pillars. She remains a Satī only for seven days before her death. Of these three days have passed, and only four remain. He must therefore hasten.

Ūdan in despair takes counsel with Lākhan. They go together to her and Lākhan entreats her not to become Satī. She remains firm in her determination, and tells Lākhan that he need not necessarily lose his life. If he wishes to save it, he can go home to Kanauj. Otherwise he must go to Delhi and fetch from there the pillars. Lākhan then tells Ūdan that they must go to Delhi and either bring back the pillars or die there.

Canto XXII

THE SANDAL PILLARS

INSTEAD of an Invocation, this canto begins with the following story:

Dēvī Śāradā is worshipped by Chauṉrā for twelve years. She then appears to him, blesses him, and says that hitherto no knight has ever yet succeeded in filling her drinking vessel to the brim.[1] So she takes him to Delhi, and is worshipped there by Prithīrāj, but even there her cup is not filled. Then she takes him to Mahōbā, where they meet Alhā and Ūdan. There she distributes *bīṟās* (rolls of betel leaf) to the three.[2] To Chauṉrā she gives two, to Ūdan five, and to Ālhā the remainder of her supply. Chauṉrā grumbles at the small number given to him, and she tells him to attend her temple next morning, when she would give him her blessing.

At break of the next day Queen Machhulā makes Alhā go off to the temple. He goes there with his sword, worships, and cuts off his own head as a sacrifice to the goddess.[3] She is much gratified by the oblation and restores him to life, at the same time conferring immortality upon him.[4] He returns home, and Machhulā then sends Ūdan to the temple. He hopes to be made immortal too, but Dēvī replies that that cannot be, the boon can be granted to only one of the two brothers. His fate is to die by the hand of Chauṉrā. Chauṉrā being a Brāhman, death at his hand will send the victim to Vishṇu's heaven.

Chauṉrā next comes to the temple. He is enraged at hearing that Ālhā has been made immortal, and threatens to rip his own belly open, so that Dēvī may become guilty of causing the death of a Brāhman. Dēvī explains that it is fated that there shall be only three immortals—two, the gods Indra and Mahadēva, in heaven ; and one, Ālhā, on the earth. It is hence impossible for her to give this boon to him. Instead thereof her blessing is that he shall slay Ūdan, and himself die by the hand of Ālhā. Thus, as Chauṉrā observes, each of the three receives a blessing—viz. Ālhā immortality, Chauṉrā to kill Ūdan, and Ūdan to die at the hands of a Brāhman.

Ūdan and Lākhan, despairing of their lives, collect their forces and

[1] It was a skull, and the drink was blood.

[2] As challenges to fill her cup.

[3] Thereby filling her cup to the brim.

[4] According to tradition, he is still alive, and will one day appear to avenge Mahōbā.

start for Delhi, reaching the river Jumna in four double marches. Lākhan is in command, and with him are Ūdan, Dhanuā Tēlī, Lalā Tamōlī, Mīrā Tālhan, Ḍhēwā, Jagnaik, the four Rājās of Gānjar, and the twelve princes of Banaudhā. The army then makes a sudden rush upon the twelve sandal-wood pillars. Lākhan has them uprooted and loaded upon carts. News is brought to Bīr Bhugantā, who hastens to the spot and stops the carts. Ūdan explains that they are wanted for Bēlā's funeral pyre, the wood of the sandal-grove previously carried off having proved too damp. The armies join battle.

Lākhan puts the carts in charge of Parsū, who is attacked by Angad. Parsū strikes down Angad with his sword, but is in turn speared by Bīr Bhugantā. Ūdan then compels Bīr Bhugantā and the Delhi army to retreat. Lākhan, on the she-elephant Bhuruhī, rushes the gate of Delhi, and declares his intention of sacking the palace and carrying off Queen Agmā in revenge for the rape of Sanjōgin (Canto I). Jagnaik, however, declares that Agmā, as Bēlā's mother, was now as sacred to him as Malhnā, Brahmā's mother, and that he will not allow Lākhan to insult her. They are nearly coming to blows, when Ūdan intervenes and pacifies both. He points out to Lākhan that the palace is now undefended, and that a Rājpūt cannot war against women. He offers to go in himself and to bring out Agmā in her litter. To this Lākhan agrees, and Ūdan enters the palace and finds Agmā. She reproaches him with warring against women, and he tells her that she is as sacred to him as Malhnā is. He tells her to put a slave-girl, dressed as her, into a litter, and to send her out to Lākhan. When the litter is brought he tells Lākhan that, now that the litter has been brought outside the door and he has taken it captive, it would be a knightly act to set it free and allow it to return. Lākhan consents, agrees that he has now taken his revenge, and sends the litter back into the women's apartments.

In the meantime Prithīrāj, on the elephant Ādibhayankar, with Chauṇrā on the one-tusker and Dhāndhū on the elephant Bhaurānand, come up with forces to rescue the pillars. After the usual challenges and Ūdan explaining as before, Dhāndhū attacks Dhanuā Tēlī, who has been put by Lākhan in charge of the carts, and strikes him down with his sword. Ūdan knocks Dhāndhū off his elephant, and is attacked by Dēbī Marāṭhā, whom he hews in two from shoulder to chine. The armies then join. After a terrible but indecisive conflict Lākhan, on his elephant Bhuruhī whirling a chain, on the east and Ūdan on the west make a concerted attack, and the Delhi army is routed. The Mahōbā army then carries off the pillars without opposition.

CANTO XXIII

BĒLĀ SATĪ

ABSTRACT

THE opening Invocation is praise of Vishṇu, tells how that god, in his incarnation as the Man-lion, protected his devotee Prahlāda, and slew the demon Hiraṇyakaśipu.

As soon as the sandal pillars arrive in the camp, Ūdan, under Bēlā's instructions, builds the funeral pyre. She puts on all her ornaments, dresses herself in bridal array, and ascends the pyre, on which has been laid the corpse of Brahmā.

News of this reaches Delhi, and Prithīrāj (on the elephant Adibhayankar) with his army hastens to the spot. They arrive just as Bēlā has mounted the pyre, and Prithīrāj exclaims that some one of the Parmāl's family must set the pyre alight, and not any of the Banāphars, who are of mean caste. Ūdan replies that Bēlā has commanded him to do it and that he will allow no one to interfere. They argue and quarrel over this, and finally Prithīrāj in a rage orders his artillery to fire. There ensues a terrible and bloody fight between the two armies (full description, as frequently before) covering twenty-four miles of ground. In single combat Mīrā Tālhan slays Bhūrā Mughul, and is himself slain by Bīr Bhugantā. Gangā (Lākhan's maternal uncle) slays Bīr Bhugantā, and is in turn slain by Dhāndhū (on Bhaurānand). Lākhan, much grieved at the death of his uncle, hastens up on his she-elephant Bhuruhī, driven by Suphnā. They join in single combat, and Dhāndhū's sword breaks and he is finished off by Lākhan. Prithīrāj rides up on Ādibhayankar and has Lākhan surrounded by nine hundred elephants, Lākhan jumps down from his howdah and gives Bhuruhī intoxicating drugs (molasses, Indian hemp, and opium). Bhuruhī, maddened, rushes forward whirling an iron chain, and breaks through the encircling ring of elephants. Lākhan smites right and left for a long time, till Prithīrāj approaches him.

In the meantime, as no one had been able to set the pyre alight, Bēlā lets her hair hang loose. A flame issues from it, and the pyre at once bursts into a blaze, so that with the corpse she is consumed.

Lākhan challenges Prithīrāj to produce some one who dare fight him. Prithīrāj urges him to cease fighting and to return to Kanauj, as he is the only heir of Jaychand. He is not fighting in his own cause and the cremation of Bēlā does not concern him. He is just as fond of Lākhan as Jaychand is, and wishes to spare him. Lākhan in answer opens his armour and displays his bare breast to Prithīrāj. No one, he says, is immortal, and if his time is come it is come, but he will not budge from the field. Prithīrāj again persuades him, 'thou art but a lad, why dost thou throw away thy life? Come over with Bhuruhī and join my forces, and then together can we sack Mahōbā.' Lākhan disdainfully, as a Rājpūt, refuses to accept the bribe. Prithīrāj then waxes wroth, and taunts Lākhan with not having been able to prevent him carrying off Sanjōgin (Canto I). Lākhan replies that then he was but three years old. He still intends to take revenge for that insult, and to humiliate Prithīrāj by setting Delhi on fire. In a rage Prithīrāj raises his bow and shoots one by one his whole quiver full of twenty-two arrows at Lākhan. They pierce his shield and all enter his chest in one and the same spot, but Lākhan sits there unmoved, as if unhurt. Prithīrāj, amazed at his heroic endurance, and seeing Lākhan's elephant charging upon his, retreats, saying to himself that he can never conquer Lākhan. As soon as he has turned his back Lākhan swoons and dies, letting his shield fall to the ground.

Chauṉṟā, seeing the fallen shield, picks it up, and hurries to where Ūdan is fighting. He cries out that Lākhan is dead and his body is already being plundered. 'I have brought his shield in token. Go and see for yourself.' Ūdan hurries off to the scene of Lākhan's last fight, and sees his corpse. He laments, 'When shall we meet again, now that the prince of Kanauj is parted from me? Ne'er will I see again my mother Dēbī.[1] Ne'er will I see again the brave Malkhān, and so, from life to life, ne'er will I see again my friend beloved. When he left Kanauj I swore to his mother that with my life would I preserve him (Canto XV), and now how can I go back and show my face in Mahōbā? Nay, let me rather die, and so wipe out my sorrow. Alive to Mahōbā will I not return.' Weeping he approaches the pyre, and thus addresses Bēlā. 'Born wast thou in Delhi to be the ruin of the clans. The light of Mahōbā became extinguished when Brahmā, thy spouse, met his fate. Lākhan, the only son of Ratībhān, has been slain in battle, and the seven sons of Prithīrāj are now no more.' Bēlā's spirit appears and comforts him. She tells him that what is fated must come to pass, and that soon each house in Mahōbā and in Delhi will hold only widows, nor will one contain a woman blessed with a spouse.

Ūdan determines to seek death at the hand of Chauṉṟā the Brāhman, and so to obtain Paradise. He, on Rāsbēndul, challenges Chauṉṟā (on the one-tusker) to single combat. They fight. At length Chauṉṟā strikes down Ūdan with a mighty sword-blow and cuts off his head, and thus Ūdan attains to Paradise.

In the confusion resulting from his death, Indal (on Hansāman) hurries to Ālhā and tells him what has occurred. Ālhā mounts his elephant Pachsāwaḍ and advances against Chauṉṟā. They fight, and finally Ālhā seizes hold of Chauṉṟā and squeezes him to death, so that no drop of his blood may fall to the earth. For Dēvī had bestowed on Chauṉṟā the boon that if a drop of his blood should fall to the earth myriads of Chauṉṟās would rise from the ground in its place.

[1] Apparently she is dead, but I have not noticed any record of the fact in the cycle.

Prithīrāj sees Chaunrā's fate, and, despairing over the fact that every one of his heroes has been slain, he discharges an arrow at Ālhā, which wounds him in the right arm, but milk, instead of blood, flows from the wound. Ālhā thereby discovers that he is immortal and wrings his hands in sorrow. 'I thought that it was Ūdan who was immortal. If I had known that it was I, he would never have died.' He charges through the intervening troops at Prithīrāj, doing great slaughter. He is about to attack him, when Indal warns him against warring against Prithīrāj, so he urges his elephant up against the other's, and carries off Prithīrāj's standard. Prithīrāj and the remnant of his army then retire defeated.

In the meantime, news of the battle has reached Mahōbā—how the armies of Mahōbā and Kanauj have been slaughtered, and how Lākhan, Ūdan, Ḍhēwā and Jagnaik have all been killed. Sunwā (Ālhā's wife) and Phulwā (Ūdan's widow) and all the other widows hasten to the field with loud lamentations. Sunwā searches among the corpses, which lie, friend and foe, heaped together. She meets Indal, and says to him, 'Have you seen Ālhā [1] and Ūdan anywhere?' Indal tells her that Ūdan has been killed, but Ālhā stops him and says that his mother has mentioned his (Ālhā's) name in his (Indal's) presence. 'If the wife of a knight does this, his Rājpūthood is destroyed. This is a sign that the first quarter of the Kali age [2] has passed away, and that we must abandon Mahōbā.' He and Indal then start off for the Kanjarī Ban.[3] Sunwā attempts to stop Ālhā and grasps his elephant's tail, but Ālhā draws his sword, cuts the tail off, rides on with Indal, and is never seen again.

Sunwā and all the other widows then throw themselves into the great blazing pit which had formed Bēlā's funeral pyre, and are all consumed. The news of this reaches Mahōbā, and Malhnā recognizes that all its men have been killed, and that all its glory is gone. She goes to her secret closet, takes the Philosopher's Stone, and with it makes her way to the lake. There she worships the stone, offers sacrifice to it, and casts it into the lake, telling it to lie there for ever, and bidding it farewell. She returns to the palace. When Parmāl hears of this climax to his woes, he refuses to eat, and after fasting for thirteen days gives up the ghost.[4] Since then no king has reigned in Mahōbā.

[1] She mentions her husband to her son by name—a gross breach of one of the strongest taboos in India.

[2] The present, or Iron, age. According to tradition, it began in 3102 B.C. and is to last 432,000 years.

[3] Or 'Forest of Lampblack', the same as the Land of Darkness, of the Legend of Alexander the Great. Here Ālhā is still waiting for the time of his reappearance.

[4] As a matter of history, he lived to be defeated by Kutbu'd-dīn Ībak in the year A.D. 1203, eleven years after the defeat and death of his enemy Prithīrāj. Prithīrāj himself defeated Parmāl in 1182.

APPENDIX

THE IRON PILLAR

AN INDIAN BALLAD

ALL who have visited the Kutb Minār at Delhi, and many who only know that wonderful column from photographs, must have remarked the Iron Pillar which stands among the remains of the palace of the last Hindū sovereign. The legend of its origin is as follows:

KING ANANGA rides afield,
  Rides to rouse the forest deer;
Knights and lords with sword and shield,
  Hounds and huntsmen follow near.

Stealing here with crafty pace,
  Bounds the cheeta on his prey;
There the hawk, from pride of place,
  Swoops upon the partridge gay.

Many an arrow deftly sped,
  Pierced the fleet-foot quarry through;
Many a brilliant pea-fowl[1] fled,
  Scared by hunter's loud halloo.

Now they seek the forest shade,
  Ere the sun fulfil his height;
As they cross a grassy glade,
  Lo they view a wondrous sight.

Midst, a lordly ram there stood,
  Tigers eight he held at bay;
Vainly roaring, to the wood
  From his charge they slunk away. 5

Straight Ananga called the sage,
  Lore of heaven and earth he knew,
'How can this such foes engage?
  Great Vyāsa,[2] tell me true.'

1 Safe from Indian hunters himself, as a sacred bird.

2 The name of the sage who arranged the Vēdas or Hindū Scriptures. The y is made a separate syllable as in Hindī. In Sanskrit it is made a semi-vowel.

'Rājā, hear, and wonder not
  Strength by weakness should be foiled;
Underneath this favoured spot
  Lies the serpent monarch coiled.

'Where the Nāga[1] rests his head,
  Teems the earth with pride and might;
He, whose foot thereon doth tread,
  Single turns a host to flight.

'Were a city reared above,
  That were queen of all the land;
Had the snake no power to move,
  Endless should that empire stand.'

Fast Ananga's men ride forth,
  Such the bidding of the King;
From the mountains of the North
  Weights of ruddy ore they bring.

Deep they dig the furnace bed,
  Fierce and fiercer blows the blast,
Lo, a stream of glowing red,
  Forth the metal bursts at last.

Now the hammer-wielders stout,
  Smiths of mighty arm, are brought;
Day and night their strokes ring out,
  Till the Rājā's work is wrought.

Goodly work of hammer-craft,
  Now the pillar rises slow;
All above a polished shaft,
  All a piercing spike below.

Where they marked the Nāga's head,
  Deep the point was driven down;
Now, all strife for empire fled,
  Earth may own a single crown.

Soon a castle clothed with might
  Round the iron pillar clomb;
Soon a city brave and bright
  Spoiled the forest-creatures' home.

[1] Snake demi-god. Śēsha is their king.

‘’Ware of wiles, I rede thee, King;
  Crafty are the serpent race;
Nought will Śēsha spare to bring
  Freedom from his irksome case.’

Trains of tribute-bearers now
  Press around the Rājā's throne;
Vassal chiefs before him bow,
  Prince of princes him they own.

Came to Court a Brāhman hoar,
  Clad in garb of cleanly white;
Sacred scrolls his left hand bore,
  Rosary of beads his right.

Singing still a sacred song,
  Hair in topknot, wreath on breast,
Steadfast pressing through the throng,
  Lifting hands, the King he blessed.

Glad of heart the Rājā rose,
  Bent and did him reverence meet;
‘Holy Sire, thy wish disclose,
  All my wealth is at thy feet.’

‘Of thy hap’, replied the sage,
  ‘Wondrous tales I hear them tell;
Now I leave my hermitage,
  Asking what in truth befell.’

‘Brāhman, ’tis a wondrous tale,
  Wondrous tale it is but true,
By yon pillar's iron nail
  Śēsha's head is stricken through.’

‘Rājā, how should mortal dare
  Deal the Nāga King a blow?
Let thy tale the children scare,
  Greybeard men are mocked not so.’

‘Evil though the age be grown,
  All is true Vyāsa spake;
’Tis the Nāga's head alone
  Doth the kings my vassals make.’

'Words are words,' the Brāhman said,
 'Faith is good, but better sight;
Be the spike in Śēsha's head,
 Lo I gage mine own to smite.'

'Fool, I hold thee to thy word,'
 Rising wrathful, cried the King;
Soon the mighty mass is stirred,
 Soon the spike doth upward spring.

Dripped the point with blood-drops red,
 Straight he drew his falchion keen;
'Now I claim thy forfeit head;'
 But the Brāhman was not seen.

Sudden earthquakes shook the plain;
 Lightning arrows cleft the air;
Ne'er shall might of man again
 Fix[1] that pillar steadfast there.

Hissing laughter rolled around;
 Spouted forth a fount of gore;
Swelled a voice of thunder-sound,
 'Foolish King, thy reign is o'er.

'None of all the Tōmar[2] race
 Hence shall sit on Dihlī's throne;
Strangers seize their forfeit place,
 Who no kindred chief will own.

'Vainly strive to face the foe
 Rival rājās one by one;
Broken is the Rājpūt bow,
 Set in clouds their glory's sun.'

[1] And thenceforward, so tradition says, the region took the name of Ḍhīlī, i.e. loose, whence Dihlī or Delhi.

[2] The king, having no sons, made his grandson Prithī, the Chauhān of Ajmēr, his heir. But Jaychand, the Raṭhōr of Kanauj, was also a grandson, and the jealousies of the cousins laid open the way for the conquest of the empire by the Muhammadans.